Best
Financial
Advertising
2

David E. Carter
Editor

ART DIRECTION BOOK COMPANY
10 East 39th Street
New York, N.Y. 10016

This book contains a large variety of advertisements for banks and savings & loan associations — over 400 different ads are reproduced here.

The purpose of the book is to give financial institutions and their advertising agencies a comprehensive source of outstanding examples of advertisements. To make the book even more useful, the ads have been placed into various categories such as savings, home improvement loans, etc.

Future Volumes

The editor and publisher plan to produce a new volume on financial advertising every two years.

To submit advertising for consideration for the next volume:

(1) send all advertisements in proof form (tear sheets will not reproduce well).

(2) include a letter giving permission for the ads to be reproduced in the book only.

(3) do not mount the ads.

(4) attach a label to the back of *each ad* with the name of the bank and ad agency.

(5) mail all material to David E. Carter, P.O. Box 591, Ashland, Kentucky 41101.

Material will not be acknowledged nor returned. People sending ads which are selected for inclusion will be notified.

Contents

Savings

I don't offer my employees a pension plan...but Bank of Delaware does.

I don't offer my employees a pension plan. Why should I, when an Individual Retirement Account at Bank of Delaware gives them such a good deal? I mean a great deal! My employees can deposit up to $1,500 a year into their account and deduct it from their income tax return. The interest earned is tax deferred until they withdraw the money, usually after retirement, and by then they will probably be in a lower tax bracket. With this tax-shelter and a high rate of return, why wouldn't they want to save for retirement at Bank of Delaware. And besides, their money is insured up to $100,000 by FDIC.

Here's a chart that shows the difference in savings between a Bank of Delaware retirement plan and a normal savings account.

See how fast your money grows			
If you invest annually	After	With our tax-sheltered plan you'll have	Without our tax-sheltered plan you'll have
$1,500	10 yrs.	$24,073	$16,019
	20 yrs.	$78,243	$45,630
$1,000	10 yrs.	$16,049	$10,679
	20 yrs.	$52,162	$30,420

Substantial penalty for early withdrawal

(This table assumes a 25% tax bracket; figures are based on 8% interest compounded daily, with an effective annual yield of 8.45% on each $1,000 added.)

Now you know why we don't have a pension plan here at Scrooge and Company.

Do yourself a favor, if you are self-employed or work where there's no pension plan... go to Bank of Delaware and protect your future. Tell 'em Scrooge sent you.

BANK OF DELAWARE

MEMBER FDIC

9

Feeling Loan-ly?

Cheer up! We'll lend you money to cut your home energy costs and Uncle Sam will give you a tax credit of up to $300. on your federal income tax.

Wouldn't you like to insulate and weather-strip your home to cut down sky-high heating bills? Install storm or thermal windows and doors? Install a more efficient burner in your furnace?

Carteret will be happy to lend you the cash to do it, and your Uncle Sam will give you a tax break of 15 percent of the first $2,000. you spend for energy-saving home improvements.

For fast, efficient service call our toll free consumer loan number or stop in at any of our 33 offices.

Dial Toll Free 800-452-9740

CARTERET SAVINGS
AND LOAN ASSOCIATION

Consumer Loans Department, 61 Myrtle Street, Cranford, New Jersey 07016
New Jersey's Largest State Chartered Savings and Loan Association
33 offices conveniently located throughout New Jersey

Double take:
Deposit $1,000, take $2,000.
Deposit $500, take $1,000.
Now in just about 6½ years.

At AmeriFirst Federal, our new Special Money Market Certificate doubles your money in just about 6½ years, faster than ever before.

10.650% a year yields 11.236% annually.*
That's the high interest rate on our Special Money Market Certificates. Interest is compounded daily, and the minimum deposit is only $100.

Earn 10.650% a year for as short as 2½ years — as long as 10.
Choose the term between 2½ and 10 years that best meets your needs. And remember, if your Special Money Market Certificate is issued for longer than 6½ years, you'll more than double your money.

Or, choose among our other shorter-term, high-rate plans.

Savings Plan	Annual Rate	Annual Yield
Six-Month Money Market Certificate: $10,000 minimum. Rate effective through February 20, 1980.	12.256%	12.256%**
One-Year Certificate $100 minimum	6.50%	6.72%
Three-Month Certificate $100 minimum	6.00%	6.18%
Regular Savings $10 minimum	5.50%	5.65%

*Rate on Special Money Market Certificates effective through February 29, 1980.

**Federal Regulation prohibits compounding interest on six-month Money Market Certificates.

By Federal Regulation, a substantial interest penalty is required for early withdrawal from any savings certificate. Rates subject to change without notice.

Special rates for Jumbo Certificates.
Come in or phone any AmeriFirst Federal Office and ask about our special negotiated rates for deposits of $100,000 or more.

The security of an AmeriFirst No-Risk savings account.
At AmeriFirst, your savings are secure, backed by over $2½ billion in assets at the South's largest Federal, and insured to $40,000 by an Agency of the Federal Government.

Open your account — or add to your existing account — by mail.
Just decide which plan is best for you, complete the coupon, and mail it with your check made payable to AmeriFirst Federal.

To: AmeriFirst Federal
P.O. Box 017777, Miami, Florida 33101
☐ I wish to open an account, or
☐ I am already an AmeriFirst customer;
my account # is _____
Amount of Deposit $_____
Type of Account
☐ Sp. Money Mkt. Term: _____ (indicate between 2½-10 years)
☐ One Yr. Cert.   ☐ 6 Mos. Money Mkt. ($10,000 Min.)
☐ 3 Mos. Cert.   ☐ Regular Savings
Name _____
Soc. Sec. # _____
Other names
if: Joint _____ or trust acct.
Acct. _____ beneficiary
Address _____
City/Zip _____ Phone _____
Note: Deposits will receive interest rates in effect on date we receive this coupon and your check.

AMERIFIRST FEDERAL
America's Number 1.

AmeriFirst Federal Savings and Loan Association. America's oldest Federal. Over $2½ Billion strong. W.H. Walker, Jr., Chairman. Member Federal Savings and Loan Insurance Corporation. **DOWNTOWN:** One S.E. 3rd Ave. (Main Office)/100 N.E. 1st Ave. **NORTHEAST:** 8380 N.E. 2nd Ave./9640 N.E. 2nd Ave./900 N.E. 125th St./18301 Biscayne Blvd. **CENTRAL:** 1400 N.W. 17th Ave. **NORTHWEST:** 16407 N.W. 67th Ave., Miami Lakes. **HIALEAH:** Westland Mall. **MIAMI BEACH:** 17395 N. Bay Rd. at Winston Towers/1025 71st St./306 41st St./ 900 Alton Rd. **SOUTH:** 2750 Coral Way/Dadeland Mall/13701 N. Kendall Dr./15101 S. Dixie Hwy. **HOMESTEAD:** 28875 S. Federal Hwy. **MONROE COUNTY:** Ocean Reef, Key Largo. **BROWARD COUNTY:** 3201 N. Federal Hwy., Oakland Park/Loehmann's Plaza at Palm-Aire, Pompano Beach/Venetian Isle Shopping Center, Lighthouse Point/Broward Mall/Universal Plaza Shopping Center. **PALM BEACH COUNTY:** 998 S. Federal Hwy., Boca Raton/Oakbrook Square Shopping Center, N. Palm Beach. **CENTRAL FLA:** 8 Orlando Div. Offices.

When you save at AmeriFirst you're really cooking.

Great kitchen gifts.

Choose from a wide selection of West Bend cookware, with Dupont's Silver-Stone non-stick surface, to ovenware by Anchor Hocking. Whatever you select you'll find it a beautiful, helpful addition to your kitchen.

To receive your choice of these 25 color coordinated items, just deposit $500 or more in a new or existing account, or renew a maturing savings certificate. Depending upon the amount of your deposit or renewed savings certificate, you get your selection as a gift or you can buy it at a big savings. One gift per account.

Here at AmeriFirst Federal, America's oldest and the South's largest Federal, you'll find a full range of no-risk, high-interest rate plans to choose from. And your savings are insured to $100,000 by an agency of the Federal Government. We'll be glad to transfer your funds for you from anywhere in the country, without charge.

So hurry in while things are cooking at AmeriFirst Federal.

AMERIFIRST FEDERAL
America's Number 1.

Visit our new Curry Ford Office.

4444 Curry Ford Road at Conway Road

AmeriFirst Federal Savings and Loan Association. America's oldest Federal. Over $2¾ Billion Strong. W.H. Walker, Jr., Chairman. Member Federal Savings and Loan Insurance Corporation. **DOWNTOWN ORLANDO:** So. Orange at Anderson – 849-6200. **AZALEA PARK:** Semoran, south of Colonial – 277-9201. **COLONIAL PLAZA:** in the Mall – 894-1591. **ORANGE BLOSSOM:** Orange Blossom Trail at Holden – 855-9331. **SILVER PINES:** Pine Hills Rd. north of Silver Star Rd. – 299-6500. **CURRY FORD:** Curry Ford Rd. at Conway Rd. **WINTER PARK:** Knowles at Welbourne – 628-1010. **KISSIMMEE:** Vine St., west of Bermuda – 846-2250. **ALTAMONTE SPRINGS:** in the Mall – 834-1919. **LONGWOOD:** 1100 Montgomery Rd. – 862-1900. **MAIN OFFICE:** One S.E. Third Ave., Miami.

Mary Plunk says don't be late! Our free place setting offer ends October 10th! The Bank of Oak Ridge's Mary Plunk urges you to make a $50 savings deposit, and get your first china or stoneware place setting absolutely FREE! Take your choice: 3-pc. durable stoneware in rich "Summertime" floral; or 4-pc. fine china in delicate "Wild Flower" pattern, both

from famous W.M. Dalton. Remember, our FREE place setting offer ends October 10th. But even after that date, you can still buy additional place settings and accessory pieces with each $25 savings deposit, at costs well under regular retail prices!

So take Mary's advice, and make your $50 deposit before October 10th. Then get into an Energy Bank savings habit, so you can complete your collection. Hurry! It's the perfect setting for saving at the Bank of Oak Ridge.

The Energy Bank

Bank of Oak Ridge

MAIN OFFICE DOWNTOWN/WEST END/ JACKSON SQUARE/CLINTON/LAKE CITY

What a dish!

OUR 25th YEAR

Member FDIC

13

VALLEY INTER/CHECK CUSTOMERS HAVE ENJOYED CHECKING CONVENIENCE WITH SAVINGS INTEREST SINCE JAN. 1, 1979.

It's as simple as ABC.

At Valley Bank, you can enjoy all the convenience of a checking account *plus* your money earns the interest of a savings account. It's a winning combination!

Banking at the Valley, with Inter/Check, you will always have a zero balance in your checking account. You make deposits to your savings account where each and every dollar starts earning interest at 5¼% which is compounded daily. It's a moneymaker!

Checks are written as always, and we automatically transfer funds from your *savings* account to your *checking* account—thus covering the amount of the check. The rest of your money remains in savings—continuing to earn interest it never earned before. Inter/Check—two accounts working together for your best interest!

Inter/Check provides you the flexibility of a regular checking account, but your money is in savings . . . earning interest every day. For full banking services—come to The Leader. Come to the Valley. Let us tell you more about this money-making plan—NOW!

"The Leader"
Valley Bank

Valley Fidelity Bank & Trust Company
Knoxville, TN

15

Civic Savings paid for our vacation

The interest we have in our savings account paid for our vacation this year, and we didn't even have to bother the principle.

So — we got a nice vacation this year, thanks to Civic Savings, and we still have our nest egg.

Civic Savings can help you — ask about one of their 12 types of savings accounts.

Add a little to your C&S
savings account regularly-
and watch it grow.

C & S Bank ⑤

The Commercial & Savings Bank
25 Court Street   Silver Bridge Plaza   Spring Valley   Member FDIC

Some good reasons to save from a good place to save- the Peoples Bank

Peoples Bank Olive Hill

Member FDIC

Get a Free "I Love Evanston" cap and scarf.

Free cold weather coverage, when you deposit $300 to a new or existing savings account.

No matter how much you love Evanston, you have to admit it gets cold during the winter. Now there's a way to fight the cold and show your loyalty. With an "I Love Evanston" cap and scarf.

Made of comfortable, washable Orlon acrylic fiber, cap and scarf sets are available in sky blue and white or navy and white.

And all you have to do to get a set for yourself or a chilly friend is deposit

$300 to a new or existing savings account at any of our three offices. Offer good only while supply lasts, so hurry. There's sure to be more cold weather coming.

Offer starts December 4, 1980.

 FirstBank Evanston ™

We care more.

First National Bank and Trust Company of Evanston, a unit of First Illinois Corporation,
800 Davis Street/901 Grove Street/1900 Central Street, Evanston, IL 60204/866-5500/273-4200/Member FDIC.
Deposits insured up to $100,000 by FDIC.

advertising supplement to Suburban Tribune

PRICELESS!

You can't buy this limited edition "I Love Evanston" tote, because its free with a $300 deposit to a new or existing savings account.

It's exclusive. It's stylish. And it's specially designed in a limited quantity to let Evanstonians express their feelings about the place they call home.

FirstBank's "I Love Evanston" totebag is also very practical. Made of rugged pale beige canvas duck, with chocolate brown lettering and a bright red heart, it's sturdy enough to carry just about anything you put in. The slim lines disguise a surprisingly large capacity (14″ across, 3″ wide, and 13½″ deep).

So hurry in to FirstBank Evanston and be one of the lucky ones to get an "I Love Evanston" totebag.

Offer good while supply lasts. Starts September 18.

 FirstBank Evanston ™
We care more.

First National Bank and Trust Company of Evanston. A Unit of First Illinois Corporation.
800 Davis Street/901 Grove Street/1900 Central Street, Evanston, IL 60204/866-5500/273-4200/Member FDIC

Deposits insured up to $100,000 by FDIC.

advertising supplement to Suburban Tribune

21

"Other banks give you a choice of savings plans. We help you choose."

Ron Anderson, Personal FirstBanker

Nowadays, most banks offer a variety of savings plans. But that only makes your decision more difficult. How do you decide what's best for you?

FirstBank has the solution. Ask Ronald Anderson, or any of our Personal FirstBankers. They can explain the differences between CD's and Money Market Certificates. Or give you the low-down on Savings Accounts and Savings Certificates. And they won't stop with an explanation, they'll advise you on what's best for your own needs.

So call Ronald Anderson or any Personal FirstBanker at 866-5680. We give you a choice and help you make a good one.

 FirstBank Evanston™
We care more.

First National Bank and Trust Company of Evanston. A Unit of First Illinois Corporation.
800 Davis Street/901 Grove Street/1900 Central Street/Evanston, IL 60204/866-5500/273-4200/Member FDIC.
All deposits insured up to $100,000 by FDIC.

Because of our London connection,

we offer 3 unique advantages in the Eurodollar CD Market.

Carroll McEntee & McGinley's Eurodollar CD package centers around a close relationship with Jessel, Toynbee & Co. Limited, a leading London discount house.

With Jessel, Toynbee's assistance, we deliver these significant advantages to you: better, quicker information for investment decisions; substantial savings in transaction costs because Jessel, Toynbee is recognized as an authorized depository by the Bank of England; and simplification of each transaction, often completed with just a phone call to CM & M.

With CM & M's package you don't need a London banker to participate in the Eurodollar CD Market. Call us for details today.

CARROLL McENTEE & McGINLEY INCORPORATED
40 Wall Street, New York, N.Y. 10005
(212) 825-6780

Your eagle eye on the government market

An investment as sound as the land they work.

The Farm Credit Banks offer you an opportunity to invest directly in America. In her land. In her farms and ranches. In the multi-billion-dollar business that is agriculture.

We're a cooperative credit enterprise owned by nearly a million American farmers and 4,000 of their marketing, supply and business service organizations. Providing credit services to farmers, ranchers and their cooperatives through the 12 Federal Land Banks, 12 Federal Intermediate Credit Banks and the 13 Banks for Cooperatives throughout the country.

We put your money where your heart is—in the heartland of America—because the land works for everyone, including

investors. And in our more than 60 years of raising billions of dollars for agriculture we have never failed to repay principal and interest on our securities.

Farm Credit Securities are backed by solid collateral—land, buildings, sophisticated equipment, livestock and other agricultural assets.

For further information on how you can invest in American agriculture, contact your investment counselor or write FISCAL AGENCY, FARM CREDIT BANKS, 90 William Street, New York, N.Y. 10038.

FARM CREDIT BANKS

26

Last Wednesday C.J.Etherington Was Spotted Leaving Mutual Federal With Silver He Didn't Pay For.

And we didn't even call the police. You see, we gave him the silver. Free or at greatly reduced prices. Just for making a qualifying deposit to his savings account.

We'd love to do the same for you. Choose from any of 14 hostess items by International Silver. All you have to do is make a qualifying deposit

to a new or existing savings account at Mutual Federal Savings. While your savings grow with us, you can enjoy the beauty and value of fine silver. Without paying a fortune for it. Now, that's an investment!

Mutual Federal Savings

Here's how to qualify for International Silver	Initial qualifying deposit for FREE gift or discount purchase			With each additional deposit of $50, you pay only
	$250 or more	$1,000 or more	$5,000 or more	
1. Goblets water, wine or sherbet	FREE	FREE		5.50
2. Chamberstick with candle	FREE	FREE	ANY	3.95
3. Bon Bon Dish	FREE	FREE	TWO	3.95
4. 10″ Round Tray	3.95	FREE	ITEMS	5.95
5. 4 Coasters	3.95	FREE	FREE	5.95
6. Relish Set	3.95	FREE		5.95
7. 3 pc. Salad Set	8.95	5.95	FREE	10.95
8. Flower Arranger	9.95	6.95	FREE	11.95
9. Pr. Candlesticks	9.95	6.95	FREE	11.95
10. Wine Rack	11.95	8.95	FREE	13.95
11. Carafe	14.95	11.95	6.95	16.95
12. Cracker n' Cheese	17.95	14.95	9.95	19.95
13. 60 oz. Casserole	19.95	16.95	11.95	21.95
14. 4 pc. Coffee Set	32.95	29.95	24.95	34.95
Eight Goblets	37.95	34.95	29.95	43.95

Norfolk, Virginia Beach, Portsmouth, Hampton, Williamsburg

What's a 'substantial penalty for early withdrawal'?

Do you lose your freedom . . . or your house, car and kids . . . or do you have to mow the lawn at your nearest United Federal office?

The answer: none of the above.

A 'substantial penalty' means not receiving some of the interest a Certificate of Deposit (CD) would have earned had the original deposit (principal) remained untouched for the full term of the CD.

Generally, this could amount to three to six months' interest depending on the length of time of the CD and the amount of principal withdrawn.

You never lose any of the money you originally deposited (principal).

This penalty for early withdrawal of any principal from a CD is a federal regulation which applies to all banks and savings and loan associations.

But a big difference at United Federal is our savings consultants. They can explain all of the facts on the many savings plans available today. In plain talk.

Visit with our savings consultants soon. You'll enjoy 'substantial benefits' by saving with the professionals at United Federal.

UNITED FEDERAL

SAVINGS & LOAN ASSOCIATION

Dothan / Ozark / Eufaula / Alabaster / Columbiana
Member Federal Savings & Loan Insurance Corporation
Your Savings Insured to $40,000
An Equal Opportunity Lender

Plain talk for savers.

Who really pays the highest interest?

You've read the claims: "We Pay High Interest," "We Pay Higher Interest," "We Pay The Highest Interest."

The fact is, the federal government establishes the same maximum interest rates on savings for all savings and loans. Likewise for all banks although a bank's interest rates are generally one-quarter percent less than a savings and loan's.

United Federal pays the maximum rate on its various savings plans. But others may not. Make sure you ask.

There is a big difference, however, in the way financial institutions add interest to your original deposit (compounding). United Federal compounds continuously. This is the most preferred technique because your money is constantly working for you. "Continuous" compounding is slightly better than "daily" compounding and definitely more desirable than "monthly" or "quarterly" compounding.

To appreciate the difference compounding can make, ask the institutions you are considering what the return on your investment (yield) will be if you put $1,000 in an account for one year.

Another big difference at United Federal is our savings consultants. Whether you have $300 or $300,000 to work with, we can help you develop a personal savings plan to meet your specific needs. Visit us soon.

UNITED FEDERAL
SAVINGS & LOAN ASSOCIATION
Dothan / Ozark / Eufaula / Alabaster / Columbiana
Member Federal Savings & Loan Insurance Corporation
Your Savings Insured to $40,000
An Equal Opportunity Lender

Plain talk for savers.

Cash Action. We pay while you save!

Cash Action. It sounds like money moving to a disco beat. In reality, it's a savings account from which United Federal can pay your bills.

With Cash Action, your money isn't sitting idle as it would be in a checking account. It's earning interest at 5½% and compounding continuously.

To get started, tell United Federal which bills you would like to set up for automatic payment.

If you want United Federal to handle a special bill just call the Cash Action number, 793-6630, Monday through Saturday from 8:00 a.m. to 8:00 p.m.

There is no service charge for Cash Action as long as your account balance is $300 or more.

And there is no limit on the number of transactions you can make.

United Federal will mail you a monthly statement to confirm all the transactions you authorized.

Visit with our Savings Consultants soon. Ask them about Cash Action.

UNITED FEDERAL
SAVINGS & LOAN ASSOCIATION

Dothan: 411 North Foster St., Northside Mall (Main Level), Circle West Shopping Center / Ozark: 101 Painter Ave. South / Member Federal Savings and Loan Insurance Corporation / Your Savings Insured to $40,000 / An Equal Opportunity Lender

Plain talk for savers.

Two kids in college is a crash course in economics. For parents.

It takes more than good grades to get through college nowadays. It also takes about $20,000.* And the way things are going, that figure could easily double before long.

But that's just the bad news. The good news is, at Home Federal Savings we can help you put your children through college without putting your budget through the wringer. Because Home Federal people like Margaret Adams and Tom Barbour have been helping their customers keep up with the higher costs of higher education for years.

"The key, of course, is to start *thinking* about college, and *saving* for college, long before your children are old enough to go off to college," explains Margaret.

"For example, if you've got a couple of pre-schoolers now, you should try to put $100 a month for each of them into a regular passbook savings account. As your money accumulates and interest is added, you can transfer part of it into one of our long-term, high interest certificates of deposit, and start the process all over again.

"Then, when they get ready to go off to college, at current

Margaret Adams and Tom Barbour of Home Federal Savings

interest rates they should have somewhere in the neighborhood of $30,000 apiece."

If your children are older, of course, you might have to employ a slightly different strategy. Either by saving a larger amount of money each month, or by having someone at Home Federal put together a combination of savings and financing programs.

"A lot of people forget that they've got a great deal of equity built up in their home," says Tom. "Well, financing your children's education is certainly an admirable way to make that equity work *for* you, instead of just sitting there. We've helped many people obtain a suitable mortgage for educational expenses, and in some cases we've even refinanced an existing loan in order to free up the cash families needed for college."

So stop by and talk with Margaret or Tom or any of our people today. Because of all the things you could give your children, a college education may well be the most important. After all, it's about the only thing nobody can take away from them.

Home Federal Savings

Charlotte: Uptown, Cotswold, Park Road Shopping Center, and Eastland. North Mecklenburg: I-77 and Highway 73. Telephone 373-0400.
*Based on average tuition, room, board, and incidental expenses at both public and private colleges, as reported by The College Scholarship Service, a subsidiary of The College Board.

Searching for the Highest Rate? You'll find it right here at Home.

10.294%.

Good thru Wednesday, Sept. 19.

6 Month Term "Money Market" Certificate*

$10,000 minimum, no additional deposits. Rate remains in effect the full 6 month term of the certificate.
For more information, call 373-0400.

*Withdrawals on Money Market Certificates prior to maturity
are subject to a substantial penalty as required by law.

Home Federal Savings

Downtown, Park Road, Cotswold, Eastland   Member FSLIC

34

CHECK OUT STATE FEDERAL'S SUPERMARKET OF SAVINGS.

NEW! 5.50%

ANNOUNCING HIGHER-INTEREST PASSBOOK ACCOUNTS; THE MAIN MEAT FOR ANY SAVINGS DIET.

Perfect for quick and easy savings, State Federal's Passbook Account earns 5½% interest! $5 minimum to open, with funds earning from date of deposit to date of withdrawal. Interest compounded daily and paid quarterly, producing an annual yield of 5.65% when earnings are left in the account to compound for one year. Existing State Federal Accounts automatically change to the new rate.

CHOICE AGED SAVINGS WITH SPECIAL TAX CUTS

8.00%

INDIVIDUAL AND KEOGH PLAN RETIREMENT ACCOUNTS

State's Individual Retirement Account (IRA) and Keogh Retirement Account—two great savings plans designed to bring home the bacon at retirement, while earning you 8% interest and a tax break today.

The IRA is a tax deductible, tax-deferred savings account for full or part-time workers without an approved pension plan. And you could qualify to deposit (and deduct) up to $1,750 each year, with the interest you earn also tax-deferred.

Keogh, for the self-employed and unincorporated, works much the same as IRA: 8% tax-deferred earnings and tax deductible deposits. Yet, you may qualify for an even bigger yearly tax break of up to $7500 each year.

Federal regulations require an interest penalty for withdrawal of IRA or Keogh funds prior to age 59½. IRA and Keogh plan accounts insured to $100,000 by the FSLIC.

SAVE BIG! WITH A JUMBO SAVINGS PACKAGE

$100,000 MINIMUM

For those who like those rare opportunities to earn even higher interest on their savings, State Federal offers an exclusive selection of Jumbo Savings Certificates, requiring a minimum deposit of $100,000 (or more) to open.

State's Jumbos feature a good choice in attractive interest rates, compounded quarterly, with terms varying from 6 months to 1 year.

For more information and current rates, call State's Jumbo Line, 583-8111, Ext. 235.

Jumbo withdrawals subject to interest penalty if made prior to maturity.

MEMBER FSLIC & USDA*
*United State's Deposit Accounts

OFFERING THE NEWEST IN FSLIC GOVERNMENT INSPECTED, GRADE A, NO. 1, UNCONDITIONALLY GUARANTEED SAVINGS PLANS, FIT FOR ANY FAMILY'S TASTES AND BUDGET.

MIX OR MATCH ACCOUNTS! STARTING JULY 1ST.

JUST ARRIVED!

4/$250

THE NEW 4-YEAR, $250 MINIMUM MONEY MARKET CERTIFICATE

The Money Market Certificate has been made even more affordable by State Federal.

With only a $250 minimum deposit required, State's newest 4-year Money Market Certificate pays an interest rate that's 1% below the average 4-year rate of U.S. Treasury securities. And you still earn ¼% more than your bank pays on this type of certificate.

While the rate on this new type of certificate changes monthly, you're guaranteed to earn the same high rate in which you opened the account for the full four years . . . with interest compounded quarterly.

Certificate withdrawals are subject to an interest penalty if made prior to maturity. Yet, like our regular savings certificates, *these penalties have been reduced at State Federal.*

WEEKLY SPECIALS OF TOP CHOICE, 6-MONTH MONEY MARKET CERTIFICATES

$10,000 MINIMUM

Feast on high interest with weekly specials on the highly-rated Money Market Certificate from State Federal (see Wednesday night/Thursday morning paper for this week's rate, or call any State office).

A State Federal Money Market Certificate can be opened in any amount over $10,000, and has a maturity of 182 days. There are still no fees or services charges, and your deposit is fully protected up to $40,000 by FSLIC insurance.

Federal regulations now prohibit compounding on Money Market Certificates. Interest penalty for premature withdrawal.

LEAVE STATE HOLDING THE BAG

Walk in to any State Federal location today, and walk out with a free heavy duty shopping bag. No deposit required. Limit one per person while supplies last.

BAG HIGHER INTEREST

—PLUS, EVERYDAY VALUES IN SAVINGS AND LOAN SERVICES

- Financial Counseling
- Savings Loans
- Conventional Home Loans
- Home Equity Loans
- Home Improvement Loans
- Transmatic Services
- Free Parking
- Notary Publics

PRICES SLASHED! ON CHOICE SAVINGS CERTIFICATES

NOW FEATURING THE NEW $250 MINIMUM DEPOSIT ON ALL OF STATE'S REGULAR CERTIFICATES.

Beef up your savings today, now that the minimum deposit requirement on all State Federal regular certificates has been drastically reduced.

With the new $250 minimum deposit, you now have four times the choices in interest earnings for the same deposit you used to pay. Plus, with any of six certificates you choose, you still earn ¼% more than your bank pays!

A SPECIAL OFFER

Open your State Federal savings certificate by July 10th, and your deposit will earn from July 1st! That's up to 10 days of free interest.

8.00%
Term: 8-10 years
Minimum: $250
Annual Yield*: 8.24%

7.75%
Term: 6-8 years
Minimum: $250
Annual Yield*: 7.98%

7.50%
Term: 4-6 years
Minimum: $250
Annual Yield*: 7.71%

6.75%
Term: 2½-4 years
Minimum: $250
Annual Yield*: 6.92%

6.50%
Term: 1-2½ years
Minimum: $250
Annual Yield*: 6.66%

5.75%
Term: 90 days
Minimum: $250
Annual Yield*: 5.88%

*When earnings are left in the account to compound for one year. Interest is compounded and paid quarterly. Certificate withdrawals subject to interest penalty if made prior to maturity. Yet, these penalties have now been reduced at State Federal.

SAFE, PROTECTED AND INSURED BY THE FSLIC ON EACH ACCOUNT UP TO

$40,000

AS ADVERTISED SPECIALS

A SUPER MARKET SELECTION OF CONVENIENT STORE LOCATIONS:

TULSA – 583-8111 Downtown, between 6th and 7th on Boston. Open 8:30 am to 4:30 pm, M-F.

Corner of 41st and Darlington, just east of Southland. Open 9:00 am to 4:30 pm, M-F. Open 9:00 am to 1:00 pm, Saturday.

Northeast corner, 31st and Mingo. Open 9:00 am to 4:30 pm, M-F.

71st Street, just east of Sheridan and next to Ziegfield's. Open 9:00 am to 4:30 pm, M-F.

BROKEN ARROW – 251-7426 709 West Washington in Sequoyah Shopping Center. Open 9:00 am to 4:30 pm, M-F.

SHAWNEE – (405) 275-1771 120 North Bell. Open 9:00 am to 4:00 pm, M-F.

State Federal Savings
AND LOAN

35

Save at Karen's

Karen Kresslov can show you how to put more of your hard-earned money into an IRA and less into the IRS.

She probably knows as much about Individual Retirement Accounts as anybody in Charlotte.

So stop by Karen's place today, or call 373-0400, and find out how to get more out of retirement than a gold watch.

HomeFederal Savings

Downtown, Park Road, Cotswold, Eastland

Save at Tom's

Tom Barbour can help you keep the wolves away when you get ready to send your little lambs off to school.

He's got three children of his own—one presently enrolled at UNC-Chapel Hill—so he really understands the idea of saving for your childrens' education.

So stop by Tom's place today, or call 373-0400. And start keeping pace with the higher cost of higher education.

Home Federal Savings

Downtown, Park Road, Cotswold, Eastland

FARM & HOME HAS JUST REMOVED THE FINAL BARRIER BETWEEN YOU AND HIGHER INTEREST.

No more minimums on certificates,* including our new 4-Year Money Market Certificate.

At Farm & Home, you can now buy Certificates of Deposit, including our new high rate 4-Year Money Market Certificate, without having to put up the hefty minimum deposit that many other financial institutions require.*

So now, you no longer need a lot of money to begin earning top interest. In fact, you can get a 4-Year Money Market Certificate, paying 8.20% interest for as little as five dollars.

The same no minimum policy applies to our full range of certificates.*

If you've shopped around, you know that many financial institutions won't let you earn today's higher interest unless you put up a lot of money. But at Farm & Home, all customers — not just a select few — can earn the highest rates allowed by federal regulations on insured accounts.

On these Certificates, you can get bonus interest,* too. Savings deposits received by the 10th of the month earn from the first of the month when left until the end of the quarter.

So if big minimum deposits have discouraged you from setting aside some money for the future, come to Farm & Home Savings, where you'll get more money for your money.

And that's not just a slogan. It's a fact that sets Farm & Home apart from many other financial institutions.

Farm & Home Savings
Association

*Federal regulations prohibit compounding, bonus interest and require a $10,000 minimum on 26-Week Money Market Certificates; and require a substantial interest penalty for early withdrawal from all certificates. Assets in excess of $2.1 billion. Home Office, Nevada, Missouri.

Getting deeper and deeper into liability insurance payments? Here's a big idea if you're exposed to professional or product risks or if you sponsor health and welfare programs.

Now, you can save yourself some money *and* improve risk management with a well-designed Self-Insured Program. In simplest terms, self-insurance is that portion of your coverage which you agree to retain as a business risk, resulting in lower cost of insurance.

Colorado National Bank is not in the insurance business. But we can help. Working with you and your benefits consultant, we'll assist in program planning, and provide the asset management, operational services and coordination you'll need. We'll also tell you about proposed legislation that may soon give tax incentives to those who self-insure.

Save yourself from the high cost of insurance. For full details on another big idea, contact a member of our Self-Insured Programs Team: John Holt, Irv Berlau or Rick Rosen. (303) 893-1862.

COLORADO NATIONAL BANK We make big ideas happen.

Member FDIC   17th & Champa St., Denver, CO 80202

41

The Big Payoff At First.

Instant Interest At First.

43

Premium Interest At First.

We'll pay you 11.75% with an annual yield of 12.4% interest on a 2½-year Payoff Savings Investment-Plus Certificate. And we'll give you the interest for the whole 2½ years *on the day you bring your money in!*

And if that's not interesting enough, we'll give you all or part of your interest in one of a long list of spectacular premiums the day you deposit your money. You can choose from a 10-speed bike to an around-the-world trip for two. It's premium interest at First. And it's the best way we can think of to present our most exciting new savings plan.

The minimum amount you can deposit is $1,000. To earn even more money on your money, you can deposit it for as long as 10 years. You can even borrow against the money you deposit.

Instant Interest.

If you'd rather, you can take your interest in cold, hard cash right on the spot. And the amount you get is why we called our plan Payoff Savings.

For instance, the immediate cash interest payment to you for a deposit of $1,000 is $254.54. For $5,000 it's $1,272.69. And for $50,000 it's $12,726.86—all on the very day you make your deposit! To find out more about Payoff Savings, please give us a call. Or drop in.

Either way, act now and get into Payoff Savings. And get the big payoff at First.

We're changing first.

FIRST NATIONAL BANK

205 W. Oak, Fort Collins, Colorado 80521, 303-482-4861
Member FDIC

Offer good for a limited time only.
Federal law requires a substantial interest penalty for early withdrawal on time deposits.
Interest and premiums received during this program are considered to be taxable income by the Internal Revenue Service.
Interest received in advance is a discounted interest rate.

How Much Is That Doggie In The Window?

Meet Obie, the sound-activated puppy that starts and stops on command.

Give Obie the order and watch him bark, walk, move his head and tail, and sit up and beg. Tell him to stop, and Obie obeys.

He's the new action sensation that "comes alive" with fun for boys and girls of all ages.*

You can give Obie (a $22.95 retail value) to your favorite boy or girl by giving us a $500 savings deposit, and $5 cash, plus tax.

You can open a new account, or add to an existing account. And you'll earn the highest legal interest for that type of account, compounded daily for maximum yield.

Come in and get the puppy that barks, walks, wags his tail, sits up and begs, starts and stops at your command, and earns you the highest legal interest, too. Only at Bank of the West.

This is a limited time offer, and may be discontinued at any time, without notice. Limited one to a customer, available only at these offices:

414 California Avenue, Palo Alto
353 University Avenue, Palo Alto
240 Third Street, Los Altos
501 Castro Street, Mountain View
717 Oak Grove Avenue, Menlo Park.

Bank of the West.

*Obie operates on 2 C cell batteries, not included. For your convenience, batteries will be available for purchase at our specified offices for the duration of this offer.

MEMBER FDIC

45

WITH THE FREEDOM
TO FAIL, COMES THE FREEDOM
TO SUCCEED.

In Andrew Jackson's time, there were safer things than defending New Orleans or crossing America in a covered wagon. Today, there are safer places to put your money than Commodity Futures.

But what opportunity. Which, as the world's leading and largest Futures exchange, is the subject we'd like to address.

If you're one of the many new people considering a Commodity or Financial Futures Contract, we advise you to listen closely when your broker tells you not to over-extend on any one trade. That increases risk and diminishes opportunity.

Successful futures traders expect to be wrong often. When wrong, they strive to exit fast. Cut losses. Or, when right, to realize gains. But always according to plan. To execute such a strategy you need a liquid market. Or put another way, the ability to get in and out fast.

And at the Chicago Board of Trade, that's precisely what we offer you.

For our information package **Call 800/621-4641. In Illinois 800/572-4217. Or ask your broker.**

 Chicago Board of Trade

47

HE WHO IS AFRAID
TO MAKE MISTAKES IS
AFRAID TO SUCCEED.

Edison, the Wright Brothers, Alexander Graham Bell. They all made mistakes before they reached their goals.

It's the same for successful Commodity and Financial Futures traders. For them, being very right once can more than compensate for several mistakes.

Successful traders follow the maxim of "cutting losses and letting profits run." They strive to identify a price movement and, if right, stay with it. If wrong, to trade rapidly. Always according to plan, of course.

Central to this strategy is a highly liquid market. One with a large volume of trading. To allow easy entry to and exit from the market.

And at the Chicago Board of Trade, the world's leading and largest Futures exchange, that's precisely what we offer you.

If you have the financial ability to participate in this market, further exploration could prove quite rewarding.

For our information package **Call 800/621-4641. In Illinois 800/572-4217. Ask your broker. Or write to our Marketing Department.**

 Chicago Board of Trade

141 W. Jackson Blvd., Chicago, IL 60604

48

NONE OF HIS INVENTIONS HAD THE DOLLAR IMPACT OF FINANCIAL FUTURES.

Invented 5 years ago by the Chicago Board of Trade.

First GNMA Futures. Then, 2 years later, Treasury Bond Futures. *So far, over 11,000,000 Financial Futures contracts have been traded. Unprecedented growth.

With this new trading vehicle a financial institution could protect against an unfavorable interest rate move; the same way those in agriculture could protect against an unfavorable commodity price move.

At the same time, vast new opportunities were opened for the knowledgeable speculator with venture capital. If interest rates moved his way, just a small shift could mean large profits. And if he was wrong, our high volume of trading (liquidity) helped him get out quickly.

Such opportunity, combined with the experience and reputation of the world's leading and largest Financial Futures exchange, explains the success of our new contracts.

Perhaps you should learn more.

*Futures contracts in U.S. Government debt are not obligations of the U.S. Treasury Department.

For our information package **Call 800/621-4641. In Illinois 800/572-4217. Ask your broker. Or write to our Marketing Department.**

 **Chicago Board of Trade**

141 W. Jackson Blvd., Chicago, IL 60604

49

IN TODAY'S WORLD, WOULDN'T WASHINGTON BE ADVISED TO HEDGE?

WITH DOUBLE-DIGIT INFLATION, WOULD HE HAVE TRADED CORN FUTURES?

Thomas Jefferson knew how to raise crops, make money and help form and guide a new nation.

But Corn Futures? Too risky?

Our answer: Whatever his decision, he certainly would have learned the facts. Not depended on word of mouth reports of tremendous profits. Or of tremendous losses.

The fact is, opportunity does exist in Corn Futures for the knowledgeable, adequately funded individual. And along with that opportunity, risk.

However, with a carefully worked out plan, there *are* ways to diminish risk.

It's a proven concept. In operation for 132 years at the Chicago Board of Trade, the world's leading and largest volume futures exchange.

Corn, Wheat, Soybean or Oat Futures. The opportunity is here.

For our information package. **Call 800/621-4641.**
In Illinois 800/572-4217. Or ask your broker.

 Chicago Board of Trade

Get a jump on tomorrow's money market.

You can. Very simply. Start doing business with a money organization that has a reputation for being out front and getting things done. Specifically, Naples Federal.

When many savings institutions discouraged high-yield, no-risk money market instruments because of "low-profit," Naples Federal not only sold them, we promoted them. Today, our customers are reaping the rewards.

When money got tight, many lending institutions had to cut off their mortgage funds. But, thanks to sound financial planning, Naples Federal had a reasonably steady flow of money available for local home buyers.

About the future. With more economic pressures, personal money management may get even tougher tomorrow than it is today. But Naples Federal can help you stay ahead of it.

Here's how. As new investment programs are created, we plan to make them available to you as fast as possible. As new financial services are unveiled, we plan to imple-

ment them quickly, with no wasted motion. As Government restrictions are modified, we plan to initiate programs that help you take advantage of these changes. Some, like Checking Accounts and Personal Loans are already available at Naples Federal.

The point is, if you're serious about getting the jump on tomorrow's money market, come to Naples Federal and team up with a leader.

Naples Federal
More than just a friendly smile.

Naples Federal Savings and Loan Association, a New York Stock Exchange Company, with offices throughout Southwest Florida.

52

Investments of $100,000 or more work harder at Dollar.

At Dollar Savings we know how important it is to keep your investment money active. Because every moment you delay, can cost you money. ⑤ So if you have $100,000 or more to invest, we'll help you design the best possible investment plan to earn the highest interest for your money. ⑤ Call me, Bob Carroll, today at

228-6851 for our current negotiated rates. Or stop in at any of our 12 convenient Columbus locations. We won't waste time in making sure your big investments work hard to earn big interest, too.

Your Dollar works harder.

Robert S. Carroll
Vice President — Sales

DOLLAR SAVINGS

Would you put your money on the bull or the bullfighter?

Merrill Lynch is currently pushing Money Market funds as a choice investment. At Naples Federal, we agree with that. Unfortunately, a little confusion is being pushed along with it: Is it better to invest in Money Market funds from Merrill Lynch, the stockbroker; or to invest in Money Market Certificates from Naples ▬▬▬▬▬ the financial institution? ▬▬ re some facts. You decide.

Brokerage firms sell Money Market funds at a daily rate and that rate can change every day. This means that you can't be sure from one day to the next how much money you're making. Or losing.

Not so at Naples Federal. For example, the rate on our new 30-month, $100 Money Market

Certificate is guaranteed for the life of the Certificate. Even if the weekly rate goes down, your rate stays up. This means you can literally lock yourself into the current high interest rate for the next 2½ years. Guaranteed.

Money Market funds purchased from private brokerage firms are not insured by a Federal agency.

But they are at Naples Federal. Our Money Market Certificates (including C.D.'s and other cash investment plans) are insured up to $40,000 by the Federal Savings & Loan Insurance Corporation and are offered at the highest interest rate you can earn under this kind of Federal Agency protection. Included under this protection are a variety of Certificates: 6-month $10,000 minimum; 30-month $100 minimum; and our jumbo $100,000 negotiable-rate Certificate.

And Naples Federal doesn't charge a fee or commission of any kind.

One final thought. Some families' plans call for more extensive investing and long-term planning than others. If yours does, we've got expert Money Consultants who can create a unique financial plan for you. A plan that offers guaranteed interest, high yield, and no risk to your capital.

Call Naples Federal now (collect) at 263-2100. We'll show you how to be bullish without the bull.

FSLIC

Naples Federal
More than just a friendly smile.
Naples Federal Savings and Loan Association with 12 Offices throughout Southwest Florida.

MONEY MARKET RATE LINE
263-2100

MAKE A HIGH-YIELD NO-RISK PHONE CALL.

This number is the Money Market Line at Naples Federal. Dial it. You'll set some high power investment machinery into motion for yourself.

For example, call on Tuesday and we'll tell you exactly what the Money Market rate is for the week. You'll know the current rate two days before the general public knows it. You can watch trends, monitor ups and downs, and anticipate how the market might go.

But our Money Market Line opens the door to something even more important.

It gives you instant contact with a Money Consultant at Naples Federal. A person who can help you create an investment program, customized to your lifestyle and circumstances. Always with an eye for locking in high-yield, no-risk investments, all insured by an agency of the Federal Government.

Some examples of our Money Market programs are: 6-month/$10,000 minimum certificate; 30-month/$100 minimum certificate; and our new $100,000 negotiable-

rate, jumbo certificate. And new programs for saving and investing are on the horizon.

How about that. A Money Market quote before half the world knows it. Also, instant contact with a Money Consultant at Naples Federal for expert investment advice. All by telephone.

It's the next best thing to being here. **FSLIC**

Naples Federal
More than just a friendly smile.
Naples Federal Savings and Loan Association with 12 Offices throughout Southwest Florida.

A Monte Carlo vacatic
Chevy Chase Savings & Lo
April 12th at Arliss

Chevy Chase is going places! On Saturday, April 12th, from 9:30AM to 2PM, we'll be opening the doors of our 12th branch office in the Arliss Shopping Center. And we're celebrating in a big way. With a dayful of festivities, free gifts and a drawing for four exciting travel prizes, including an 8-day vacation for two in Monte Carlo. At Chevy Chase, we want you to go places with us!

High-Spirited Activities

The festivities will get off to a flying start at 10AM, Saturday, April 12th with free kites. Courtesy of the clown who'll be on hand for your amusement. We'll

have cotton candy for sweet tooths. A Dixieland Band for jazzy accompaniment. And a "Moon-bounce" air pillow that'll have your kids literally jumping for joy.

Open an account at our Arliss Grand Opening and take home a free canvas tote bag. Attractive and sturdy, it's perfect for long trips or every day errands. And there's no minimum deposit needed to get one.

Take Off with Great Travel Prizes

Enter our Grand Prize Drawing with the coupon attached and you could win any one of the following fabulous prizes. Drawings will take place at 11:00, 12:00, 1:00 and 2:00 on April 12th, 1980. You don't have to make a deposit to enter or be present to win.

First Prize: 8-Day Vacation for Two in Monte Carlo (Drawing at 2:00)

It's the French Riviera's most luxurious resort. Monte Carlo, Monaco. Spend your days soaking up the Mediterranean sun, snorkelling, sailing and waterskiing. Or playing golf on Mon Carlo's magnificent 18-hole course stretching 3,000 feet above th sea. At night you' enjoy the world famous Mon Carlo Casino, superb restaurants, posl nightclub and the fine in entertainment. Our

Money in our bank

MONEY MARKET CERTIFICATE

is worth more than corn in your bin.

Assuming you have 5,000 bushels of corn in storage, you could sell it today for about $2.10 a bushel, or $10,500.00.

By investing in a First Security 6-month money market certificate at 13.549%, you'll earn $709.38 when the C.D. matures this October. This is a return of over 14¢/bushel.

Your corn is now worth $2.24 a bushel on today's market.

Your corn could deteriorate during 6 months of on-farm storage and cost you 6 cents per bushel. By selling on today's market you save that 6 cents and

Your corn is now worth $2.30 on today's market.

If your corn is stored at the elevator, 6 months storage charges would amout to about 12¢/bushel. By selling now,

Your corn is now worth $2.36 on today's market.

Use your own pencil; we think you'll find your money in our bank is worth more than corn in your bin.

FIRST SECURITY BANK + TRUST COMPANY

Charles City, Marble Rock, Ionia. Member FDIC.
Substantial interest penalty for early withdrawal of certificates.

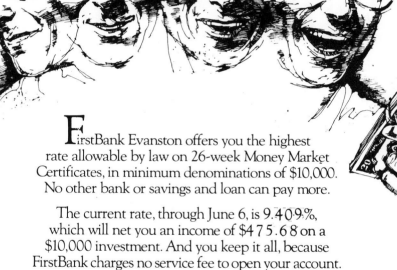

AMERICAN SAVINGS MAKES DOLLARS AND SENSE OUT OF THE NEW SAVINGS REGULATIONS.

New government savings regulations and guidelines are now in effect. By understanding how they work, you can make more money.

The regulations are complicated, interest rates change monthly, sometimes weekly. It really takes an expert to understand them. American Savings has more than a hundred professional Savings Counselors behind our <u>Earn More Desks</u>. They will explain the regulations to you and show you how to take advantage of them.

Stop by and see one of our Savings Counselors today. They'll give you the best financial advice you've ever had.

PAYING THE HIGHEST INTEREST RATES ALLOWED BY LAW SINCE 1950.

AMERICAN SAVINGS

26 convenient locations to serve you in 19 South Florida cities
In Dade, 673-5566. In Broward, 485-0200. In Palm Beach, 392-6960.
American Savings & Loan Association of Florida. Assets exceeding $1.6 billion.
Your savings insured to $40,000 by an Agency of the Federal Government.
Listed and traded on the New York Stock Exchange

61

A free Centra
...just fo

Cen
N

If your sw
Smucker'
dishes an
toppings.
those chill
When you d
with any o
Timex Wa
Pen. A
for be
si

Ches
1192 Boyls
Other offic

*Except NOW
value. Federal

Bank bunny openers.

...nk/Chestnut Hill and CentralBank/
...m will be giving away gifts to
...itors beginning Thursday, March
...Just deposit $250 or more into any
...or existing savings account*, and
...give you a free bunny... just in time
...ster.

...oth wins out, you can have the
...ae Twosome instead — two sundae
... 6-oz. jars of Smucker's ice cream
...u can choose a 72" x 90" blanket for
...of-winter evenings.

...$5,000 or more, you can walk away
...ne following: A man's or woman's
...allmark's classic Chrome Felt-Tip
...iece Corning Ware Wildflower set,
...cooking and serving. Or, a complete
...piece set of Homer
...lin Ironstone Dinner-
...e, which is both durable
...d attractive.

...sit our Chestnut Hill
...Needham office
...y and take home
...of our free gifts just
...peners.

...Hill Cooperative Bank is now...

63

Invest $500 or more in Western's Special 2½ Year Savings Certificates.

They're guaranteed. They're safe. And we pay more than commercial banks.

2½ years now earns (Feb.1-Feb.29)

10.65%
interest rate

11.43%
annual yield*

Western's rate is ¼% higher than conventional commercial banks. Interest is compounded daily for an even higher yield, and credited monthly.

If you choose, you can have the interest payment sent to you monthly when $5,000 or more is invested, or quarterly, semi-annually or annually when $2,500 or more is invested. You are insured by the Federal Deposit Insurance Corporation for up to $40,000 per ownership. No fees are charged. And your certificate can be renewed automatically after 2½ years at the interest rate in effect at that time.

So why settle for less from other investments such as commercial bank certificates or money market funds? Visit any Western office today.

*Due to leap year, Western pays you 366 days of interest during the first year on all certificates purchased prior to March 1, 1980. The annual yield for the remaining term would be 11.40%.

Federal law applicable to all banks requires that certificates redeemed before maturity will be subject to substantial penalty.

Western
SAVINGS BANK

Member Federal Deposit Insurance Corporation

65

PETERSON BANK PAYS YOU 15% ON A $100,000* C.D.

Tell your chauffeur we're
at 3232 W. Peterson.

Chicago, Illinois 583-6300 • Member FDIC

*Subject to substantial penalty if withdrawn prior to its six month maturity. Federal regulations prohibit the compounding of interest during term of deposit.

68

Uncle Nat Played Santa For Three Generations

And He Never Worried About Paying For It

Before the days when anyone thought about something like a Christmas Club, our Uncle Nat was playing Santa Claus for the whole family. His Santa outfit was makeshift and the whiskers had not quite turned white, but oh how we believed.

Every Christmas there were more children and then came the grandchildren. The year before he died Uncle Nat played Santa to his three great grandchildren. They came all the way from Omaha.

And Nat always had a little present for everyone no matter how many or how old we were. We learned later that he used a special Savings Account designated "Santa Fund."

Today, at the Burlington Savings Bank there is a special convenience known as a Christmas Club. It pays 5½% interest, compounded continuously and lets you end up with anywhere from $50.00 to $1000.00 for next year's Christmas Shopping.

We urge you to open one of these accounts, because Christmas shouldn't be filled with worry about how you're going to pay for it.

We learned that from Uncle Nat.

When you choose to open your account at the Burlington Savings Bank, the two premiums pictured below are available while supplies last.

SYRUP PITCHER
$10 initial deposit

TRIVET
Initial deposit less than $10

 Burlington Savings Bank MEMBER FDIC

71

82

Government Securities.
We originated the idea of trading them in <u>odd lots.</u>

"We love our freedom!"

For growth, flexibility and security.

It's easy to see why people are so enthusiastic about their Freedom Savings accounts. ☐ They like the steady, risk-free financial growth. They appreciate the independence a Freedom Savings account gives them, the easy access to their funds. And they value the security of insur-ance to $100,000 per depositor. ☐ That's why Freedom Savings accounts are included in so many sophis-ticated investment programs. ☐ Make Freedom Savings your family financial center. If you appreciate growth, flexibility and security, you'll love your freedom!

Freedom Savings

When you hear what you can earn on $100,000 in a 30-day certificate, you'll love your freedom!

If you have $100,000 or more to invest right now, call W. Robert Seitz at 273-5767 in Tampa or 1-800-282-7702 (toll-free) outside Tampa. He'll discuss our current rate on 30-day $100,000 certificates and remind you how FSLIC insurance protects your funds to $100,000 per depositor. You'll like what he has to say. And you'll love your freedom!

Federal regulations impose a substantial penalty for early withdrawals from certificates of deposit.

FREEDOM SAVINGS. **Where saving sets you free.** *BRANDON 1101 W. Brandon Blvd., Brandon Mall/*CARROLLWOOD 10821 N. Dale Mabry, Tampa/*DALE MABRY SOUTH 721 S. Dale Mabry, Tampa/*DOWNTOWN 500 Franklin Street, Tampa/*EAST HILLSBOROUGH 1920 East Hillsborough, Tampa/*FOWLER AVENUE 1720 E. Fowler Ave., Tampa/GANDY BOULEVARD 4411 Gandy Boulevard, Tampa/HILLDALE 5205 N. Lois Ave., at Hillsborough, Tampa/*TOWN 'N COUNTRY 7545 W. Hillsborough, Tampa/*WESTSHORE PLAZA 350 Westshore Plaza, Tampa /AUBURNDALE 111 Havendale Blvd./WINTER HAVEN 1120 First Street, South   *24-hour Freedom Machine locations.   24 locations across Florida. Over $1 billion in assets.

War Bonds.
Then Savings Bonds.
Now another change.

New Federal regulations will affect your Series E Bonds.

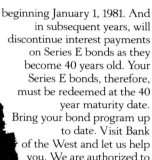

One of every three American households has U.S. Series E Bonds — some dating back 40 years! Now, as of January 2, 1980, these bonds are being discontinued. However new bonds are being introduced to take their place and offer you new investment opportunities.

In addition, Bank of the West wants you to know that the U.S. government will cease paying interest on bonds purchased in 1941, beginning January 1, 1981. And in subsequent years, will discontinue interest payments on Series E bonds as they become 40 years old. Your Series E bonds, therefore, must be redeemed at the 40 year maturity date. Bring your bond program up to date. Visit Bank of the West and let us help you. We are authorized to redeem the old bonds and sell the new issues.

BANK OF THE WEST

$10 million in assets and growing

P.O. Box 310 • Parker Road and Main Street • Parker, Colorado 80134 • 841-4000
Open Monday through Friday, 7am to 6pm, Saturday from 9 to Noon.

Member FDIC

SERIES EE

COLLECT 10 GRAMS OF PURE SILVER ABSOLUTELY FREE

Yours when you deposit $10,000 or more at Majestic. Or get five grams free with a deposit as low as $5,000. Even with lower deposits, you can purchase these valuable, American-made silver ingots at exceptionally low cost. And that's just one example of the kinds of values you can expect when you invest your savings at Majestic.

Complement your ingot with sterling silver jewelry. Choose elegant 14k. solid gold jewelry. Or choose from a broad array of appliances, blankets, electronic items, luggage or tools—all made by the most respected manufacturers— your assurance of value. There are more than 70 choices in all, many of them free with qualifying deposits at Majestic.

I invite you to visit any of Majestic's 40 convenient branches. And take advantage of over 70 ways to get the greatest value for your savings and checking dollars.

Illustration enlarged.

Majestic Savings
WE TAKE PRIDE

88

Jan. 21-Feb. 19 Aquarius

You are highly intelligent, curious, unpredictable and a lot of fun to be with. You respect individuality so it's no wonder you have many, many friends. We're hoping you'll accept our offer of a dollar to open a new savings account at our bank. Since more famous people were born under your sign than any other, someday we can brag that you are our customer.

Capricorn Dec. 22-Jan. 20

People can always count on you. You have a strong sense of responsibility and your feet are firmly planted on the ground. You have high ambitions and you're sensible about money. C'mon into our bank and we'll give you a dollar to start a new savings account.

Sagittarius Nov. 23-Dec. 21

People flock to you because of your zest for life and your unique combination of wit, intelligence and fiery drive. You're also a free spirit who doesn't stay put in one place too long. So while you're still in Hunterdon County, c'mon into our bank and open a new savings account. We'll put a dollar in it for you.

Feb. 20-March 20 Pisces

To help others is your first instinct. In fact, you frequently subdue your own needs to brighten other people's lives. You are blessed with an active imagination, so imagine how large your savings account will grow when you open a new one at our bank with the dollar we'll give you.

Scorpio Oct. 24-Nov. 22

You were born for success and you know it. You are supremely confident and have a passionate nature which is tempered by exquisite self-control. Your many commitments may have kept you from opening a savings account so we're hoping that, with this reminder and a dollar, you'll start a new one at our bank.

March 21-April 20 Aries

You have boundless energy and enjoy conquering new, exciting challenges. We know you're an incurable optimist and much too busy forging ahead to stop and put something aside for a rainy day. So we'll give you a dollar to open a new savings account at our bank.

HUNTERDON COUNTY NATIONAL BANK
Member FDIC

Libra Sept. 24-Oct. 23

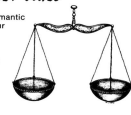

You are charming and romantic and no one can resist your smile. You seek fairness and weigh every side of an issue carefully before making a decision. We're hoping you'll decide to open a new savings account at our bank, and we'll even give you a dollar to start it.

April 21-May 21 Taurus

You are a tower of strength, sensible and practical in all your decisions. Your steadfast determination and thrifty nature give you enormous potential for amassing great wealth. You probably already have a savings account, but we'll give you a dollar to open a new one at our bank.

You are home-loving, kind, and sensitive to other people's feelings. You regard wastefulness as a crime and money clings to you. We know you love the water so we'll help you save for that boat you've always wanted. C'mon into our bank and get your dollar to open a new savings account.

Virgo Aug. 24-Sept. 23

You are analytical, logical and very honest. Your financial future is important to you so you are a natural saver. C'mon into our bank and we'll give you a dollar to open a new savings account. We know you'll keep on adding to it.

May 22-June 21 Gemini

You're more clever than almost anybody and you dazzle folks with your lightening-fast mind. You enjoy change, so - quickly, before you change your mind, come in to our bank and open a new savings account. We're waiting with a dollar to start it for you.

Cancer June 22-July 23

Leo July 24-Aug. 23

You are wise, generous, and courageous, and you travel through life first class. People are impressed by your obvious superiority. You are a born leader, so lead your family and friends to our bank. We'll open a new savings account for each of them with a dollar.

FREE! Beautifully illustrated posters of each Zodiac sign. Come in and ask for yours.

Fid-ick or ef-dee-eye-see

Maybe you warned your kids against four-letter words, but you can use this one even in a church vestibule. The long handle for FDIC is Federal Deposit Insurance Corporation and it means that your savings and checking deposits at our bank are covered against loss by federal insurance.

The chance-taking days of stuffing money in a mattress are long gone. We are too intelligent to put our nest egg in jeopardy and too smart to fall prey to a fast buck with no guarantees and a lot of "if" clauses that cover the other guy but not us. That's like taking a suit to a drycleaners where they're not responsible for buttons, shrinkage, zippers, color-fastness, pants, vests, etc. Will we ever get our suit back in the same condition? And then if we don't claim it by a certain time, they're not responsible for even acknowledging its existence. FDIC gives you certainty in an uncertain world. Coverage is now provided for up to $100,000 per depositor. By setting up an assortment of individual, joint and trust accounts, husband and wife may have insured accounts with us totaling half a million dollars and a family of four can increase their protection to $1,400,000.

There is, however, no insurance on money market funds which are issued by mutual fund organizations and frequently touted as high-yielding substitutes for savings accounts. And the yield the funds pay fluctuates daily. Unless you have a Ph.D. in calculus, you might find it difficult to determine your actual yield.

So the next time you see that four-letter word by our name — no matter how you pronounce it — you can sit back and relax. Your money is safe with FDIC.

MEMBER FDIC

HUNTERDON COUNTY
NATIONAL BANK

NUMBER FOUR IN A SERIES.

90

To heir is human.

People have been having babies for millenniums — it's the most natural thing in the world.

But there's no one quite so special as your child. From that first breath it was clear your son or daughter would be an individual capable of anything.

Maybe he or she will be a marine biologist — an archeologist — a diplomat — a surgeon — President of the United States — a geologist — a famous poet — president of I.B.M. — Chairman of the Board of Hunterdon County National Bank.

Your child is so smart, he just might choose Princeton or Harvard or Stanford or Brown or ...well, anyway, you can bet your boots his education will be expensive.

Right now's the time to set up a College Savings Plan — a tax-sheltered way to save for his college education.

Come in to your neighborhood branch (we have 10) of Hunterdon County National Bank. We're a member of FDIC so your deposits are completely protected.

With our Hunterdon County National Bank College Savings Plan you can contribute up to $3,000 a year (or $6,000 if both parents contribute) to an account in your child's behalf.

"Up to" is the maximum. You can start your plan with as little as $25 and then add $10 or so a week.

Any interest on this account is taxed to the child, which usually means no taxes at all.

Plus, you don't have to be a parent to contribute. Any adult may make a gift of up to $3,000 a year ... grandparents, other relatives, guardians or even just friends.

To heir (or grandheir) is human. To give, divine.

HUNTERDON COUNTY
NATIONAL BANK

SECURE!

At Gem City your savings are safe. For a lot of reasons.

Every dollar of savings up to $100,000 per depositor is insured by an agency of the Federal government. For a certain combination of family accounts, you can even be insured up to $500,000 at Gem City.

But just as important, Gem City has earned its reputation for 93 years as a sound, well-managed financial institution. That's why Gem City has always been able to pay a high rate of interest on your savings investment.

High return, sound organization and insured security. That's batting a thousand.

Gem City Savings
making things happen for you.

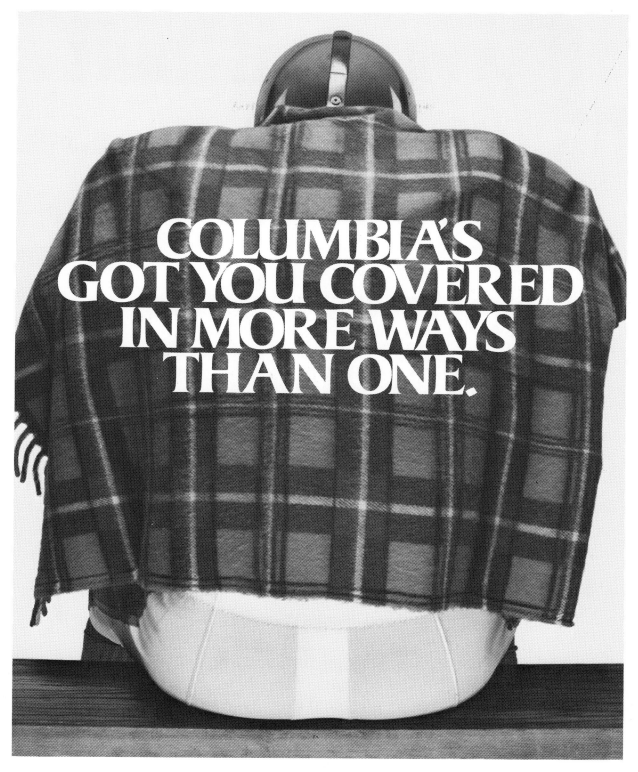

COLUMBIA'S GOT YOU COVERED IN MORE WAYS THAN ONE.

Only Columbia Savings offers you the convenience of 42 Colorado locations. So you're covered with personal service, guaranteed savings plans and loans almost everywhere you go in our state.

And only Columbia offers you such great incentives to save. Like this exclusive Bronco Plaid stadium blanket by Faribo. It's yours absolutely free with a $1,000-$4,999 deposit. Or get two free when you deposit $5,000 or more.

It's just one of the gifts you can choose when you save at Columbia. We've got all your wishes

covered—with over 50 special gifts, like digital clock radios, irons and cookware. All free or at a very low cost just for saving at Columbia.

We'll be with you in even more ways very soon. Watch for Columbia checking accounts offering daily interest—and more.

 **Columbia Savings**
We're with you. In more
places, more ways than anyone.

EQUAL OPPORTUNITY LENDER

93

If you want high interest without risk, we're with you.

Your savings are guaranteed safe at Columbia.

At Columbia, when we say "we're with you," we mean just that. We understand that you want the greatest possible return on your money, with the greatest possible security. That's why Columbia's Money Market Certificates offer the highest rates available.* And all Columbia accounts are insured up to $100,000.

High interest and maximum security aren't the only ways your money works hard for you at Columbia. Our unbeatable range of name brand popular gifts makes saving a very rewarding experience. Come in to any one of our 41 convenient locations and find out for yourself just how much Columbia is with you.

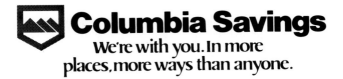

Columbia Savings
We're with you. In more places, more ways than anyone.

*Call any convenient Columbia office for our current Money Market Certificate rates.

One of the little pleasures of saving at Columbia.

Free with our 6-Month Money Market Certificate.

11.074%
Annual Rate

11.545%
Effective Annual Yield*

No other savings and loan pays you higher interest— 11.074% if you invest $10,000 between 9/25/80 and 10/1/80.

And no other savings and loan offers you a better incentive to save — fashionable silver ingot jewelry absolutely free. † It's a very limited offer, exclusively from Columbia Savings.

Choose the 4-gram ingot mounted on a gold-plated money clip or gold-plated keychain. Or choose the 5-gram ingot. It makes a perfect addition to any necklace or charm bracelet.

All three are 99% pure silver. And all three are gifts of lasting value to give to someone special or keep yourself.

Or you can choose from over 40 other free premiums when you get your 6-Month Money Market Certificate at Columbia Savings.

We're with you with great savings plans and exclusive gifts at 42 convenient Colorado locations.

 **Columbia Savings**
We're with you. In more places, more ways than anyone.

95

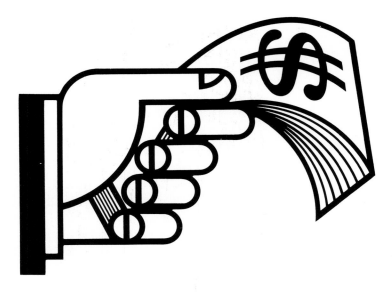

4 Good Reasons To Save at Home Federal.

1. ■ Convenience. Home Federal has three convenient locations: downtown Ashland, Flatwoods and South Shore. All have handy drive-in windows to serve you faster.

2. ■ Highest Interest. Home Federal pays you highest interest on all types of savings plans — everything from passbook accounts to savings certificates.

3. ■ Experience. Home Federal was founded in 1889. And our staff includes people with many years experience in helping people plan savings programs.

4. ■ Helping the area grow. When you save at Home Federal, you're helping your community grow, because Home Federal re-invests the money in the community in the form of mortgage loans.

HomeFederal Savings&Loan

Ashland   Flatwoods   South Shore

Hug, squeeze and love it again.

The KB&T Christmas Cub is back.

Free with $500 deposit or a savings certificate.

The KB&T Christmas Cub was such a hit last Christmas that we've brought it back for another season.

To get your free Cub, just deposit $500 in a KB&T Regular or Golden savings account. Or purchase a KB&T savings certificate.

You can also get a Christmas Cub* for just $5 when you open a KB&T Christmas Club account. And additional bears are available for $5 when you make a $300 savings deposit.

Offer available at our Main Office, 107 Capital Street, or the KB&T MiniBank Center, Virginia and Laidley Streets.

We are the bank that bears interest.

KB&T

* Ribbon not included.

TWO WAYS TO EARN FAT CAT INTEREST:

FAT CAT
LOOPHOLE CERTIFICATE
12.000%

FATTER CAT
MONEY MARKET CERTIFICATE
12.256%

Even if you can't scrape up $10,000 for a Money Market CD you can still earn Fat Cat interest with First National's Loophole Certificate. You can earn it on deposits between $3,000 and $9,000 for six months.

HERE'S HOW IT WORKS:
Just bring any amount from $3,000 to $9,000 to First National. We'll loan you enough to make up the difference between your deposit and the $10,000 needed to buy the six-month Loophole Certificate. Your deposit is the only security needed for the loan. Six months later the loan is automatically paid back and your original deposit has netted Fat Cat interest. See the chart for this week's Loophole Certificate and loan figures.

Earn Fat Cat interest on a small deposit while you can. Hurry to any First National branch or the lobby of the main bank. Or call 371-7264.

FOR EXAMPLE, ARE YOU EARNING
10.583%
ANNUAL INTEREST ON
$4,000
FOR SIX MONTHS?

Here's the other way to earn Fat Cat interest. The Money Market Certificate earns more interest, but you must have the $10,000 yourself. No loan is involved in this one. That's why you earn the full amount. The Money Market Certificate is a six-month CD and requires a minimum deposit of $10,000.

THIS WEEK'S RATE WILL PAY
$611.12
ON $10,000 FOR SIX MONTHS.

THE LOOPHOLE CERTIFICATE
12.000%
Six-month rate available now through February 20.

You Deposit	We Loan You	Interest You Earn on Certificate	Interest You Pay on Loan	Your Net Earnings	Loophole Annual Interest Yield*
$3,000	$7,000	$598.36	$452.50	$145.86	9.777%
$4,000	$6,000	$598.36	$387.86	$210.50	10.583%
$5,000	$5,000	$598.36	$323.21	$275.15	11.067%
$6,000	$4,000	$598.36	$258.56	$339.80	11.388%
$7,000	$3,000	$598.36	$193.92	$404.44	11.619%
$8,000	$2,000	$598.36	$129.28	$469.08	11.791%
$9,000	$1,000	$598.36	$ 64.64	$533.72	11.926%

*Based on 366-day year.

Federal law requires that we charge a minimum of 1% over the deposit rate. Federal regulations currently set the maximum loan rate at 13%. Therefore, the maximum interest payable through February 20 on the Loophole Certificate is 12%.

When you think of money, think First.
 FIRST NATIONAL BANK IN LITTLE ROCK

98

Now you can earn current 2½-year C.D. interest rates for 5 years.

So your money works harder... twice as long.

Even a small amount of money works hard to earn big interest at Dollar. And with our 2½-year Certificate of Deposit you can receive that interest rate for 5 years. So you can be assured of today's high interest rate later, too...even if the rate goes down in the meantime.

Ⓢ Our 2½-year C.D. pays you high money market rates with only a $500 minimum deposit.* And your money is now insured for up to $100,000 by an agency of the Federal government.

Ⓢ So stop by any nearby Dollar office soon. We'll make sure that all of your savings earn the highest possible interest rate now... and later.

*Early withdrawal is subject to a substantial penalty. New rates set every two weeks.

Branch Manager

Right now, with the 2½-year rate, your money can be earning:

00.00%
Annual Rate

00.00%
Annual Effective Yield

There's a Dollar Savings office near you:

MAIN OFFICE:
Gay at High St.
228-6851

ARLINGTON:
1756 W. Lane Ave. at Brandon
481-8187

EASTMOOR/BEXLEY:
2951 E. Main St.
236-5065

FIFTH/NELSON:
2344 E. Fifth Ave. at Nelson
253-7218

GERMAN VILLAGE:
673 Mohawk St.
444-6866

HILLIARD:
3750 Main St.
876-9946

PICKERINGTON:
266 Hill Road N.
837-5591

SUNBURY:
45 E. Granville St.
965-3931

TRI-VILLAGE:
1177 Olentangy River Rd. at Third
294-6361

WALNUT HILL:
6121 E. Livingston Ave. at Brice
864-1162

WESTERVILLE:
579 S. State St.
891-1451

WORTHINGTON:
200 W. Wilson Bridge Rd.
436-3653

Your Dollar works harder.

DOLLAR SAVINGS
Member F.S.L.I.C.

102

103

"Actually, your money will multiply a lot faster with a Met Bank 30 Month Treasury Certificate."

There are a lot of ways to make money quickly. But the safest, easiest way is to invest in a Met Bank 2½ Year Treasury Certificate.* You can participate with as little as $1,500, so you earn the highest yield without tying up a lot of money for a long time. Call us today for the current interest rate. Because we're experts in the care and feeding of savings. *Early withdrawal requires a substantial interest penalty.

At St. Paul Federal, they showed me how little my life savings were really worth.

When I moved to Oak Park from out of state, one of the first things I wanted to do was transfer my savings. That's when I found out how dumb I'd been for the past 10 years.

Because, when I talked to St. Paul Federal about a savings account, the officer asked me, "Are you sure you want just a savings account?"

"Sure I'm sure," I said. "What else would I want?"

"Do you have kids?"

"Two."

"Well, you can get savings certificates that can mature when they're ready to go to college—that way you get a higher rate of interest, in fact the highest allowed by law."

"Do you have a pension plan where you work?"

"If only," I complained.

"We can fix you up with your own Individual Retirement Account, with no taxes to pay on it until you start getting the income. Meanwhile, the interest keeps building up the principal. Are you planning to save up for something else?"

"Two weeks of peace and quiet," I said.

"For that you need a regular savings account, so you can take the money out any time you want, without a penalty."

As we talked, I began to realize that, for the past 10 years, I hadn't used my money wisely at all. My savings had been lying around in a commercial bank and they could have been worth a lot more today if I'd only had this talk 10 years ago.

Then, I realized another thing. A busy officer of a busy Savings & Loan Association had just taken 20 minutes of his time to talk to me about my financial affairs. He didn't have to do that—all I came in for was a regular savings account.

Frankly, I don't expect humanity from a banker. I still can't quite believe it. Do you think he thought I was somebody else?

 # St. Paul Federal Savings
We give you more for your money than money.

105

Save for a free gift.

Save now.

We want your business. We want you to save with us. And frankly, we're prepared to do more than just say "thank you" for it. So, when you deposit $500 or more into a new or existing account at Naples Federal, it automatically qualifies you to go on a shopping spree with us. For free gifts!

Shop now.

Shop for gifts that are attractive, useful and valuable. Gifts with names you know and trust. Like Corning Ware, Sanyo, Westclox, Oneida. Gifts that make your table sparkle, help you with kitchen chores, wake you in the morning, make you a mathematical whiz, you name it. (Any of these products would make a nice gift during the holiday season.) And there's more. You can also select gift certificates from Publix, Burdines or Maas Bros., and popular S&H Green Stamps. We made sure your shopping spree has plenty of variety!

Start now.

Shop the chart first. It shows you the many gifts to choose from. Notice that all gifts are free, with a qualifying deposit.

This offer is good from November 10th through December 31st. So, right now is the right time. Bring your qualifying deposit into any office of Naples Federal today and start shopping.

FREE GIFT ITEMS	First Deposit to a New or Existing Savings Account qualifies you for a FREE GIFT as follows:			
	$500 to $999 deposit	$1000 to $4999 deposit	$5000 to $9999 deposit	$10,000 or more deposit
Rubbermaid 5-bowl Food Keeper Set	Free	Free		
Westclox Electric Alarm Clock	Free	Free	Any Two	Any Two
Corning Ware 2-piece Set	Free	Free		
Bibb 72" x 90" Blanket		Free		
Kimball End-Grain Cutting Board		Free	Free	
$5 Gift Certificate*		Free	Free	
Westclox Digital Alarm Clock			Free	Free
Oneida Silver Hostess Snack Tray			Free	Free
Corning Ware 6-piece Starter Set				Free
Oneida 12" Silver Round Tray				Free
Sanyo Lithium Powered Calculator				Free
$10 Gift Certificate*				Free
S&H Green Stamps	600 Stamps	1200 Stamps	1800 Stamps	3000 Stamps

*Your choice of a certificate from Publix, Burdines or Maas Brothers.
- Offer good only while supply lasts.
- One gift per family, please.
- Deposit should remain in account for at least 90 days.
- Sorry, no mail or phone orders.
- Offer does not apply to deposits made to Advantage Checking™ Accounts.
- **Offer good at any Naples Federal office.**

Naples Federal
More than just a friendly smile.

Naples Federal Savings and Loan Association, a New York Stock Exchange Company, with offices throughout Southwest Florida.

The best thing to happen to savings since the pig.

First came the piggy bank. Not a bad place to save. Except money didn't earn any interest. And it wasn't really all that safe.

Next came the savings account. Much better. Money did earn interest. And it was insured. Problem was, inflation took the money away faster than interest could build it.

So people tried the stock market, corporate bonds, gold. Their investments grew faster than inflation. Unfortunately, they shrunk just as fast.

There is a better alternative. Not really new. But it's dependable as well as profitable. The First Bankers. We can put your money into the kind of high interest investments you've been hearing about. We probably know some you haven't heard about, too. And, with The First Bankers, they're all insured. The point is, we understand all the financial ins and outs that can make the difference between profit and loss. Money is our business. Our only business. Always has been.

Savings isn't as simple as it used to be. Not in these hard times. You need an expert to advise you. And we want to be that expert.

 THE FIRST BANKERS
MEMBERS FDIC

We want to work with you.

107

GET FAT FOR LESS THAN TEN GRAND.

THE LOOPHOLE CERTIFICATE

Even if you can't scrape up $10,000 for a Money Market CD, you can still earn Fat Cat interest with First National's Loophole Certificate.

HERE'S HOW IT WORKS:

Deposit between $3,000 and $9,000 at First National, and we'll loan you enough to make up the difference between your deposit and the $10,000 needed to buy the Loophole Certificate. Your deposit is the only security needed for the loan. Six months later the loan is automatically paid back and your original deposit has netted Fat Cat interest. (See the chart below.)

Start earning Fat Cat interest on a small deposit today. For more details, come by any First National branch or the lobby of the main bank. Or call 371-7264.

THE LOOPHOLE CERTIFICATE
13%

Six-month rate available now through March 26.

You Deposit	We Loan You	Your Net Earnings	Annual Interest Yield
$3,000	$7,000	$159.57	10.667%
$4,000	$6,000	$229.38	11.501%
$5,000	$5,000	$299.18	12.000%
$6,000	$4,000	$368.99	12.333%
$7,000	$3,000	$438.80	12.572%
$8,000	$2,000	$508.61	12.750%
$9,000	$1,000	$578.42	12.889%

FOR EXAMPLE, ARE YOU EARNING 12% ANNUAL INTEREST ON $5,000 FOR SIX MONTHS?

Federal law requires that we charge a minimum of 1% over the deposit rate. Federal regulations currently set the maximum loan rate at 14%. Therefore, the maximum interest payable through March 26 on the Loophole Certificate is 13%. Federal regulations also prohibit the compounding of interest during the term of the deposit. Substantial penalty for early withdrawal.

When you think of money, think First.

FIRST NATIONAL BANK IN LITTLE ROCK

MEMBER FDIC

THE LOOPHOLE GETS BIGGER.
11.985%

FIRST NATIONAL LETS YOU EARN LIKE A FAT CAT ON A SMALL DEPOSIT.

Is your money earning between 9.72% and 11.90%? If not, wake up! Take advantage of First National's Loophole rates on six-month Money Market Certificates while you can.

FIRST NATIONAL'S FOUND A LOOPHOLE AND HERE'S HOW IT WORKS:

Just bring any amount from $3,000 to $9,000 to First National. We'll loan you enough to make up the difference between your deposit and the $10,000 needed to buy a six-month Money Market Certificate. Your certificate is the only security needed for the loan. Six months later, the loan is automatically paid back and your original deposit has netted Fat Cat interest. See the chart for examples of Loophole Certificate and loan figures.

Earn Fat Cat interest on a small deposit while you can. Hurry to any First National branch or the lobby of the main bank. Or call 371-7264.

FOR EXAMPLE, ARE YOU EARNING
10.54%
ANNUAL INTEREST ON
$4,000
FOR SIX MONTHS?

---

*Federal law requires that we charge a minimum of 1% over deposit rate. Federal regulations prohibit the compounding of interest during the term of the deposit. Substantial interest penalty is required for early withdrawal.

11.985%

Six-month Money Market CD rate available now through February 13.

LOOPHOLE CERTIFICATE RATES

You Deposit	We Loan You	Interest You Earn on Certificate	Interest You Pay on Loan*	Your Net Earnings	Loophole Annual Interest Yield
$3,000	$7,000	$597.61	$452.50	$145.11	9.72%
$4,000	$6,000	$597.61	$387.86	$209.75	10.54%
$5,000	$5,000	$597.61	$323.21	$274.40	11.03%
$6,000	$4,000	$597.61	$258.56	$339.05	11.36%
$7,000	$3,000	$597.61	$193.92	$403.69	11.59%
$8,000	$2,000	$597.61	$129.28	$468.33	11.77%
$9,000	$1,000	$597.61	$ 64.64	$532.97	11.90%

When you think of money, think First.

 FIRST NATIONAL BANK IN LITTLE ROCK

110

Bring a friend to Chicago's Bank and get a free Sony Betamax.

When your friend deposits $50,000 in a 2½-year Super-Saver CD at The First National Bank of Chicago, you get a $1,250 cash award. Or a free Sony Betamax. Or a free Kimball Organ. Or a free mink and leather coat. Or a selection of other gifts totaling 1,250 points from our holiday catalog.

Your friend can deposit less, but the more he puts into 2½- or 5-year Super-Saver CDs or 6-month T-Rate CDs, the more you get in cash or gifts.

So bring your friends to Chicago's Bank. See all 45 gifts on display on our Plaza level. Then get the highest available bank interest for your friends, and cash or gifts for yourself. Free.

Call The Bring-A-Friend Hotline, 732-5126, for gift catalog and details.

 FIRST CHICAGO
The First National Bank of Chicago

Rules and Regulations:
Gifts/cash available to individuals only, 18 or older, who are not members of the depositor's household. Funds must be new to the Bank (the Bank will make this determination). T-Rate CD renewals are not eligible, nor are deposits made before November 10, 1980. The Bank reserves the right to withdraw this offer at any time. Supply limited. Merchandise will be shipped to you direct from our supplier. Items are not available for pickup at the Bank. Allow 4-6 weeks for delivery. A copy of the warranty on any product is available free upon request in writing to Premium Coordinator, The First National Bank of Chicago, Two First National Plaza, Chicago, Ill. 60603.

	Your Cash Award—OR GIFT POINTS		
DEPOSIT	6-Month T-Rate CD*	2½-Yr. Super Saver**	5-Yr. Super Saver**
$3,000	—	$ 75	$150
5,000	—	125	250
7,000	—	175	350
10,000	$50	250	500
15,000	75	375	750
20,000	100	500	1,000
25,000	125	625	1,250
50,000	250	1,250	2,500

*Rate: 14.167%. Yield: 14.883%. Available Nov. 20 to Nov. 26. 182-day Maturity. Yield subject to change at renewal. Minimum deposit $10,000. Interest not compounded.

**Rate: 11.75%. Yield: 12.65%. Available Nov. 13 to Nov. 26. Compounded daily. 2½- or 5-year maturity. Minimum deposit without award: $500.

Substantial penalty for early withdrawal; also, depositor would forfeit amount of award paid to the referring friend.

Member FDIC. Also available at our Banking Centers at Wabash & Monroe, Michigan & Chicago and the expanded Loop facilities at The Xerox Centre.

Bring a friend to Chicago's Bank and get a free microwave oven.

When your friend deposits $15,000 in a 2½-year Super-Saver CD at The First National Bank of Chicago, you get a $375 cash award. Or a free microwave oven. Or a free color TV. Or a free Toro lawn mower. Or a selection of other gifts totaling 375 points from our holiday catalog.

Your friend can deposit less, but the more he puts into 2½- or 5-year Super-Saver CDs or 6-month T-Rate CDs, the more you get in cash or gifts.

So bring your friends to Chicago's Bank. See all 45 gifts on display on our Plaza level. Then get the highest available bank interest for your friends, and cash or gifts for yourself. Free.

Call The Bring-A-Friend Hotline, 732-5126, for gift catalog and details.

FIRST CHICAGO
The First National Bank of Chicago

Rules and Regulations:
Gifts/cash available to individuals only, 18 or older, who are not members of the depositor's household. Funds must be new to the Bank (the Bank will make this determination). T-Rate CD renewals are not eligible, nor are deposits made before November 10, 1980. The Bank reserves the right to withdraw this offer at any time. Supply limited. Merchandise will be shipped to you direct from our supplier. Items are not available for pickup at the Bank. Allow 4-6 weeks for delivery. A copy of the warranty on any product is available free upon request in writing to Premium Coordinator, The First National Bank of Chicago, Two First National Plaza, Chicago, Ill. 60603.

Your Cash Award—OR GIFT POINTS

DEPOSIT	6-Month T-Rate CD*	2½-Yr. Super Saver**	5-Yr. Super Saver**
$3,000	—	$ 75	$150
5,000	—	125	250
7,000	—	175	350
10,000	$50	250	500
15,000	75	375	750
20,000	100	500	1,000
25,000	125	625	1,250
50,000	250	1,250	2,500

*Rate: 14.167%. Yield: 14.883%. Available Nov. 20 to Nov. 26. 182-day Maturity. Yield subject to change at renewal. Minimum deposit $10,000. Interest not compounded.

**Rate: 11.75%. Yield: 12.65%. Available Nov. 13 to Nov. 26. Compounded daily. 2½- or 5-year maturity. Minimum deposit without award: $500.

Substantial penalty for early withdrawal; also, depositor would forfeit amount of award paid to the referring friend.

Member FDIC. Also available at our Banking Centers at Wabash & Monroe, Michigan & Chicago and the expanded Loop facilities at The Xerox Centre.

114

This is no time to be locked into ordinary yields.

This is no time to settle for bank certificates or investments that lock you into a set rate.* With today's uncertain economy this certainly is no time to lock up your money for years and years. Especially when, with **Delaware Cash Reserve,** you can get high money market dividends and prompt, no-penalty liquidity.

Delaware Cash Reserve is the money market fund that lets you take advantage of every fluctuation of the money market without tying up your money. You get high money market dividends, credited daily. And the minimum investment is only $1,000 with no sales charge! Whenever you need cash, you can withdraw all or

part of your investment with no penalties for early withdrawal. In fact, your money stays so liquid, you can even elect to write checks (minimum $500) and continue to collect dividends until the checks clear. You decide when and how much to withdraw—nobody else holds the purse strings when you invest in **Delaware Cash Reserve.**

Don't lock up your money. Don't be locked into ordinary yields. Get money market dividends and no-penalty liquidity with **Delaware Cash Reserve.** For current information and a free prospectus call toll free anytime **1-800-523-4640.** In Pennsylvania **1-800-462-1597.**

In Pennsylvania: Free of personal property taxes.

*Of course, your principal is insured in a bank and does not vary, but your investment has a fixed return.

Invest in the Money Market Fund from The Delaware Group

7 Penn Center Plaza
Phila., Pa. 19103

Call anytime toll free 1-800-523-4640. In Pennsylvania call 1-800-462-1597, or return this coupon for a free prospectus containing more complete information including management fees and expenses. Read it carefully before you invest or send money.

Name _____

Address _____

City _____ State _____ Zip _____

Phone: Business _____ Home _____

Delaware Cash Reserve, 7 Penn Center Plaza, Phila., Pa. 19103 G84

115

You don't have to be a big shot to invest in Delaware Cash Reserve. Just smart.

No contest, right? You want—and deserve—all you can get for your money and with **Delaware Cash Reserve** you don't have to be a Wall Street Whiz to get it. It's as easy as putting money in a bank, except instead of 5½%* passbook interest, **Delaware Cash Reserve** gives you those high money market dividends you've been reading about. Money market dividends, credited daily, plus prompt, no-penalty liquidity.

Right! You don't have to tie up your money to earn a little extra when you invest in **Delaware Cash Reserve.** If you need money for an emergency, you can withdraw part or all of your money when you want with no penalty at all! You can even elect to write checks ($500 minimum) on your account and continue to collect dividends until the checks clear.

Add it up: High money market dividends, no-penalty liquidity that gives you full control of your money—and the security of knowing your money is being handled by one of the nation's oldest money managers.

All you need is a $1,000 initial investment. No sales charge. No charge for the phone call either.

Call toll free anytime
1-800-523-4640
In Pennsylvania,
1-800-462-1597

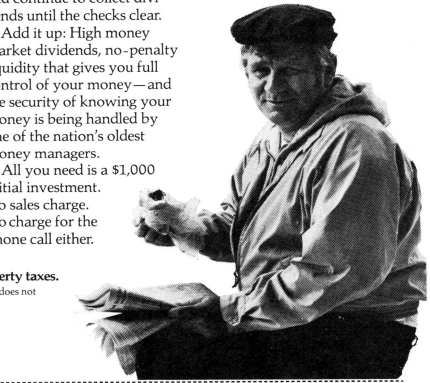

In Pennsylvania: Free of personal property taxes.

*Of course, your principal is insured in a bank and does not vary, but your investment has a fixed return.

The Money Market Fund From The Delaware Group

7 Penn Center Plaza
Phila., PA 19103

Return this coupon for a free prospectus containing more complete information including management fees and expenses. Read it carefully before you invest or send money.

Name_____

Address_____

City_____ State_____ Zip_____

Phone: Business_____ Home_____

Delaware Cash Reserve, 7 Penn Center Plaza, Phila., PA 19103   Q03

© Delaware Management Company, Inc. 1980

You figure it out.
$1,000 at 5½% in a bank, or $1,000 at 00.00% in Delaware Cash Reserve?

You know the interest banks are paying on savings accounts. You know from the financial pages what the money market is doing. You figure it out. Do you want your money in a savings account earning a maximum of 5½%*, or in **Delaware Cash Reserve,** the money market fund that pays high money market dividends, credited daily.

Did you say, "but how about savings certificates?" Yes, the bank will pay you more on certificates— **provided** you don't mind having your money tied up under penalty for early withdrawal. And if you're after

the bank's high-interest certificates, forget it. $1,000 won't do you any good at all.

But with **Delaware Cash Reserve,** $1,000 (with no sales charge) is all you need to earn the same high money market dividends we pay our $100,000 shareholders— and your money is

so liquid you can redeem anytime without charge or penalty. Or, you can elect to have the convenience of a checking account so you can pay bills, taxes, etc., just by writing a check of $500 or more and continue to collect dividends until the check clears.

You figure it out. Then call us for current information and a free prospectus. Call toll free anytime **1-800-523-4640.** In Pennsylvania, call **1-800-462-1597.**

* This was the 7 day average net annualized yield on _____ . Yield is a function of type and quality of investment, portfolio maturity, and the Fund's operating expenses (some of which are being temporarily borne by the Fund's investment advisor). Yield cannot be guaranteed over any given period. Also, principal is not insured. The average portfolio maturity on this date was _____ days.

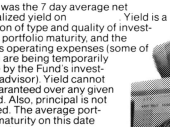

In Pennsylvania: Free of personal property taxes.

*Of course, your principal is insured in a bank and does not vary, but your investment has a fixed return.

Invest in the Money Market Fund from The Delaware Group

7 Penn Center Plaza
Phila., Pa. 19103

Call anytime toll free 800-523-4640. In Pennsylvania call collect 1-800-462-1597, or return this coupon for a free prospectus containing more complete information including management fees and expenses. Read it carefully before you invest or send money.

Name _____

Address _____

City _____ State _____ Zip _____

Phone: Business _____ Home _____

Delaware Cash Reserve, 7 Penn Center Plaza, Phila., Pa. 19103 G83

How to help offset interest on your monthly bills

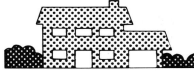  

It's not just inflation that's killing you. It's the accumulated interest you pay out every month—on the mortgage, your car or business loans and, what is it now on your charge accounts? 15% 18% More? What you need is a way to help offset the high cost of credit. And you have it.

Just use Delaware Cash Reserve as a "high interest checking account"
Delaware Cash Reserve is more than a money market fund that pays high dividends, credited daily. To smart money managers everywhere...individual and business...the Fund's checking account option is the easy way to earn the something extra to help offset big interest charges. How? By keeping a non-interest bearing checking account to a minimum. By paying bills from Delaware Cash Reserve, where your money earns high

dividends and checks can be drawn that earn daily dividends until they clear.

It's easy. Here's how it works.
1. Open a Delaware Cash Reserve account with as little as $1,000—no sales charge—and sign up for the checkwriting option.
2. Begin earning high money market dividends, credited daily, from your first deposit.
3. Each pay period—instead of depositing money into your non-interest bearing account—add it to your Fund investment to earn more daily dividends.
4. Once a month look over your bills. Lump small bills together and draw one check ($500 or over) to your bank checking account to cover them. For single bills that are $500 or more, write a Fund check just as you would on any ordinary checking account with one difference: all

your Fund checks will continue to earn daily dividends until they clear.
5. Add up your earned dividends. Subtract them from the interest you've paid out. See? Even a bank* NOW account couldn't offset that much interest on your bills!

Easy in, easy out—no sales or withdrawal charges and no penalties!
Of course you can use Delaware Cash Reserve's liquidity and high yield for long-term investment, but to start earning "the something extra" to offset the interest on your monthly bills right now, mail the coupon below, or better still call toll free anytime:
1-800-523-4640.
In Pennsylvania,
1-800-462-1597.

In Pennsylvania: Free of personal property taxes.

*Of course, principal is insured in a bank, but rates and penalties are fixed.

The Money Market Fund From The Delaware Group

7 Penn Center Plaza
Phila., PA 19103

Return this coupon for a free prospectus containing more complete information including management fees and expenses. Read it carefully before you invest or send money.

Name_____

Address_____

City_____ State_____ Zip_____

Phone: Business_____ Home_____

Delaware Cash Reserve, 7 Penn Center Plaza, Phila., PA 19103   Q04

© Delaware Management Company, Inc. 1980

119

The Investment Your Bank Won't Tell You About.
Delaware Cash Reserve.

These days your bank is talking big about short-term money market certificates* that earn interest pegged to the Treasury Bill rate. Provided, of course, you don't withdraw early at a substantial penalty. The last thing your bank wants you to hear about is **Delaware Cash Reserve.** Especially now that the bank can't compound interest daily.

For one thing, **Delaware Cash Reserve** is the money market fund with no minimum holding period. You can withdraw all your money, or part of your money, any business day. With all your dividends. Without any penalty. For another thing, **Delaware Cash Reserve** earns money market dividends and credits them daily, taking advantage of every interest change in the market. And would your bank want you to know that you can elect to use **Delaware Cash Reserve** like a checking account? You can write checks ($500 minimum) on your fund to pay taxes, tuition, bills, even salaries and expenses—and your check continues to earn daily dividends until the check clears.

What's more, there's no sales or redemption charge, but there's an additional benefit: your money is handled by one of the nation's oldest money managers.

And here's the clincher. You can have all this for one-tenth the cost of a bank certificate: $1,000 initial investment.

Of course your bank won't tell you about **Delaware Cash Reserve.** But we will. Mail the coupon below, or call toll free **1-800-523-4640** for a prospectus and current information. (In Pennsylvania call collect **215-988-1333**.)

In Pennsylvania: Free of personal property taxes.

*Of course, your principal is insured in a bank and does not vary, but your investment has a fixed return.

The Money Market Fund From The Delaware Group

7 Penn Center Plaza
Phila., Pa. 19103

It's time to get it together. Checking and Savings at AmeriFirst.

And time to get a Timex, too.

Now's the time to move your savings and checking accounts to AmeriFirst Federal. You can choose from a beautiful assortment of 12 men's and women's Timex watches, including precise quartz and LCD's in gold and silver finishes. Or select a handy travel or electric snooze alarm. There's even an elegant pen and pencil set for people who already have plenty of time on their hands.

Just deposit $500 or more in a new or existing AmeriFirst Federal checking or savings account or renew a maturing certificate. Depending on the amount of your deposit, you can receive your selection as a gift…or you can buy it at a special low price. One gift per account.

It pays to have your checking and savings at AmeriFirst. At AmeriFirst you earn 5¼% a year interest compounded daily on your checking funds, plus high interest on a wide variety of savings plans. You also get a single monthly statement, itemizing both your checking and savings transactions. And no matter where you open your account, you can do business at any of our 45 convenient offices throughout Florida.

AmeriFirst Check service is free each month when you maintain a minimum checking balance of $500 or more, or a total balance of $10,000 or more in all accounts listed on your single monthly statement. If your checking balance falls below $500 and your combined balance is less than $10,000, your monthly service charge is only $3.

You'll also enjoy the peace of mind of doing business here at the South's largest Federal, where your funds are backed by over $3 billion in assets.

Savings, checking, and a Timex. The time to get it all together is now. At AmeriFirst Federal.

	First deposit to a new or existing checking and/or savings account qualifies for one gift or one purchase as follows:					With each additional deposit of $100 or more PAY ONLY
	$500 to $999	$1,000 to $4,999	$5,000 to $9,999	$10,000 to $19,999	$20,000 or more	
1. Papermate Chrome Pen & Pencil	Gift	Gift	Gift	Gift	Gift	$4.95
2. Westclox Travel Alarm	$2.95	Gift	Gift	Gift	Gift	5.95
3. Timex Electric Snooze Alarm	2.95	Gift	Gift	Gift	Gift	5.95
4. Timex Woman's Round Cavatina	8.95	$6.95	Gift	Gift	Gift	11.95
5. Timex Woman's Sportster	8.95	6.95	Gift	Gift	Gift	11.95
6. Timex Man's Silver LCD	8.95	6.95	Gift	Gift	Gift	11.95
7. Timex Man's Gold LCD	8.95	6.95	Gift	Gift	Gift	11.95
8. Timex Woman's Gold Oval Cavatina	10.95	8.95	$6.95	Gift	Gift	14.95
9. Timex Woman's Twin Band	10.95	8.95	6.95	Gift	Gift	14.95
10. Timex Man's Gold LCD — Black Band	10.95	8.95	6.95	Gift	Gift	14.95
11. Timex Man's Silver LCD — Silver Band	10.95	8.95	6.95	Gift	Gift	14.95
12. Timex Woman's Gold LCD	15.95	13.95	11.95	$9.95	Gift	20.95
13. Timex Woman's Gold Dial	15.95	13.95	11.95	9.95	Gift	20.95
14. Timex Man's Silver Deluxe LCD	15.95	13.95	11.95	9.95	Gift	20.95
15. Timex Man's Gold Quartz	15.95	13.95	11.95	9.95	Gift	20.95

Quantities limited. Some items may become unavailable. No rainchecks or phone or mail requests. No gifts for internal transfers. Savings deposits for gifts must remain 60 days. One gift per account.

AMERIFIRST FEDERAL
America's Number 1.

MEMBER
FSLIC
Federal Savings & Loan Insurance Corp.
Your Savings Insured to $100,000

AmeriFirst Federal Savings and Loan Association. America's oldest Federal. Over $3 Billion strong. W.H. Walker, Jr., Chairman. Member Federal Savings and Loan Insurance Corporation. **DOWNTOWN:** One S.E. 3rd Ave. (Main Office)/100 N.E. 1st Ave. **NORTHEAST:** 8380 N.E. 2nd Ave./9640 N.E. 2nd Ave./900 N.E. 125th St./18301 Biscayne Blvd. **CENTRAL:** 1400 N.W. 17th Ave. **NORTHWEST:** 16407 N.W. 67th Ave., Miami Lakes. **HIALEAH:** Westland Mall. **MIAMI BEACH:** 17395 N. Bay Rd. at Winston Towers/1055 Kane Concourse/1025 71st St. /306 41st St./900 Alton Rd. **SOUTH:** 2750 Coral Way/341 Almeria/Dadeland Mall/13701 N. Kendall Dr./15101 S. Dixie Hwy. At Cutler Ridge Mall. **HOMESTEAD:** 28875 S. Federal Hwy. **MONROE COUNTY:** Ocean Reef, Key Largo. **BROWARD COUNTY:** 3201 N. Federal Hwy., Oakland Park/Loehmann's Plaza at PalmAire, Pompano Beach/Venetian Isle Shopping Ctr., Lighthouse Point/Broward Mall/Universal Plaza Shopping Ctr./1740 East Hallandale Blvd. **PALM BEACH COUNTY:** 998 S. Federal Hwy., Boca Raton/Oakbrook Square Shopping Ctr., N. Palm Beach. **CENTRAL FLA:** 10 Orlando Div. Offices. **WEST COAST:** Sunshine Mall, Clearwater/244 Shopping Ave., Sarasota/551 U.S. Bypass 41, Venice/1928 College Parkway, Ft. Myers/2073 Ninth St., North, Naples.

121

Saving at Chicago's Bank gives you a nice warm feeling.

Choose a jacket, vest, blanket or scarf when you save $500 or more at Chicago's Bank.

Stay warm all winter with a 100% goose down jacket or vest, or a 100% wool blanket, stadium blanket or scarf. Free or at great savings when you save at The First National Bank of Chicago. Just deposit $500 or more in any new or existing savings account or NOW account, or buy a high-interest CD. Then enjoy that nice, warm feeling. At Chicago's Bank. Call 732-6000 for details.

ITEM	DEPOSIT LEVELS		
	$500 1,499	$1,500– 4,999	$5,000 OR MORE
A. 100% Down-Filled Nylon Jacket— Navy Blue,Men's/Women's Sizes XS, S, M, L, XL	$59.95	$49.95	$39.95
B. 100% Wool Blanket—Blue, White, Tan, Cocoa, Full Size, 80" X 90"	29.95	19.95	9.95
C. 100% Down-Filled Nylon Vest— Brown/Tan (Reversible) Men's/ Women's Sizes XS, S, M, L, XL	29.95	19.95	9.95
D. 100% Wool Stadium Blanket— Green or Red Tartan Plaid, 52" X 62"	14.95	4.95	FREE
E. 100% Wool Scarf—Earth-Tone Plaids, 8" X 72"	9.95	FREE	2 FREE

Substantial interest penalty for early withdrawal from time accounts. Supplies are limited and The First reserves the right to withdraw this offer at any time without notice. All persons taking advantage of this offer must comply to standards established by The First National Bank of Chicago based upon Federal Regulations regarding premium promotions. Deposits made before January 2, 1981, do not qualify. To assure your satisfaction, and for proper fit of jackets and vests, all merchandise must be selected and picked up at the Bank; sorry, no mail orders, shipping or merchandise returns. Offer expires February 27, 1981.

FIRST CHICAGO
The First National Bank of Chicago
Member FDIC

122

America's oldest Federal has a brand new name—AmeriFirst Federal. It's a name that reflects our heritage and traditions as the nation's oldest Federal. One that reflects our Association as it is today—the South's largest Federal with over $2½ Billion in assets—serving many communities throughout South and Central Florida.

It all started back in 1933, when Dr. W. H. Walker went to Washington and came home with Charter #1—for the first Federal savings and loan association in America. He named his company First Federal of Miami and established a standard of service that made First Federal a leader from the beginning.

But soon, many other First Federals were opening for business. Today, there are more than 40 different First Federals in Florida alone, and hundreds more nationwide. Sometimes it gets kind of confusing.

As we continue to expand our services statewide, it's important that we have a name that will set us apart. One that's not easily confused with anyone else.

So, First Federal of Miami is now AmeriFirst Federal.

But, only our name has chan[...]

You'll find the same friendly people, the same convenient lo[...]tions, and the same security an[...]insurance for your savings ac[...]

First Federal of Miami grew up with Florid[...]

counts. And most importantly, you'll find the same traditions [...]

Dr. W. H. Walker, founder of America's first Federal.

Our Charter #1, the first issued.

The people of First Federal of Miami a[...]

of your savings accounts or home loans.

America's Number 1.

And if you're not one of our customers, we'd like to invite you to become one. After all, when it

comes to your savings and home loan, why settle for anything less than America's Number 1.

...e that Dr. Walker established ...r customers have enjoyed ...er 46 years: A real interest ...ing people save. And help-

...deral executives and civic leaders—1951.

...ople with mortgage financ-
...they can own their own
...
...u're already a First Federal
...mi customer, there is
...g you need to do—there
...hange in the status of any

The opening of our first branch office.

Our headquarters building—nothing's changed but the name.

...roud to present our brand new name.

FIRST
...RAL

...Office) 100 N.E. 1st Ave. **NORTHEAST:** 8380 N.E. 2nd Ave./9640 N.E. 2nd Ave./900 N.E. 125th St./18301 Biscayne Blvd. **CENTRAL:** 1400 N.W. 17th Ave.
...Dr./15101 S. Dixie Hwy. **HOMESTEAD:** 28875 S. Federal Hwy. **BROWARD COUNTY:** 3201 N. Federal Hwy. Oakland Park/Lochmann's Plaza at Palm-Aire/
.../Oakbrook Square Shopping Center, N. Palm Beach. **CENTRAL FLA:** 8 Orlando Div. Offices.

125

Introducing the

It's like any other checking account except for three big differences:

1. Your checking funds earn 5¼% a year interest compounded daily. The highest rate allowed by law.
2. You get a single monthly statement that itemizes all transactions for both your AmeriFirst Check account and all savings accounts opened under the same account number. Paid checks are returned with each statement. It's like a complete book-keeping service.
3. Only the AmeriFirst Check is backed by America's oldest and the South's largest Federal.

AmeriFirst Check service is free each month when you maintain a minimum checking balance of $500 or more, or a total balance of $10,000 or more in all accounts listed on our single combined monthly statement. If your checking balance falls below $500 and your combined balance is less than $10,000, your monthly service charge will be only $3. (For Senior Citizens aged 62 or older, there's no service charge regardless of balance.)

You get free personalized wallet-style checks, too when you keep a total of $10,000 or more in the checking and savings accounts listed on your combined statement.

So now you can enjoy the convenience of having both your savings and checking accounts at AmeriFirst; it can save you time and effort. And no matter where you open your account, you can do business at any of the 45 convenient AmeriFirst offices located throughout Florida.

It all checks out to a lot of differences. 5¼% a year interest on your checking account. One consolidated monthly statement. And the convenience, security, and peace of mind of doing business at the South's largest Federal where your funds are secure, backed by over $3 billion in assets.

Stop by now and open your checking account at the one place where you get all these big differences. AmeriFirst Federal.

America's oldest Federal has a brand new name—AmeriFirst Federal. It's a name that reflects our heritage and traditions as the nation's oldest Federal. One that reflects our Association as it is today—the South's largest Federal with over $2½ Billion in assets—serving many communities throughout South and Central Florida.

Dr. W. H. Walker, founder of America's first Federal.

It all started back in 1933, when Dr. W. H. Walker went to Washington and came home with Charter #1—for the first Federal savings and loan association in America. He named his company First Federal of Miami and established a standard of service that made First Federal a leader from the beginning.

Our Charter #1, the first issued.

But soon, many other First Federals were opening for business. Today, there are more than 40 different First Federals in Florida alone, and hundreds more nationwide. Sometimes it gets kind of confusing.

1 First Federal of Miami
Over $2½ Billion Strong-Largest in the South

As we continue to expand our services statewide, it's important that we have a name that will set us apart. One that's not easily confused with anyone else.

So, First Federal of Miami is now AmeriFirst Federal.

But, only our name has changed.

You'll find the same friendly people, the same convenient locations, and the same security and insurance for your savings

First Federal of Miami grew up with Florida.

accounts. And most importantly, you'll find the same traditions

First Federal executives and civic leaders—1951.

of service that Dr. Walker established and our customers have enjoyed for over 46 years: A real interest in helping people save. And helping people with mortgage financing so they can own their own homes.

If you're already a First Federal of Miami customer, there is nothing you need to do—there is

America's Number 1.

no change in the status of any of your savings accounts or home loans.

And if you're not one of our

Our headquarters building— nothing's changed but the name.

customers, we'd like to invite you to become one. After all, when it comes to your savings and home loan, why settle for anything less than America's Number 1.

The people of First Federal of Miami are proud to present our brand new name.

AMERIFIRST FEDERAL

General Institutional Image

This bank president is out to make Citizens Central a household word.

R. Carlos Carballada, president of Citizens Central Bank, won't try to teach your babies how to say Citizens Central. All he wants to do is to help you with your household chores if you're the lucky winner in Citizens Central Bank's hand-for-a-day contest.

All you do is fill out the coupon. Just deposit it at any Citizens Central Bank office. And you've got a chance to win the services of Mr. Carballada or one of his seven branch officers.

Mr. Carballada isn't any slouch and neither are his branch officers. So keep your hand-for-a-day busy all day. He'll do laundry, cut the lawn, wash windows or the car. He'll even babysit your kids.

Last year, Mr. Carballada worked for Chuck Dominessy doing stock boy chores in his pharmacy. The year before that, Ed Fontaine got a real kick out of watching him milk cows and clean the barn. This year he may be cleaning something else.

Any homeowner can win this year's hand-for-a-day contest. Just stop in at any Citizens Central office and drop off your coupon today.

The drawing will be held on Saturday, June 30th. Winners can claim their hands on Thursday, July 12th.

"Hand-for-a-day." An exclusive, not-so-big-city service from the country bank.

Return to any Citizens Central office no later than Saturday, June 30th.

Name _____

Address _____

City/Town _____

Telephone No. _____

Do you live in a home? _____ or apartment? _____

How many in your family? _____

Citizens Central
A Charter
New York Bank

The country bank with big city services.
Arcade, Delevan, Rushford, Silver Springs, Yorkshire, Elba, Lyndonville.

Member F.D.I.C.

The name that counts is yours.

The fact that Cleveland Trust is now AmeriTrust may take some getting used to at first.

For us as well as for you.

But the new name doesn't change anything as far as you're concerned.

Your old Cleveland Trust passbooks, accounts, checks, VISA and FastCashier cards, and loans are still as good as ever.

It's *your* name that counts. Not ours.

AmeriTrust.

A great new bank was born in 1894.

When Cleveland Trust began serving Cleveland, the boundaries of our city stopped about a mile east of Wade Park and a mile west of Edgewater Park.

But our city grew and prospered, and as it did, Cleveland Trust kept expanding to help finance this growth, both business and personal, through depressions, wars and panics, bad times and good.

The communities kept getting bigger and bigger, until the "neighborhood" we serve today is all of Ohio, MidAmerica — the industrial heartland of the United States — and beyond.

But, until now, you wouldn't have known it by our name.

CLEVELAND TRUST

And again in 1979.

So now we'll be known as AmeriTrust of Cleveland, a new name for a bank that was 85 years in the making.

AmeriTrust. A five billion dollar bank holding company with 120 offices in Ohio.

AmeriTrust. A family of 10 affiliate banks, now with a common identity.

AmeriTrust. A new name for the banks that are making things happen in MidAmerica.

Thanks largely to the good neighborhood we grew up in.

Meet the bank that trust built.

Meet AmeriTrust of Cleveland, a new name for Cleveland Trust, Ohio's largest bank.

The name is new, but it inherits an 85-year legacy of trust in its customers and the citizens of Cleveland.

Enough trust to pioneer branch banking, continuously building new offices to serve Cleveland as the city stretched and grew.

A "Trust for all Time"— the Cleveland Foundation established in 1914, as the nation's first community trust fund.

A trust in people symbolized by keeping its doors open to customers wishing to withdraw their deposits during the panic of 1933 when many Cleveland banks failed.

A trust in Cleveland's future that has spent over $55 million to restore and enlarge its downtown headquarters and build new branches in the last 10 years, and is committed to more.

AmeriTrust may represent a new name in MidAmerican banking, but it's hardly an overnight success story.

It took a bank like Cleveland Trust to build it. And a city like Cleveland to make it possible.

AmeriTrust

AmeriTrust
CHARLES FLETCHER

134

After 85 years, we made a name
for ourselves.

AmeriTrust

We started corporate life as Cleveland Trust.

Since then we've become one of America's largest bank holding companies with over $5.5 billion in assets and $7 billion in trust assets. Our lead bank lends up to $40 million to a single customer.

In profitability and capital strength, our performance is about double the large bank average for 1979. In the last 16 years, our dividends paid have grown faster than all but four of the top 50 in America.

Our family of banks has grown in scope as well as size, with 120 offices plus national and international capabilities in innovative lending and cash management.

Now, we have a name to take us to a new horizon. AmeriTrust. A major financial institution attuned to all of today's financial needs and preparing for all of tomorrow's.

You'll remember the name. Just think of America. And trust.

The bank on the North Coast

The North Coast of America
MidAmerica to the world.
AmeriTrust Corporation:
the $5.5 billion family of banks wi
helps keep MidAmerica's comm
Innovative financing that
in Illinois, grows corn in I
in Minnesota, pours steel
AmeriTrust began corporate life
85 years ago. We've grown with the time
Now our name reflects our broader bus
Today, your banking needs may
But tomorrow, you may need the bank
in America's heartland. With its wealth
things happen for you in MidAmerica.

ernational shoreline that links

offices that **that's making**
mming.
actors **things happen in**
nes ore

eland Trust **Mid America.**
merica.
rizons.
l serviced by a West or East Coast bank.
North Coast that's totally in touch with business
es and ideas, AmeriTrust wants to make

AmeriTrust.
900 Euclid Avenue, Cleveland, Ohio 44101

"You can't miss it, Gridley, Long Island is somewhere east of Shea Stadium."

WORLD WIDE BANK INC.

Does your banker know Long Island as well as he knows Manhattan island?

Most big city banks use Long Island as a training ground for their young calling officers.

If they prove themselves, it's back to their Manhattan headquarters to work on a Fortune 500 account.

At Long Island Trust, our calling officers get ahead by helping their Long Island customers get ahead.

After all, our business is on Long Island. Not Manhattan island.

We're dedicated to Long Island.

We've been helping local businesses for over 50 years. In fact, over 95 percent of our loans are made to Long Islanders.

When you take out a loan with us, your application doesn't commute to Manhattan for approval.

Our headquarters are in Garden City. And for a regional bank, we're among the largest in the country, with close to a billion dollars in assets.

Our officers know their customer's business.

We have senior lending officers throughout the Island. So they're always available to approve a loan request.

Our officers know a lot about Long Island business, too. In fact, many are specialists in Long Island industries.

So whether you're a fisherman in Montauk, an electronics manufacturer in Suffolk, or a retailer in Garden City, come into Long Island Trust. We're the bank that works for you.

Long Island Trust
A LITCO BANCORPORATION SUBSIDIARY   MEMBER FDIC
The Island's largest bank.

A new tree to come to for shelter.

A new tree to come to for shelter.

After 60 years we're changing our name.

We're not changing our goal. We still want to be your savings institution.

A new tree to come to for shelter.

After 60 years we're changing our name.

We're not changing our goal. We still want to be your savings institution.

BB&L is now Brazos Savings.

We're branching out. But our roots still run deep in the Brazos Valley.

BRAZOS Savings

Brazos Savings Association of Texas

Main Office: 2800 Texas Avenue/Bryan, TX 77801/779-2800

141

142

"THIS COULD BE THE BEGINNING OF A BEAUTIFUL RELATIONSHIP."

O pening a savings or checking account at Hospital Trust can be the beginning of a lasting and meaningful relationship. Hospital Trust can provide all the banking services you need — now and later when you go out to conquer the world.
We have 24-hour Automatic Teller Machines. Master Charge. Visa. Tuition loans. Auto loans. Traveler's Checks. NOW Accounts. And all the corporate and trust services so dear to the hearts of lawyers, accountants and M.B.A.'s.

YOU FEEL BETTER BANKING AT HOSPITAL TRUST.

"How Come My Letter From Home Was Only A Letter From Home?"

No money. Just a letter. That's when you appreciate having a little extra
tucked away in a Hospital Trust checking or savings account.
It's convenient. Hospital Trust has 37 offices throughout Rhode Island.
And we have Automatic Teller Machines so you can make withdrawals
from your account any time of the night or day.
You can even arrange to have dear old Dad remit your allowance directly to your account.

You Feel Better Banking At Hospital Trust. ⊞

A simple guide to a no-risk, high-interest, high-yield investment from Home Federal

Increase your initial deposit by over 100%!

Most of the things we enjoy most in our lives are simple and uncomplicated. We think you'll agree, Home Federal's 8% investment account is no exception. Deposit $1,000 or more for 8 years and 8 months, and we *guarantee* you double your money. No brokerage or attorneys fees. No complications. Visit Home Federal today and find out how easy it is to earn high interest in complete safety.

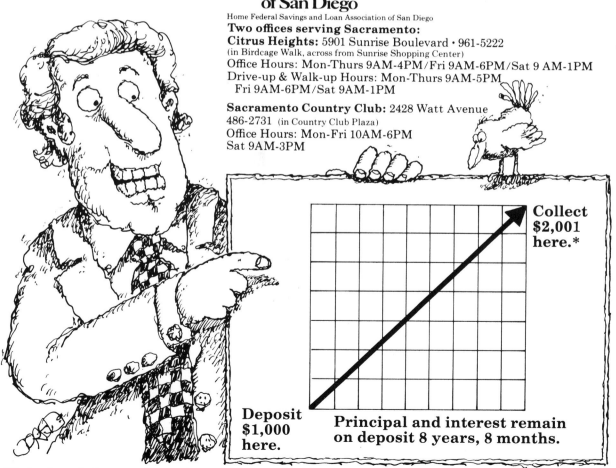

HOME FEDERAL SAVINGS
of San Diego

Home Federal Savings and Loan Association of San Diego

Two offices serving Sacramento:
Citrus Heights: 5901 Sunrise Boulevard · 961-5222
(in Birdcage Walk, across from Sunrise Shopping Center)
Office Hours: Mon-Thurs 9AM-4PM/Fri 9AM-6PM/Sat 9 AM-1PM
Drive-up & Walk-up Hours: Mon-Thurs 9AM-5PM
 Fri 9AM-6PM/Sat 9AM-1PM

Sacramento Country Club: 2428 Watt Avenue
486-2731 (in Country Club Plaza)
Office Hours: Mon-Fri 10AM-6PM
Sat 9AM-3PM

Collect $2,001 here.*

Deposit $1,000 here.

Principal and interest remain on deposit 8 years, 8 months.

*Federal regulations require a substantial interest forfeiture for early withdrawal of term accounts. Principal and interest must remain in the account for the full term to achieve this growth.

145

You should get more for saving than a certificate

Join the Home Federal Investor Club.

Any savings institution will provide a good interest rate on a deposit of $2,500 or more. But, if that's all you're getting for your money, withdraw it and bring it to Home Federal. A $2,500 deposit here entitles you to membership in the Investor Club, use of the Investor Club lounge and a giant portfolio of special services—with no service charges. You should get more for saving than a certificate. And you do. At Home Federal.

HOME FEDERAL SAVINGS
of San Diego

Two offices serving Sacramento:

Citrus Heights: 5901 Sunrise Boulevard • 961-5222
(in Birdcage Walk, across from Sunrise Shopping Center)
Office Hours: Mon-Thurs 9AM-4PM/Fri 9AM-6PM/Sat 9AM-1PM
Drive-up & Walk-up Hours: Mon-Thurs 9AM-5PM/Fri 9AM-6PM/Sat 9AM-1PM

Sacramento Country Club: 2428 Watt Avenue • 486-2731
(in Country Club Plaza)
Office Hours: Mon-Fri 10AM-6PM/Sat 9AM-3PM

Home Federal Savings and Loan Association of San Diego

Here's how to defer taxes as you slide gracefully into a lower tax bracket

1. open

If you are not presently covered by a pension plan, open an Individual Retirement Account (IRA) at Home Federal.

2. defer

Each year, you can contribute 15% or $1,500 (whichever is less) to your IRA retirement fund.

And, you can subtract your annual contribution from taxable income on both your Federal and State income tax returns.

3. enjoy

You continue to defer taxes right up to the time you're in a more comfortable tax bracket. Start as early as 59½ or as late as 70½. It's your decision.

Ready to get started? Open your IRA account at Home Federal now.

HOME FEDERAL SAVINGS
of San Diego

Two offices serving Sacramento:
Citrus Heights: 5901 Sunrise Boulevard • 961-5222
(in Birdcage Walk, across from Sunrise Shopping Center)
Office Hours: Mon-Thurs 9AM-4PM / Fri 9AM-6PM / Sat 9AM-1PM
Drive-up & Walk-up Hours: Mon-Thurs 9AM-5PM / Fri 9AM-6PM / Sat 9AM-1PM

Sacramento Country Club: 2428 Watt Avenue • 486-2731
(in Country Club Plaza)
Office Hours: Mon-Fri 10AM-6PM / Sat 9AM-3PM

Home Federal Savings and Loan Association of San Diego

When you're out
We're in

The beauty of Saturday hours
at Home Federal Savings

Most of the people we know are tied up on business during business hours. Which is why we extended our business hours beyond yours—to include Saturdays. When you're easily able to get out and about, we're in. Ready to serve. With a smile. We also set up special hours to give you a chance to catch us on your way home during the week, if you need us. If the idea of customer hours appeals to you, drop in this Saturday and find out how Home Federal can give you more than time. We have a lot of great ways to help you save money, too.

HOME FEDERAL SAVINGS
of San Diego

Two offices serving Sacramento:
Citrus Heights: 5901 Sunrise Boulevard • 961-5222
(in Birdcage Walk, across from Sunrise Shopping Center)
Office Hours: Mon-Thurs 9AM-4PM/Fri 9AM-6PM/Sat 9AM-1PM
Drive-up & Walk-up Hours: Mon-Thurs 9AM-5PM/Fri 9AM-6PM/Sat 9AM-1PM

Sacramento Country Club: 2428 Watt Avenue • 486-2731
(in Country Club Plaza)
Office Hours: Mon-Fri 10AM-6PM/Sat 9AM-3PM

Monday—Tied up all day.

Tuesday—Lunch with boss.

Wednesday—Lunch at desk.

Thursday—Panic. No lunch.

Friday—Surprise visit from corporate H.Q.

Saturday—You're free. We're open.

Home Federal Savings and Loan Association of San Diego

149

On Saturday,
if you need Home Federal,
we'll be there.

Home Federal is open on Saturday from 9:00 AM to 1:00 PM.

So, if your Saturday schedule includes getting caught up on things financial, we're the best place for you to keep your money.

Unlike most other financial institutions, we always have plenty of time for you, even on the weekend.

Enjoy your Saturdays. Relax, shop and play. And when you're passing the intersection of Poway or Pomerado Roads, remember this.

If you need Home Federal, we'll be there.

In Poway at 12411 Poway Road. Call 748-1133.

Lobby hours:
Monday-Thursday
9:00 AM-4:00 PM
Friday 9:00 AM-5:30 PM
Saturday 9:00 AM-1:00 PM

Walk-up hours:
Monday-Thursday 4:00-5:00 PM
Friday 5:30-6:00 PM

Drive up hours:
Monday-Thursday
9:00 AM-5:00 PM
Friday 9:00 AM-6:00 PM
Saturday 9:00 AM-1:00 PM

HOME
FEDERAL
SAVINGS
of San Diego

Home Federal Country. There are futures building here.

150

To reserve a free room in Poway, call Home Federal.

When community organizations need a place to meet in Poway, they call 748-1133 and ask for Dottee Campbell, Home Federal Office Manager.

Because Home Federal has a special community meeting room that seats up to 60, classroom style. And, it's available free of charge to any community group (subject to prior scheduling).

The YMCA, Chamber of Commerce, Soroptomists, Real Estate Board, School Board, Water District and Sheriff's Department are among the groups who are taking advantage of this facility.

If your group could benefit by use of our free meeting space, call Home Federal. Don't be bashful if you're not a Home Federal customer. The room is here to benefit the entire community.

To reserve a free room in Poway, call Home Federal Savings of San Diego.

In Poway at 12411 Poway Road.
Call 748-1133
Lobby hours:
Monday-Thursday 9:00 AM-4:00 PM
Friday 9:00 AM-5:30 PM
Saturday 9:00 AM-1:00 PM
Walk-up hours:
Monday-Thursday 4:00-5:00 PM
Friday 5:30-6:00 PM
Drive-up hours:
Monday-Thursday 9:00 AM-5:00 PM
Friday 9:00 AM-6:00 PM
Saturday 9:00 AM-1:00 PM

HOME FEDERAL SAVINGS
of San Diego

Home Federal Country. There are futures building here.

Home Federal Savings & Loan Association of San Diego

151

Drive up, walk up or trot up — 6 days a week

Savers on horseback. It could only happen here in Poway. And it's no problem at Home Federal. Because making things convenient for our savers is what we do best.

So whether you drive up, walk up or trot up to our handy location at Poway and Pomerado Roads, we're ready.

Even on Saturday.

In Poway at 12411 Poway Road. Call 748-1133

Lobby hours:
Monday-Thursday
9:00 AM-4:00 PM
Friday 9:00 AM-5:30 PM
Saturday 9:00 AM-1:00 PM

Walk up hours:
Monday-Thursday 4:00-5:00 PM
Friday 5:30-6:00 PM

Drive up hours:
Monday-Thursday
9:00 AM-5:00 PM
Friday 9:00 AM-6:00 PM
Saturday 9:00 AM-1:00 PM

HOME FEDERAL SAVINGS
of San Diego

Home Federal Country. There are futures building here.

Home Federal Savings & Loan Association of San Diego

How to pay 5 bills with one phone call and no postage

When it's bill-paying time, call Home Federal. Tell us who you want to pay and how much to pay them. We write the checks and deliver them. It's that simple.

Paying bills is only one of the things you can do with a $1,000 minimum balance Money Mover account.

You can move cash from your bank checking account to a Home Federal Savings account and back again. So, when you're not spending, those checking dollars earn 5½% interest at Home Federal.

You can also transfer funds to your broker, as fast as a phone call, to take advantage of an exceptional opportunity.

Money Mover. It saves time, trouble, energy and money . . . while you earn more interest than is paid at any bank.

In Poway at 12411 Poway Road.
Call 748-1133.

Lobby hours:
Monday-Thursday 9:00 AM-4:00 PM
Friday 9:00 AM-5:30 PM
Saturday 9:00 AM-1:00 PM
Walk up hours:
Monday-Thursday 4:00-5:00 PM
Friday 5:30-6:00 PM
Drive up hours:
Monday-Thursday 9:00 AM-5:00 PM
Friday 9:00 AM-6:00 PM

HOME FEDERAL SAVINGS of San Diego

Home Federal Country. There are futures building here.

153

You can buy more than high interest in our money market.

Home Federal T-Certificates are 26-week, $10,000 minimum balance investments.

For investing that amount, you'd expect high Money Market interest. Which is exactly what you get at Home Federal. And, that's just the beginning.

For openers, your investment is guaranteed . . . there are no brokers or attorney fees . . . and your account is insured to $40,000 by an agency of the federal government.

You defer taxes, too. The interest earned on our Series B T-Certificates does not have to be declared until you file your 1980 income tax return.

And, you automatically receive membership in our exclusive Investor Club. A complete portfolio of services with no service charges, including: a personal safe deposit box, document copying and travelers checks and money orders.

Visit us today, or call for the current rate and yield on T-Certificates. And remember that high interest is only the beginning at Home Federal Savings.

In Poway at 12411 Poway Road.
Call 748-1133.

Lobby hours:
Monday-Thursday 9:00 AM-4:00 PM
Friday 9:00 AM-5:30 PM
Saturday 9:00 AM-1:00 PM
Walk up hours:
Monday-Thursday 4:00-5:00 PM
Friday 5:30-6:00 PM
Drive up hours:
Monday-Thursday 9:00 AM-5:00 PM
Friday 9:00 AM-6:00 PM

HOME FEDERAL SAVINGS
of San Diego

Home Federal Country. There are futures building here.

Home Federal Savings & Loan Association of San Diego.

154

Home Federal Country
There are futures building here.

It's a warm, comfortable feeling, being helped by someone you trust.
That's why so many Californians look to Home Federal
to help them plan for their future.
The security of our guaranteed investments makes the future predictable ... and bright.
Come visit Home Federal Country.
There are futures building here.

HOME FEDERAL SAVINGS
of San Diego

Choose a banker guaranteed for the life of your business.

We're piggish on Pike County.

We're bullish on America too, but Pike County is the area Farmers State has always been known to root for. Farmers State Bank has a lot of confidence in the people of Pike County and in what they are doing. That's because we know Pike Countians are energetic, hard working and progressive. That's the way we want people to see us over at the bank. All the energies, interest and progressive banking services we can muster will always be devoted to keeping Pittsfield and Pike County on the grow.

Farmers State, and our number of customers are growing too. There's a "stick-together, help-one-another" feeling you ought to check out if you're not banking at Farmers State. From a complete range of checking and savings plans, including convenient drive-up and bank-by-mail to lending services for a wide range of needs, Farmers State offers the most comprehensive banking services in the area. And, we're constantly adding to them with new services like the 24-Hour TellerPhone and our Corntribution Wagon for community fund raising and support of special occasions like Pig Day. Pig Day . . . Pike County . . . You . . . and Farmers State. When you think about it, who wouldn't be Piggish on Pike County?

Farmers State Bank

Pittsfield, IL 62363   217-285-5585

A change for the better.

158

"WE CAN PROMISE THE WORLD. AND DELIVER IT."

Meet a tough, professional banker.

Dick Harding is manager of Pacificbank's International Department. He's serious about his job. Good at what he does. And his knowledge of international banking comes first-hand because, like other senior staff members, he's put in time overseas.

"Pound for pound, we have more off-shore banking experience than any other bank in the State. We know our way around the world because we've been there".

Dick will tell you that Pacificbank offers the best of two worlds when you're doing business abroad.

"We're the State's third largest full service bank, and because of our size, we can be more responsive, make faster decisions, and give our customers more personal attention".

At the same time, Pacificbank can match international services with the biggest banks in the country, because they're part of Western Bancorporation, a $25 billion multi-bank holding company.

"We have six representative offices overseas. And access to Western Bancorporation branches around the world. And because we're all part of the same organization, we can get more done, faster for our clients".

Dick Harding is a tough, professional banker. Like others in his department, he knows that import-export trade is burgeoning in the Northwest. And he's ready to help Washington companies make the most of it.

Call (206) 292-3340. Ask for Dick Harding. When it comes to banking abroad, he knows the territory.

Pacificbank

A TOUGH, PROFESSIONAL BANK.

Richard Harding, vice president and manager of Pacificbank's International Department, with Taky Kimura, Great Empire Trading Company.

159

"IN PENSION AND PROFIT-SHARING, THE BOTTOM LINE IS PERFORMANCE.

AND WE'RE THE TOPS."

Meet a tough, professional banker.

Bob Smith is the man to talk to about Pacificbank's pension and profit-sharing capabilities. He'll tell you that Pacificbank manages employee benefit trusts for a diverse group of companies. And the Bank's track record is second to none among Washington banks.

"Last year, Pension & Investments magazine (August 28, 1978) put us in the Number Two spot nationally of 196 banks and insurance companies for equity investment performance over the last nine years."

Among others, Frank Russell Co., Inc. concurs. They ranked Pacificbank eighth nationally of 113 banks in equity investment performance for the eight years ending December 31, 1978.

"Better performance, even a little better, can make a big difference in a company's employee benefits over the years."

Bob Smith is a tough, professional banker. He knows performance is only part of a successful pension and profit-sharing relationship. There has to be personal attention and good service, and Bob's ready to deliver that, too.

Call 292-3731. Ask for Bob Smith. He's a good investment in your company's future.

Pacificbank

A TOUGH, PROFESSIONAL BANK. ™

A Western Bancorporation Bank.   Member F.D.I.C.

Pacificbank's Bob Smith, Director of Marketing for Employee Benefits, with Ben J. Smith, Jr., President of Seattle Mortgage.

THE BANK OF HIGHWOOD WOULD.

Ten Highwood Avenue, Highwood   433-3000

THE BANK OF HIGHWOOD MAY LOOK SMALL. BUT UNDERNEATH, IT ISN'T.

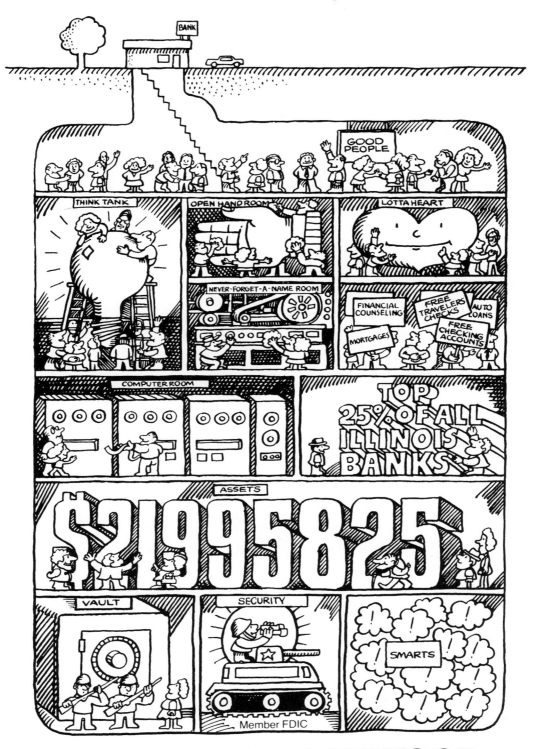

THE BANK OF HIGHWOOD
Neighborhood bank for the whole North Shore

In our business
if anything happens to either one of us
we could be out of business.

IT HELPS TO KNOW SOMEONE WITH MONY.

A partner dies.

Or becomes disabled.

Either could be disastrous to any business. But, with the help of someone with MONY, Mutual Of New York, you can plan on doing business as usual if the unusual should occur.

MONY agents have the professional skills to design a program especially for you and your partners.

They'll take into account the specifics of your business, its potential for growth and other change, and the families involved.

They'll draw on services like AIDS, a computerized illustration system, to analyze various solutions to insurance problems. And a Home Office Consulting Service to help them develop insurance programs for even the most complex business, estate and tax situations.

In short, MONY insurance specialists provide the expertise and personal service that few insurance companies can deliver.

They could help keep you in business. So talk to someone with **MONY**

The Mutual Life Insurance Company of New York, 1740 Broadway, New York, N.Y. 10019

We've become so used to living on our two incomes
if anything happened to either of us
the family would be in trouble.

IT HELPS TO KNOW
SOMEONE WITH MONY.

Families that depend on two incomes have become the rule today. Unfortunately, families where both incomes are fully protected are still the exception.

If there are two wage earners in your household, it will help to know someone with MONY, Mutual Of New York.

MONY agents realize that to protect you completely it is essential to look at your combined total income.

They'll help you design a plan that's right for you, based on your needs, obligations and life-style. And one with the flexibility for change in the future.

In short, our insurance professionals will provide you with the expertise and personalized service few insurance companies can deliver.

So call us today. Because whatever happens, it helps to have **M$NY**

JIMMY GOT PLASTERED LAST NIGHT.

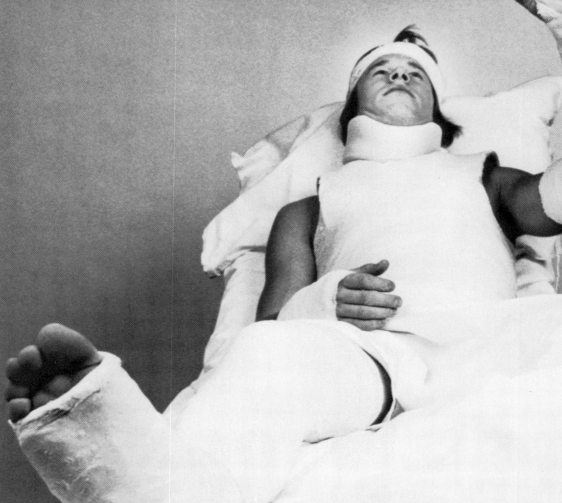

Don't Drink and Drive.

 Prepared as a public service by Colonial Bank.

KAREN GOT SMASHED
LAST NIGHT.

Don't Drink and Drive.

Prepared as a public service by Colonial Bank.

How Budgeting Can Set You Free.

Have you ever found yourself wondering where the money's gone at the end of the month? Probably more often than you'd care to admit. Worse yet, if you're like most people, you have no idea how much you've spent, or on what. But like most people, you probably think the alternative — living on a budget — would be about as liberating as a straightjacket, right? Wrong.

No Muss. No Fuss. No Guessing.

Living on a budget doesn't have to be a pain. On the contrary, budgeting has a way of taking you out of the dark. It can tell you exactly where you stand from one month to the next. There's no guessing. No wondering where all the money went. Probably for the first time, you feel in control of your life...and less controlled by your debts.

Making a List and Checking it Twice

Basically a budget is a list. It tells you what you're going to spend your money on during the month. For most, the list is broken down into income, fixed expenses (these are the ones you can't avoid — like your rent or mortgage, gas for the car, utilities, taxes, payments and savings) and variable expenses (these are the ones that make up your day-to-day living expenses — like groceries, dinners out, the new roof, the shoes for Joey, the night at the movies and the kids' allowances).

To figure out what your budget is, subtract the total amount of fixed expenses you currently have from your take home pay. What's left is the amount of money you have to spend on variable expenses over the coming month.

If the total for variable expenses is more than the amount you have to spend, check your list again. Something's got to go.

Little White Lies Will Get You in the End

When you're figuring your expenses, be honest with yourself. Put down what's real, not what you'd like things to be. You won't stay on your budget long if it becomes "hard work", so keep it simple. Don't figure down to pennies. Be flexible. If you leave yourself too little leeway you're sure to fail.

Sock it To Your Savings

Pay yourself first. That's the golden rule of any budget. Every month, when you sit down to pay your bills, write your savings account a check, too. Before you know it, those small monthly saving "expenses" you've socked away will amount to a chubby little nest egg.

Remember though, be honest. Put down a total you can reasonably expect to save each month. If you get a raise, try saving half of it. Chances are, you won't miss it.

A Quick Way To Test the Water

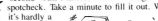

We've put together what we call the 60 second "Am-I-In-Hot-Water ?" budget spotcheck. Take a minute to fill it out. While it's hardly a substitute for the more detailed budget sheet, it should tell you fairly fast whether or not you're holding your own or drowning financially.

The 60 Second "Am-I-in-Hot-Water ?" Budget Spotcheck

Monthly Take Home Income	$ _____
Fixed Expenses	
Mortgage	$ _____
Utilities	$ _____
Loans (auto or other)	$ _____
Installment payments (including credit cards)	$ _____
Savings (for insurance payments, taxes, future and emergency needs)	$ _____
Total Fixed Expenses	$ _____
Amount available for Variable Expenses (subtract Fixed Expenses from take home income)	$ _____
Variable Expenses	
Food	$ _____
Household Maintenance	$ _____
Transportation	$ _____
Recreation (dinner out, vacation etc.)	$ _____
Miscellaneous (Clothing, Medical etc.)	$ _____
Total Variable Expenses	$ _____

If your total variable expenses exceed the amount you had available for variable expenses, you're in hot water.

This is part of a continuing series of inflation-fighting ads from Bank of Commerce to help you make the most of your money.

Watch for other ads on subjects like college financing, planning your expenses, shopping for new and used cars, and credit opportunities for women.

Bank of Commerce
7th & Boulder, Tulsa, Oklahoma
584-3321

The Bank that Means Business

Member FDIC

How to Tell If That New Dream House Is Really the House You've Already Got

So the old dream house has turned into a nightmare of crowded bathrooms and leaks in the roof. That once modern kitchen is starting to look like something from a 20-year-old ad. And instead of over-stuffed chairs in the living room, it's the living room itself that's overstuffed. With family.

Welcome to the ranks of American families who have outgrown their houses. Families who find themselves starting off in search of that new dream house. It's natural enough. So natural, in fact, that the great majority of people in this situation don't look closely enough at their options.

Step #1.

When you put your house up for sale, people will be trooping through, sizing the place up, saying, "This place has great possibilities." So, if you're thinking of selling and moving on — that's the first thing to look at. The possibilities.

Make a list of your "if only's". "If only the kitchen were bigger." "If only we could open up some of the living rooms a bit." "If only we could add a half bath." "If only we could add a bedroom." "If only we could put in a den." "If only we had a fireplace." And so on. All those "if only's" could well become real improvements to the house you think no longer meets your needs.

Step #2.

"Ah," you say. "Remodeling costs like everything." Have you looked at mortgage rates and home prices lately?

After you've listed all the things you really want and need in a house, it's time to look at some hard facts and figures.

First Things First.

Before you can begin to think about reworking your house, you have to consider your house's structure and what kind of shape it's in. And the best place to begin is the foundation. If mortar is soft and crumbly, your foundation might need anything from complete rebuilding to a fairly substantial repair job.

In poured concrete foundations, some cracking is normal. Open cracks, on the other hand, usually mean a failure that will get worse.

In the case of wood used in the foundation, check wood beams for rot. Prying against the grain with a knife, the wood should splinter cleanly. Since termites aren't so easily detectable, it's best to have your house gone over by a professional exterminator.

Make notes of your observations, so you can point them out to a contractor later on.

Your Home From a Bird's-eye View.

Pay particular attention to the roof, chimney, window casings, and frame of your house. For example, that once straight roof line could well have begun to sag — a sign that the roof, or possibly the frame itself, is out of kilter.

In the case of roofing material, look for brittleness in asbestos shingles and signs of rot in your wood shingles.

Carefully examine your chimney for loose mortar or unusual settling. Again, make notes you can discuss with a contractor.

If These Walls Could Talk.

Quite often, they would tell you they're getting old and tired. Look closely at the alignment of walls, floors, door frames, and window frames. And, again, make notes of anything that is in obvious need of repair, as well as anything that is questionable.

Never Overlook the Obvious.

Furnace, water heater, air conditioning, appliances, plumbing, wiring, duct work, even insulation. They all have to be considered. Have a professional check them out for you.

When it comes to insulation, the amount and type of insulation you'll need will depend upon what improvements you will be making. Insulation is another point to discuss with a contractor, but it pays to read up on the subject, too.

So the Place Needs Work.

Remember, your house has "possibilities". Discuss them with an expert. A contractor.

But, before you do, ask around. A contractor's best reference is his work. Talk to friends who have had work done. Ask who did their work and start the process off with people who have been recommended as qualified.

Armed with what improvements you would like to make, along with what improvements you need to make — sit down and have a long talk with your contractor. Have him re-check everything you checked. Talk with him about materials, design, and so forth.

Then, get a second opinion. Or even a third. And get detailed estimates of time and cost.

Don't Let the Big Numbers Scare You Off.

When does your remodeling project become too expensive? A good general rule is that the improvement should not exceed two-thirds the cost of a comparable new house. And even at that, remember — you're not talking about a comparable new house. You're talking about upgrading yourself to a better house.

Here's a simple computation you can do, using your contractor's estimate, your mortgage rate, the value of your present house, and the price of the house you were thinking of moving into. Very often, considering selling and closing costs, plus loan origination "points," a home improvement loan may be a better buy.

Value of present home	$_____
Less loan balance	$_____
Down payment available for new home	$_____
Cost of new home	$_____
Less down payment	$_____
Amount to be mortgaged	$_____
Monthly mortgage payment for 30 years (less taxes and insurance)	$_____
Monthly payment for improvement loan for 10 years	$_____
Plus present mortgage payment (less taxes and insurance)	$_____
	$_____

It really pays to get the most from your home investment. That can mean getting the most from your home. And whether it takes a lot of remodeling or a little. Whether you're going to have a contractor do the work, or do some of it yourself. Remember — we'd like to help you get the most from your home investment at Bank of Commerce.

This is part of a series of inflation-fighting ads from Bank of Commerce to help you make the most of your money. Watch for other ads on subjects like planning your expenses, buying a new car, and making money from gas-saving tips.

bc Bank of Commerce
7th & Boulder, Tulsa, Oklahoma
584-3321

The Bank that Means Business

Member F.D.I.C.

How to Cut Uncle Sam Out of Your Will

If you're like most of us, you're probably planning to leave your estate to your family. And Uncle Sam is planning to take some for himself. Now, thanks to trusts, you can make sure he doesn't get any more than he has to.

You Giveth. Estate Taxes Taketh Away.

Every year, millions of Americans sit down with their lawyers and prepare a will as a means of protecting their families. What they don't realize is that a will alone may not be enough to assure their family's full financial protection — especially with today's spiraling inflation and growing tax burden.

If There's a Will, There's a Way.

More and more families have turned to trusts as a way of protecting their loved ones.

Why trusts? Well, for one, an individual's estate is likely to last longer and be worth more over the long run if it's left in trust.

For another, it assures family members that beneficiaries will always be cared for — no matter how good or bad their health is.

And probably the biggest consideration of all, putting the estate in a trust can reduce the estate taxes your heirs are expected to pay Uncle Sam.

For Example:

To show you what we mean, let's take an example. Say Mr. and Mrs. Smith own property worth $300,000; their present plans call for Mr. Smith's share of the property to pass outright to his wife following his death. The couple has agreed that at Mrs. Smith's death everything remaining will be paid to their children.

Under today's new tax laws, no estate tax will be due on Mr. Smith's estate when he dies. That means, following his death, Mrs. Smith will have the full $300,000 to live on.

But, when Mrs. Smith dies, the estate no longer enjoys its favorable tax status. As much as $37,200 will have to be paid in estate taxes before Mrs. Smith's property is distributed to their children.

Had Mr. Smith left a portion of his property in trust for his wife's benefit, he could have virtually eliminated the estate taxes due at her death as well as at his own. The result: $37,200 saved for his children.

A Good Thing That Gets Better.

While the estate tax savings alone can make setting up a trust appealing, it's not the half of it. In addition to the tax break, a properly drawn up revocable trust makes sure you never lose control of your assets. The trust can be amended — even cancelled — at any time, by you. You can add or withdraw property. If you've got life insurance tied to your trust, you can borrow on your policies, or cash them in. Best of all, the whole trust arrangement can be adapted to events that you can't foresee at the time the trust is first set up. In addition, assets held in a revocable living trust avoid probate proceedings.

Figuring Out What You're Worth.

Take a minute to fill in the net worth estimate above. Once you've finished, round off the bottom figure and match it to those listed beneath it. It should give you a fair assessment of how much you're worth and how much you could save your family in estate taxes by setting up a trust.

Estimating Your Estate's Value

Assets

Bank Accounts	$ _____
Life Insurance...(Face Value)	_____
Current Value of Stocks and Bonds	_____
Market Value of Business Interest	_____
Pensions & Annuities	_____
Real Estate, Including Home	_____
Personal Property	_____
Other	_____
Total Assets	$ _____

Liabilities

Mortgage balance due	$ _____
Other loans due	_____
Total Liabilities	$ _____

Total Assets	$ _____
minus	
Total Liabilities	$ _____
equal NET WORTH	$ _____

Total Net Worth	Trust Can Save For Children, Up To
$250,000	$21,400
350,000	52,600
425,000	55,100
500,000	70,800

Making Sure *What* You Leave Behind Goes to *Who* You Leave Behind.

No one wants to think about dying. People don't even like to talk about it. And often it's the family who's left to pick up the pieces.

Making sure they're cared for is where the Bank of Commerce can help. Our people are trust experts. Working with you, your attorney, accountant and life underwriter, we can help you set up an estate plan that insures *what* you leave behind goes to *who* you leave behind. If you'd like to know more, come by or call us.

This is a part of a series of inflation-fighting ads from Bank of Commerce to help you make the most of your money.

Watch for other ads on subjects like home improvements, planning your expenses, buying a new car and credit opportunities for women.

Bank of Commerce
7th & Boulder, Tulsa, Oklahoma
584-3321

The Bank that Means Business.

How Women Can Rate With Creditors When They Don't Have A Credit Rating.

Used to be, women had a tough time getting credit and building a financial identity. And it's no wonder. The single working woman had to sit through questions like, "How soon are you planning to marry?" before the question of her financial ability was even brought up. As for the married woman — her financial identity was tied to her husband's. Completely.

But these days, with women taking a more active role in the economy, financial attitudes toward them — particularly toward working women — are undergoing a big change.

No Husband. No Money. No Credit.

In days past, when a woman married, she gave up any financial identity she might have had. Which probably was no problem as long as she had a husband to co-sign loans and apply for credit. But without him — especially if she didn't earn a salary outside the home — she found herself in real financial trouble. Credit was not something she could have without a husband.

But now the role of a married woman is recognized in all joint credit accounts, even when the wife is a full-time homemaker and doesn't earn a salary outside the home. When an account is opened, names of both husband and wife are forwarded to the credit bureau. That way, by using the account, a wife builds a credit history of her own.

Please, Make Me Worthy

When you're being considered for credit, creditors look at two things: One. Your ability to pay the loan back. (What they're talking about here is your income.) And two. Your willingness to pay the loan back. (Here's where your credit history comes in.)

If you're working, the first one should be no

problem. As for your local credit bureau probably has one on file. If not, they'll usually set one up for you for little or no cost.

This file spells out the details of most every credit relationship you've had. It lists the name of the credit grantor, the date the account was opened, the last transaction, the high amount of credit extended, the balance owed, any amount past due...everything a creditor would want to know and wouldn't hesitate to ask.

More Than One Way To Get There

If you've never married or you're divorced or widowed, and want to establish credit, there are a number of ways to go about it. One way is to apply for an account with a local merchant, dress shop or department store, or for one of the major universal credit cards.

Another is to obtain a small installment loan — the kind you repay in regular monthly payments. Here at Bank of Commerce, we

make all kinds of installment loans. For cars. For trips. For that new shag carpet in the living room. Even a business loan. Whatever it is, if you can meet the financial requirements — male or female — you'll get your loan. We'll make the paperwork fast, the payment plan as simple as we can. That you have our word on.

It also helps to have some money socked away in a savings account. That shows a potential creditor that you not only have some rainy day resources, but you can also manage your money well enough to have something left now and then at the end of the month. Here again, we'd be happy to help you set up the right kind of account to fit your situation.

They Can Still Say No, But Keep Trying.

Remember, if you get rejected for credit the first time out, don't be discouraged. Keep applying. But do it one store at a time.

If your request for credit is successful and you obtain a credit card, or an installment loan, bear in mind that it's a privilege, not a right. No one can be forced to give you a charge account. They just can't say no because you're a woman or divorced or single.

This is part of a continuing series of inflation-fighting ads from Bank of Commerce to help you make the most of your money.

Watch for other ads on subjects like home improvements, college financing, buying new and used cars, and expense planning.

Bank of Commerce
7th & Boulder, Tulsa, Oklahoma
584-3321

The Bank that Means Business.

How To Make Dollars and Sense Out Of Those Gas-Saving Tips.

They're cropping up everywhere. Those helpful-hints booklets dedicated to getting you more from the gasoline you buy. Some of them are good. Others are just plain crazy. And the advice ranges from tune-ups and tires to how much you can save by driving with your windows up.

If you're like most of us, you've got to wonder at some of the advice. And when it's expressed in percentages of fuel saved or mileage increased, it's hard to see any tangible gain from mending your driving ways.

Sorting Through the Advice.

While we're not going to tell you which tips to take and which to ignore, we *can* help you when it comes to saving gas. By presenting the money side of the gas-saving issue. Armed with that, along with one of the many good brochures available, you can more easily determine which tips will—or will not—save you money.

Getting It Down To Gallons and Cents.

Here's what you need and here's what you do: Go get a pencil and notepad, and put them in your glovebox. Then, summon up some real dedication. Write down everything. Every fill-up — the number of gallons and the cost. Every trip — the number of miles to and from. Keep a scrupulously accurate record for one month.

How To Use Your Own Cost Study.

Let's say that you've logged 1,000 miles in your month of keeping travel records. That's a fairly average number of miles to drive in a

month. By dividing the number of gallons of gas you've purchased into the number of miles you've driven, you learn that your car is taking you 25 miles on a gallon of gas. With gas at right around $1.10 a gallon, it's costing you $44.00 a month in gasoline.

Now then. Let's see how many cents we can shave off that $44.00 you're spending each month for gas.

When You Burn Gas, Make Sure You Burn It All.

Naturally enough, a car that's not in tune will waste plenty of gas. So, getting tuned up is the first piece of gas-saving advice we'll try.

By keeping your car in tune, you can get as much as 9% more out of the gas you buy. That figures out to be $3.96 over the course of a month. And now it's costing you $40.04. Let's see how much farther down we can go.

Rolling Easier.

Make it easier for your car to roll along. The second tip you might want to try is getting a set of radial tires for your car next time you need tires. Testing has shown that radials will increase your gas mileage as much as 10%. Remember now, we've already cut $3.96 off your monthly gas bill. So saving 10% of what's left means saving $4.00. Now your gas bill is down to $36.04.

Keep Constant Speeds, and You Keep On Saving.

The results of this tip will vary a great deal, all depending upon how you drive and where. Some estimates say that you can save as much as 20% by driving 55 as opposed to 65 or 70 on the open road.

Of course, 100% of your driving is not done on the open road. In the city, most estimates say you can save 10-20% by avoiding jackrabbit starts, trying to anticipate so you can keep as constant a speed as possible, and generally driving at modest speeds.

As we mentioned, the results will vary. A great deal. But, spend a month making a dedicated effort to drive conservatively. Staying at

the speed limit. Pacing yourself in traffic. And let's say, conservatively, that you save another 15%. You've just shaved off another $5.04, and you've got that monthly gas bill down to $30.64.

More Common Sense Will Save More Gas.

Then there are the intangibles. Those gas-saving tips that really amount to just plain old common sense can cut your monthly gas bill even more. To mention a few:

● Carpooling. Since you've already got good records on your monthly gas consumption and its cost, it will be easy to see how much gas can be eliminated by not driving to work every day. There's been a lot of talk about carpooling. And it's a great idea. If there's not a carpool at work — start one. Tack up a note at the water cooler or coffee pot, get one going, make new friends, and save lots more gas and money.

● Trip Center. Here's a little family project that can save you plenty of gas, money and time. Especially on busy weekends. Post a little chalkboard in the kitchen. Have every family member write down his or her errands for the day, and then try to schedule as many of them for one day as you can.

● Public Transportation. One of the greatest gas savers there is. And while you're saving gas and money, you can use the time to work, read, or talk with friends while someone else fights the traffic.

● Think. That's the most important thing. Drive sensibly. Drive less whenever possible. Keep your car at its peak of efficiency. And you'll just keep subtracting from that monthly gas bill. Your car is getting to be a bigger and bigger investment all the time. And the point to all this is that, as a big investment, you need to use the money you spend to buy and operate an automobile to the best of your advantage. The tips in this ad will help you get started toward making the most of your car. And when new-car time rolls around, we can help you make the most of your money again with an auto loan or custom leasing program.

This is part of a series of inflation-fighting ads from Bank of Commerce to help you make the most of your money. Watch for other ads on subjects like home improvements, planning your expenses, buying a new car and credit opportunities for women.

bc Bank of Commerce
7th & Boulder, Tulsa, Oklahoma
584-3321
The Bank that Means Business

Member F.D.I.C.

172

When you're out of work, you're out of luck. Unless you've got more than a credit card.

Saving for a rainy day is something your parents might have done, but it's totally out-of-date in today's economy.

"Oddly enough, quite often I'll recommend to my customers that they buy something on credit, instead of saving for it," says Merle Baucom of Home Federal Savings.

"Take a small appliance, a $200 to $300 item, for example. By the time you squirrel away the money to buy it, inflation has caused the price to go up by 50 to 100 per cent.

"In cases like that, people are usually surprised when I tell them they'd be better off using their credit card. Because Home Federal doesn't even have credit cards."

Merle Baucom of Home Federal Savings

But, even though saving for a rainy day is not always a good idea, saving for a *flood* might be the smartest thing you'll ever do. Merle explains the difference:

"As I said, using credit intelligently is one of the keys to managing money. But a credit card won't do you a bit of good when the unexpected happens — like a serious illness, an accident, losing your job, or anything that interrupts your normal income. Because even though your paycheck comes to a halt, the bills just keep coming. And if the situation should last long enough, you could very well find yourself in a financial hole that's just too deep to ever crawl out of."

The answer, of course, is to set aside enough money out of every paycheck to take care of the times when there *is* no paycheck.

Admittedly, that's easier said than done. But it *can* be done, no matter how hopeless it may look to you. Because at Home Federal, we've got a variety of savings plans, and one of them is bound to suit your pocketbook and your goals.

We'll give you the highest federally insured interest rates you can find anywhere in North Carolina and the soundest advice you can find anywhere in the world.

So stop by and talk with Merle, or any of our other people, about our emergency savings plans. But, please, do it soon. Before the unexpected happens. Unexpectedly.

HomeFederal Savings

We try to help people withold taxes from Uncle Sam. Instead of the other way around.

The way we figure it, you could use the money just as much as the government could. Maybe more. So, we've made it a habit in recent years to help our customers put more of their hard-earned money into a Keogh or IRA, and less into the IRS.

IRA, of course, is short for Individual Retirement Account, and it's designed for people who aren't covered by a pension plan where they work. Keogh, or HR-10, is a retirement account for self-employed people and their employees.

With a Keogh or IRA from Home Federal, you get a three-way tax break while you're building your own retirement program. Andy Anderson explains:

"First, you get a break on your state and Federal tax returns. Because you can put as much as 15 per cent of your income — up to $1,500, or $1,750 if you include your spouse — into your IRA, and you can deduct that amount from your gross income when April 15 rolls around. The same applies to the Keogh, except the limits are higher — $7,500 or 15% of your income, whichever is less.

Andy Anderson of Home Federal Savings

"You get another break on the interest your account earns. Because, unlike other savings accounts, you don't have to pay taxes on that interest each year.

"And the third tax break comes when you start withdrawing your money, anytime after age 59½. Because by that time, you're likely to be in a lower tax bracket."

But the important thing is that we're talking about a significant amount of money.

"Say you're 33 years old, for example," says Andy. "If you put in $1,500 each year, you'd put a total of $49,500 into your account by the time you reached 65. But because of the compounding effect of the interest, at current interest rates you'd have more than *a quarter of a million dollars** built up in your retirement account."

We encourage you to call Andy, or any of our other people, for a no-obligation analysis of your particular situation. But we encourage you to do so as soon as possible. Because retirement may seem like a long way away, but it gets a little closer every day.

HomeFederal Savings

Charlotte: Uptown, Cotswold, Park Road Shopping Center, and Eastland. North Mecklenburg: I-77 and Highway 73. Telephone 373-0400.
Assuming a level annual contribution of $1,500 on the first day of each year and a constant return of 8 percent, compounded daily, a Keogh or IRA after 33 years would yield an account balance of approximately $253,000. As with all time deposits, a substantial penalty is required for early withdrawal.

MEMBER
FSLIC
Federal Savings & Loan Insurance Corp.
Your Savings Insured to $40,000

Introducing a new service from Home Federal

Home Federal Country.
Where tomorrows start today.

If you're not prepared for the future, changes in your lifestyle can cause immeasurable harm.

Marriage, income loss or gain, sudden disability, divorce or death . . . all bring serious consequences.

Careful planning can minimize the effects of sudden change and help make the future more secure.

The question is, where can you find the help and direction you need to plan wisely?

Home Federal can help you

We have a confidential advisory program called Special Organizational Services (SOS). You don't have to be a customer to participate and there is no cost or obligation involved.

All you need do is visit any Home Federal office in San Diego County and ask for the SOS advisor.

A specially trained person will help you with a series of free booklets designed to get you organized now.

One is for personal organization and record keeping. Another will assist you in money management. And the third provides for careful retirement planning.

In addition to valuable information, the booklets themselves become part of your planning, as they include spaces for recording information for later reference.

Help for existing situations

If you need help due to a recent death, divorce or disability come to Home Federal for free, no-obligation SOS advisory service.

A specially trained person will help you determine what information, legal papers and benefits you may need. Without complication or confusion.

We promise, although we may not have a ready answer to every question, we'll try to find out who does.

SOS can help you get organized

The SOS service clearly does not replace the services of insurance agents, accountants or attorneys.

In fact, we recommend you use them when necessary.

What we do offer is help. Step-by-step direction to help you deal with your problems.

The sooner, the better

Come to Home Federal today for free assistance in planning for the future now . . . or after the fact assistance in dealing with immediate problems. SOS can help you — The sooner the better.

The largest San Diego-based Savings and loan Association

HOME FEDERAL SAVINGS
of San Diego

SOS. A free community service offered exclusively by your full-service family financial center. Home Federal Savings.

Alpine 2124 Arnold Way, across from Post Office • 445-2629
Carlsbad 2580 El Camino Real, across from Plaza Camino Real Ctr. 729-0917
Chula Vista 501 "H" St., at 5th • 427-7280
Clairemont 5825 Balboa Ave., across from FedMart • 565-8262
College Center 6080 El Cajon Blvd. at College • 583-1292
Coronado 1000 Orange Ave., between 10th St. & Isabella • 435-4141
Del Mar 2690 Via de la Valle, in Flower Hill Ctr. • 481-7151
Downtown San Diego 7th & Broadway • 238-7612
El Cajon 200 S. Magnolia, at Douglas • 440-1611
El Cajon/Parkway Plaza East, near Thrifty • 442-9411
Encinitas 221 West "E" St., at 3rd • 753-5536
Encinitas/Village Square 1452 Encinitas Blvd. • 436-7411
Escondido 250 W. Valley Pkwy., at Escondido Blvd. • 746-2222

Escondido/Valley Parkway 1516 E. Valley Pkwy., across from The Vineyard • 741-1494
Grossmont Center 5506 Grossmont Ctr. Dr., west of Grossmont Hospital • 461-9907
Imperial Beach 1100 Palm Ave., at 11th • 424-8196
Jamul Lyons Valley Rd. & Highway 94 • 461-4850
Julian 2007 Main St. • 765-0112
Kensington 4078 Adams Ave., west of Public Library • 280-8871
La Jolla Downtown 1005 Pearl Street, corner of Pearl and Girard • 459-0222
La Jolla Village 3211 Holiday Ct., across from B of A • 455-0440
Lawrence Welk's 8975 Champagne Blvd. • 749-3287
Midway-Rosecrans 3333 Rosecrans, Loma Square Ctr. • 223-2216
Mission Hills/Hillcrest 265 W. Washington, at Albatross • 293-7940
Mission Valley 5111 Mission Center Rd., at Camino de la Reina • 238-7867

North Park 3921 30th St., off University • 299-6572
Pacific Beach 1000 Garnet Ave., at Cass • 483-4800
Pine Valley 28789 Hwy. 80 • 473-8731
Poway 12411 Poway Rd., at Pomerado • 748-1133
Ramona 1308 Main St., at 13th • 789-0221
Rancho Bernardo 16789 Bernardo Center Dr. • 485-6360
San Marcos 186 S. Rancho Santa Fe Rd., at Grand • 727-5160
San Ysidro 390 E. San Ysidro Blvd., at entrance to Safeway Shopping Ctr. 428-5541
Southeast San Diego (Real Estate Loans only) 43rd and Keeler • 263-6617
Spring Valley 619 Sweetwater Rd., Spring Valley Ctr. • 462-2390
Sweetwater Town and Country 1510-D Sweetwater Rd. at 805 • 474-8376
Tierrasanta 10795 Tierrasanta Boulevard • 571-7696
University Towne Center (opening soon)

Home Federal Savings & Loan Association of San Diego

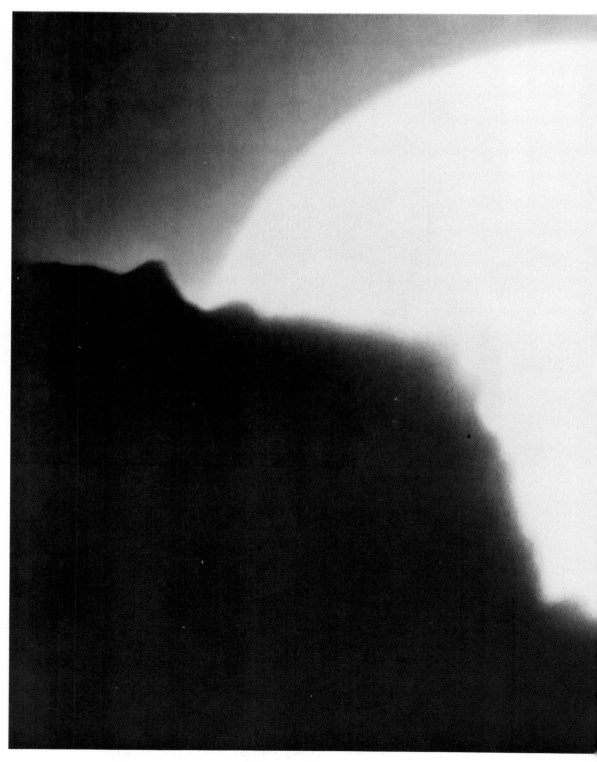

At Security Bank, our symbol stands for more than just the sun setting behind a rim of solid rock. It sums up our philosophy of banking. It says that when you walk through our doors, you're number one under the sun. That kind of attitude won't show up on a monthly statement or a loan application. But all the same, you can bank on it. Because we back it up with a solid base of financial resources, and a wide range of services.

Personal banking. For example, we have a variety of plans to help get you into the savings habit; personalized checking accounts that add convenience to your money management; loan services to help

you realize your plans and ideas; the Security 24 automatic teller machine that makes banker's hours obsolete; bank cards designed to eliminate the risk of carrying cash; convenient drive-in and Saturday banking at Security West; individual retirement plans that look out for your future; and a wide range of other special services designed to fit the needs of almost everyone.

Business banking. In any commercial venture, we think the best opportunities for success come when knowledgeable, experienced people in your business work with knowledgeable, experienced people in ours. That's why whatever business you're in, our specialized bankers make it their business to speak your language

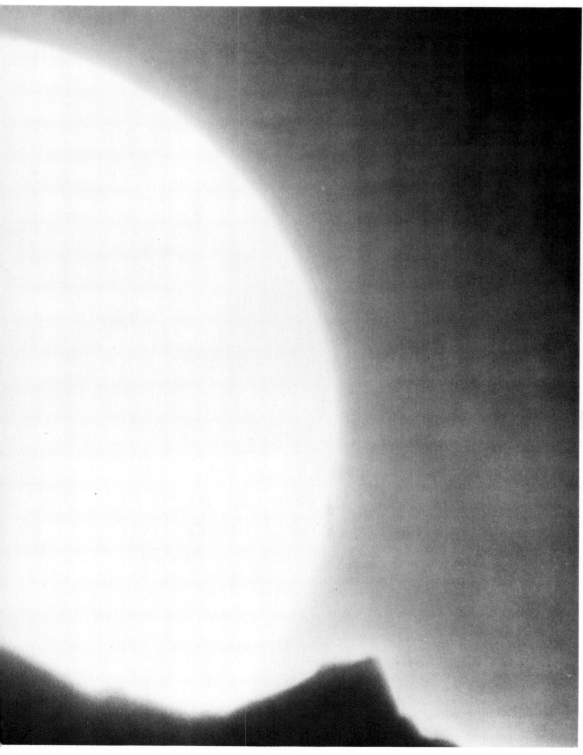

We've been
around the square
a long time.

When the trolleys ran.
And the cotton bloomed.
And the streets were brick.
And the circus came.
Citizens First National was
there! Helping: that's really
what it is all about today.
They're kinda old-fashioned,
that way. For they still
remember when the square
was a square. You see
…Citizens First National
was there! First place in the
hearts of their
many friends.
You might say.

CITIZENS
FIRST NATIONAL BANK OF TYLER

We've been around the square a long time.

When the trolleys ran. And the cotton bloomed. And the streets were brick. And the circus came. Citizens First National was there! Helping that's really what it is all about today. They're kinda old-fashioned, that way. For they still remember when the square was a square. You see …Citizens First National was there! First place in the hearts of their many friends. You might say.

CITIZENS FIRST NATIONAL BANK OF TYLER

"A small business needs a bank it can talk to, president to president."

Our president, Bob Newman, believes in people who run small companies with big ideas.

There is a bank on Wall Street
where the president makes it his business
to help small companies grow as they
haven't grown before.
Its name is The Merchants Bank and Trust Company.
And it isn't in New York.

Merchants.
The Wall Street bank in Norwalk.

The Merchants Bank and Trust Company, 59 Wall Street, Norwalk, Connecticut 06852. (203) 852-5552
Deposits Insured by The Federal Deposit Insurance Corporation

Announcing the grand opening of Farm & Home's new Downtown San Antonio office.

ONE GRAND OPENING. ONE GRAND PRIZE.

Stop by during grand opening at our new Downtown office, and you could get a lot more than a warm and friendly welcome. You could walk out a thousand dollars richer.

What grander grand prize than a grand? One thousand dollars in cash to spend any way your heart desires, or a one thousand dollar savings account. So, come on in and get acquainted during our Grand Opening Week, May 14 to 18.

After 45 years in the same location, we're back where we started.

Our new building's in the same place our old one was. The corner of Travis and Jefferson. Just as convenient, and more up to date.

So stop by and try your luck at our grand. The rules are as simple as saying "Hello." All you have to do to be eligible is drop in and fill out an entry blank. Anyone over 18 can enter, and there's no obligation. Deadline for entries: 3:00 p.m., Friday, May 18.

The grand prize drawing will be held Friday afternoon, May 18. And you don't have to be there to win.

"Baby Grand" prizes every day.

Even if you don't win our Grand Opening Grand, you'll have plenty of chances every day to cash in on our hospitality.

We're giving away $250 worth of savings accounts in daily drawings. Plus there'll be plenty of refreshments for everyone who drops by.

Come in today.

We'll be happy to show you around our brand new office. And, if you're interested, we'll even show you how your savings can earn more at Farm & Home than they do at some other financial institutions.

It may surprise you to learn that not everybody pays the high annual rates Farm & Home does.

In fact, Farm & Home pays the highest annual rates allowed by federal regulations. And we offer a variety of savings plans to fit your needs.

Earn with insured safety.

Accounts are insured to $40,000 by the Federal Savings and Loan Insurance Corporation. And they're backed by the strength of Farm & Home's 85 years of experience and more than $1.9 billion in assets.

All of which adds up to more money for your money at Farm & Home Savings.

Come see for yourself. Today.

MORE MONEY FOR YOUR MONEY.

Farm & Home Savings
Association

202 Jefferson
San Antonio 78286
Phone 225-6771

184

Home office Nevada, Missouri

When Lucille B. Smith moved to Fort Worth in 1912, her mother told her to "find a good home, a good church, and a good bank."

From her "Lady Bird Chair," where the First Lady had sat during a 1965 visit, Lucille B. Smith conducts the latest tour of her life.

"I discovered America on Sept. 5, 1892," she begins with characteristic creativity. Then goes on to say as a little girl in Crockett, Texas, she wanted only to "do big things."

And that she has.

She invented the first hot roll mix in the United States. And later, her legendary "chili bisquits."

She set up the first commercial foods and technology department at the college level at Prairie View A&M. She published a popular cookbook.

In 1966, Fort Worth celebrated Lucille B. Smith Day, following her sending hundreds of fruitcakes to American troops in Vietnam.

In 1970, Gov. Preston Smith appointed her to the Governor's Commission on the Status of Women, claiming she "had done more for people — not a race — but people, than any other black woman in Texas history."

Surrounded by plaques, photographs and momentos of her gilded career, the mother of three, grandmother of 14 and great-grandmother of 10, fondly recalls the days she and husband, Ulysses, came to Fort Worth.

"Before U.S. and I moved here in 1912," Lucille says, "my mother gave me three important instructions.

"First, find a decent place to live. Rent only until you can buy. We did just that, and soon paid $50 down on our first home.

"Second, she said to find a good church. That was St. Andrew's United Methodist.

"Now, third, she said, find a good bank. Well, it so happened that our church kept its money at the Continental National Bank. So U.S. and I said we believed we'd try that bank.

"And do you know that the very first time we went in, with just a few dollars to open our first little checking account, I fell in love.

"Everyone there had a smile in their voices. They treated our little dab of money like a whole lot.

"They may have a different building now, but those smiles are the same. That smile is what drew me to CNB and it's kept me there all these years."

Happy Thanksgiving, Mrs. Smith. From all of your friends at CNB.

Continental National Bank
made another friend today.

Member FDIC,
Member Southwest Bancshares, Inc.
Seventh at Houston.
Open 8 a.m. to 6 p.m. Monday through Friday,
Mini and Motor Banks also open 8 to 2.

MERCANTILE NATIONAL BANK OF ARLINGTON

Grand
O · P · E · N · I · N · G

YOU'LL · FIT · RIGHT · IN

R U L E S

1 It's easy to win! Just bring your piece of the puzzle into Mercantile National Bank of Arlington during our GRAND OPENING, February 11-15.

2 If the number on your puzzle piece matches any of those on our list of WINNING NUMBERS, you win! (Check with our Contest Coordinator to see what you've won.) One in every 10 puzzle pieces is a winner. Hundreds of prizes to be given away! And the poster is yours to keep!

3 Join your neighbors. And join the celebration. At 707 E. Lamar Blvd. We're open 9 a.m.-6 p.m., Monday through Friday during Grand Opening week only.

P R I Z E S

1st Prize Sleek new bicycles. Hold onto your handle-bars! There's fun and **fit**ness in these beautiful 10-speeds from Schwinn.

2nd Prize Snappy roller skates. Join the roller craze and **fit** yourself into a pair of these super skates.

3rd Prize Wonderful warm-ups. Suit yourself in a good-looking warm-up in the color and **fit** you want.
    And lots more! Big league baseball caps. Head outdoors in an all-around cap that adjusts to **fit** any size.
    T-shirts by the yard. What else is so **fit**ting for any sport or activity. Hundreds to be given away!

"If they'd let me write this ad, I'd put $8.8 million worth of new customers right up there in the headline."

That's our President, Joe King, talking.

And, as you can see from our year-end financial statement, 1979 was a very good year for Home Federal.

Particularly when you consider that we achieved such admirable growth in an economy fraught with uncertainty, tight money, and continued talk of a recession. In spite of the fact that things were tough all over, more people entrusted their life's savings to Home Federal than ever before.

We appreciate the confidence our depositors placed in us during 1979, and we hope you'll join them in 1980. Because we might have gotten $8.8 million worth of new customers, but we've still got room for a few more.

Assets	December 31, 1979	December 31, 1978	Increase (Decrease)
First Mortgage Loans.	$265,112,862.14	$228,649,580.62	$ 36,463,281.52
All Other Loans.	4,439,117.03	2,328,257.28	2,110,859.75
Cash, U.S. Government and			
Other Agencies.	24,928,047.21	27,830,672.40	(2,902,625.19)
Fixed Assets Less Depreciation.	3,113,204.72	2,618,480.68	494,724.04
Prepayment to Secondary FSLIC Reserve .	315,913.51	365,562.50	(49,648.99)
Real Estate Owned.	0	0	0
Deferred Charges and Other Assets.	532,061.37	474,602.45	57,458.92
TOTAL ASSETS.	$298,441,205.98	$262,267,155.93	$ 36,174,050.05

Liabilities and Net Worth	December 31, 1979	December 31, 1978	Increase (Decrease)
Savings Accounts.	$222,052,099.06	$213,215,451.79	$ 8,836,647.27
Advances from FHLB.	15,000,000.00	5,000,000.00	10,000,000.00
Securities Sold Under			
Repurchase Agreement.	23,996,875.00	12,751,250.00	11,245,625.00
Loans in Process.	16,462,694.57	13,779,616.30	2,683,078.27
Other Liabilities.	3,224,819.24	1,920,144.15	1,304,675.09
Specific Reserves.	22,176.59	19,973.19	2,203.40
General Reserves and Surplus.	17,682,541.52	15,580,720.50	2,101,821.02
TOTAL LIABILITIES & NET WORTH.	$298,441,205.98	$262,267,155.93	$ 36,174,050.05

Home Federal Savings

Organized 1883. Telephone 373-0400.
Uptown, Cotswold, Park Road Shopping Center, Eastland Area, North Mecklenburg at I-77 and Highway 73.

MEMBER
FSLIC
Federal Savings & Loan Insurance Corp.
A U.S. Government Agency

IT'S ALL DOWNHILL FROM HERE.

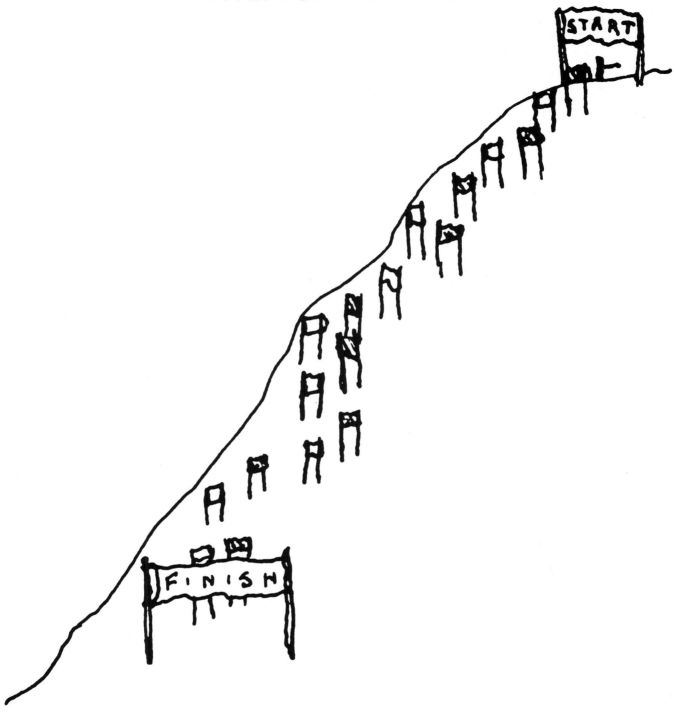

GOOD LUCK TO THE U.S. SKI TEAM
FROM THE COLORADO NATIONAL BANKS.

Members F.D.I.C.

Another big idea: Guaranteed Rate Contracts for Employee Benefit Plans.

Colorado National Bank is first in the Rocky Mountain region to offer a Guaranteed Rate Contract (GRC) investment to companies with pension and profit-sharing plans.

This means your company's employee benefit plan can be guaranteed over many years with a consistently high interest rate.

GRC's provide stability and high yield. The long-term value of an employee benefit plan is quickly forgotten when security markets go into decline. So, many companies and their employees demand more stability in their plans.

If you can deposit at least $50,000 in assets from your plan, you can participate in the best qualified plan investment alternative yet, providing:

- Safety of principal (unlike stocks and bonds).
- Guaranteed high interest rates over extended time (unlike Certificates of Deposit).
- Flexibility to meet your plan's requirements (like stocks, bonds and Certificates of Deposit).

Two flexible GRC plans. Both versions of our GRC give you and your employees long-term high yield. Here's how they work:

- With a deposit of $100,000, your plan will yield 9.2% per annum over 10 years.
- With a deposit of over $50,000, your plan is expected to yield over 9% the first year, with each yield and one-fifteenth of principal reinvested each year for 15 years. This roll-over plan gives you, in effect, the benefit of new money rates every year.

So, if you want your plan guaranteed, call, write or visit us about Guaranteed Rate Contracts. Irv Berlau or Mike Huntoon, Colorado National Bank, P.O. Box 5168, Denver, Colorado 80217. (303) 893-1862.

COLORADO NATIONAL BANK
Member FDIC

We make big ideas happen.

189

Finding energy as an independent was a big idea. Colorado National Bank helped make it happen.

Max H. Ernest III, President, XO Exploration
"To operate as an independent in the oil business, it's absolutely essential to work closely with your bank. Meeting our working capital needs must be done quickly by people who know the business. Without Colorado National Bank, we simply couldn't operate."

John Ferry, Vice-President, Colorado National Bank
"The kind of financing needed in the energy and minerals business requires a unique understanding. Especially when you're talking to independent oil operators and miners who need to get into production. We've been with XO since they opened in 1972. Today they're successfully operating in 5 states."

COLORADO NATIONAL BANK

Member FDIC

Independents in the oil business account for a large share of our nation's production. So we're vitally interested in helping companies like XO and other natural resource related businesses with their big ideas. At Colorado National Bank, we can't think of a better way to make our financial resources work harder. If you've got a big idea, give John Ferry a call at 893-1862. He'll help you make it happen.

We make big ideas happen.

"When we began our oil and gas exploration company, our first major discovery was the Energy Department at Fort Worth's CNB."

Dick Lowe, president, American Quasar Petroleum Co.

R. L. (Dick) Lowe, president, American Quasar Petroleum Co., backed up by **Dean Cochran,** vice president, CNB's Energy Dept. Behind them, AQP's 15,620' gas well, the #1 Kusch, in Grayson Co., Texas.

From the Canadian Rockies to the Mississippi Gulf Coast, American Quasar Petroleum and Continental National Bank have covered a lot of ground together in the search for oil and gas.

The company's founders began their long association with CNB by banking there as individuals. So, in 1969, when they wanted to form their own exploration company, it was only natural for them to turn to CNB for assistance.

"When we were first trying to get started in the oil and gas business, Continental National Bank was behind us all the way," Dick Lowe remembered. "They found us a partner to help share some of the debt, and the resulting money helped us get started."

Today, AQP has grown to be one of the largest independents in the energy business.

And its subsidiary, Can-Am Drilling Programs, is the largest limited partnership public drilling fund in the world.

Success. It comes from having a banking friend who's interested in helping you achieve it for yourself.

Continental National Bank

made another friend today.

Open 8 a.m. to 6 p.m. Monday through Friday, Seventh at Houston, Fort Worth, Texas. (817) 334-9000. Mini and Motor Banks also open Saturday 8 to 2.
Member FDIC, Member Southwest Bancshares, Inc.

191

One of the oldest buildings in Salinas is now the newest bank in Salinas.

The newest bank in town is now open, in the Forrester Building, at 371 Main Street, downtown.

We've refurbished it and furnished it with great care, striving to make it a community showpiece, recapturing a part of Salinas' past. Because we're committed to being a part of Salinas' future.

For more than 105 years we've prided ourselves on bringing new banking ideas and innovative bank services to the West. And we're very pleased and proud of this opportunity to now offer them to Salinas.

We hope you'll stop by soon and see us. We think you'll really like what you see.

You'll like banking that's more convenient.

It's not always easy to do your banking during "bankers hours." That's why we keep longer hours, making it much easier to do your banking with us.

Our walk-up window is open 'til six every weekday; so you can stop here on your way home from work, instead of taking time away from work.

When you come into our bank, you'll discover it's faster getting out of the bank.

And when you can't come into our bank, we have bank-by-mail and night depository services to help you with your banking.

You'll like banking that's easier.

We have a banking plan that's easier to keep track of, and easier to use, than any plan you've ever used before. It's called One-Book-Banking. And it's available only at Bank of the West.

In one handy book you get checks and checking account deposit slips. You also get savings account deposit and withdrawal slips, preprinted with your name and account number. Plus you get a check register, a savings register, and an automatic payment/deposit reminder register. All in one book.

And at Bank of the West, you get a monthly report on all your basic banking activities, all on one report.

Our One-Statement-Banking makes recordkeeping easier and more accurate.

You'll like banking that's more responsive.

No one checking plan can suit everyone. That's why we offer a wide choice of checking plans and check styles; so you can have the plan that best suits you.

You can have checking plans that you are charged for in relation to your check usage. You can have plans with a flat minimum charge no matter how much you use them. You can have plans that are free of service charges. You can even have a plan that earns you money on the money you would normally keep in your checking account.

You can also have freedom from worry with overdraft protection, and the convenience and time-saving of automatic transfers.

Our choice in Savings programs is equally as wide as our choice in checking plans. So you can save for whatever you want, at the pace you want to save. We have Regular Plans, for readily available funds that still earn you interest. We have longer term certificates for fixed amounts. And longer term open deposit accounts so you can add to initial amounts.

And every savings plan we have pays you the highest interest the government will allow us to pay for that particular plan. Where the law will allow us to, we also compound your interest daily, so you can realize the maximum legal yield.

At Bank of the West, we have the convenience of three credit cards available to qualified customers: our exclusive Gold Card, the American Express Gold Card, and VISA.

And when you need a loan for any good reason, there are a lot of good reasons to get it from us. Compare our rates with any other bank's rates and you'll discover the best reason: a loan from us will probably cost you less.

You'll like banking that's more comprehensive.

At Bank of the West, full service is total service. In addition to all the advantages of all the services highlighted above, we offer a great many more. Leasing for personal or corporate purposes. Trust services for individuals and businesses. Complete business services for all sizes of businesses. And more.

And all of our services are offered with professionalism and a sincere appreciation of the opportunity to serve.

We'd like to be of service to you. Come see us. You'll see how much better banking can be.

Bank of the West

193

Save time – use the
Civic Savings drive-in window.

There are lots of reasons for using the Civic Savings Drive-in window. Some people don't want to find a parking place, others are in a hurry. Me — I don't want to leave my car.

Whatever your reason, you can save time by using the drive-in window at Civic Savings.

CIVIC
SAVINGS

Ohio River Road	507 Chillicothe Street	507 Emmitt Avenue	738 East Main Street
Wheelersburg	Portsmouth	Waverly	Jackson
574-2524	354-6611	947-7718	286-6355

128 years ago, we helped farmers with their banking needs.

We still do.

THE BANK
PEOPLES DEPOSIT BANK

195

On January 2,1979 First Nation
HOW THE WE

The year is 1874. Automobiles and airplanes and phonographs and electric lights are little more than tinkerers' dreams. The ring of a telephone is still more than a year away. And Custer still has 2 years before making his last stand.

The place is San Jose. James Lick is making plans to put an observatory atop

kick up dust, while horses and their riders were kicking out in disgust. Marconi was sending wireless messages across the ocean, while KQW was beaming the world's first regularly scheduled radio broadcasts from San Jose. And Al Jolson was belting out tunes in the Unique Theater on Santa Clara Street for $75 a week.

First National Bank

Mt. Hamilton. The Valley's farmers are planting a record 800,000 lb. tobacco crop. A group of local businessmen are getting ready to drill for oil in Moody's Gulch.

And another group of local businessmen have just started a bank for the stated purpose of lowering the high interest rates being charged for loans (up to 10% a month!).

The bank is Farmers National Gold Bank. One of only 10 such banks ever chartered in the U.S.

Just six months after opening for business, Farmers National Gold Bank moves its business from a small upstairs office to a large two story building on the Southwest corner of First & Santa Clara Streets. And in 1880, changes its name to the First National Bank of San Jose.

Today, that same bank occupies that very same corner, in a nine-story headquarters for its 37 offices in Santa Clara, San Mateo and Alameda Counties.

The early 1900's. Those were exciting days! The Wright Brothers were just getting off the ground. Cars were beginning to

was doing a very brisk business – it seems the prune orchards were clearly gaining dominance over the wheat and tobacco fields of the Valley. Disaster strikes San Francisco. In those dark nights of 1906, San Jose residents can see the flames from atop the Valley hillsides. Under the same darkness of night, the savings of numerous San Francisco citizens and businesses are moved by their banks down to First National for safekeeping – the vaults are literally overflowing with gold, coin and currency.

In 1910, First National dedicates its new 9-story building – then the Valley's tallest structure.

During the first World War, First National's central location made it an ideal spot for selling liberty and war bonds.

At war's end, an unparalleled boom began. Stutz, Pierce-Arrows and Packards were the pride (or envy) of nearly every

American.

Lindbergh was making the world smaller. Flappers and hipflasks and speakeasies and all that jazz were all the rage.

And it all went bust in the biggest in history. People went jobless and ho less, and lost their life savings as nume banks and financial institutions went u

millions to local businesses and residents determined to make our economy go again.

And once again we went to war, and First National again served as a purchase point for bonds.

The forties also saw First National embark on an agressive

program of leadership in the banking industry – seeking to bring customers new ideas and innovations to make banking easier, more convenient, and more responsive.

At the very end of the decade, First National introduced the very first drive-up teller windows in the area.

In 1953, the Bank introduced the first bank credit card in the West.

In 1961, First National's customers were among the first in the country to benefit from the speed and accuracy of electronic check processing.

Later, in the sixties, we brought Westerners the first Auto Leasing plan, and we brought out the West's first credit card that was also a check guarantee card. And we issued our cards to married women in their first names, rather than

their husbands'.

The sixties also saw us introduce the ease of single statement banking and automatic loan payments.

Early in the seventies, we started staying

open later – the first major bank in the area to do so.

Most recently, we were also the first bank in the West to offer consumer loan rebates. And throughout our history, whenever banking regulations have permitted, we have always been among the very first in the West to pay customers the highest interest rates on their savings.

Which brings us to today. Today, we're the 14th largest bank in California, with assets over $500,000,000. We have grown far beyond San Jose, with 37 offices in 16 cities in 3 counties.

It is our goal to continue growing, by continuing to do what we've always tried to do: offer our customers the best ideas in banking, with a sincere appreciation for their interest in banking with us.

Since 1874 we have been serving people in the West, growing with the West. For over 104 years we have been a leader in banking services for the West.

So it seemed very natural for us to become…

ot at First National – not one lost one cent – the depression ved.

ica began rebuilding. And so did Clara Valley. During the thirties forties, First National loaned out

Bank of the West

Member FDIC. All deposits insured to $40,000

**When Union troops
were in Central Kentucky,
we were The Bank.**

**People have been
banking on us
since 1850.**

THE BANK

PEOPLES DEPOSIT BANK
& TRUST CO.

Member FDIC

When Lincoln was president, we were "The Bank."

People have been banking on us since 1850.

THE BANK
PEOPLES DEPOSIT BANK & TRUST CO.

Member FDIC

The Bank
Paris, Ky.

When postage was 2¢, we were "The Bank."

People have been banking on us since 1850.

THE BANK

PEOPLES DEPOSIT BANK & TRUST CO.

Member FDIC

We will not fold, spindle, or mutilate you.

Have you ever tried talking to a computer? Do you miss talking to the people who are concerned? Then it's time you talk to the people at the largest, independent, home-owned bank in Northern New Mexico. The Bank of Santa Fe.

Sure we have high speed computers and the latest in banking industry equipment too. But, our greatest asset at The Bank of Santa Fe is our experienced staff, who are always at your disposal.

Our people are experienced in taking care of your financial needs and your money. Our people are always ready, willing and able to help.

Our people, who are your neighbors and friends, do not think of you as just a number!

Are you tired of getting the "fast shuffle" at the other banks? At The Bank of Santa Fe our personal service has not been folded, spindled or mutilated. Our people take pride and extra care in treating our valued customers with old fashioned courtesy and warmth... never out of style at The Bank of Santa Fe.

Come in and visit with our people anytime...we'd like to get to know you even better!

The Better Bankers

The bank of Santa Fe

TEN CONVENIENT DRIVE-UP WINDOWS.

Main Office
241 Washington Avenue

State Capital
422 Old Santa Fe Trail

St Michael's Drive
809 St Michael's Drive

DeVargas Center
East Parking Lot Area

Call 983-3374
For All offices
For your convenience.

FDIC
Each depositor insured to $40,000
FEDERAL DEPOSIT INSURANCE CORPORATION

Know someone who's moving to Delaware? Tell Alice!

If you know someone who is moving to our State, you can help make their move a lot easier. Just contact Alice Kelley of Bank of Delaware's Newcomer Service and tell her about them. She'll be happy to help them get acquainted with Delaware before they move. Bank of Delaware has already helped more than a thousand families relocate, and they've all been grateful for our help. Our Newcomer Service helps take some of the problems out of moving with the "Welcome to Delaware" kit.

This complimentary kit is a collection of useful facts and information about housing, schools, taxes, restaurants, shopping centers, banking services and much, much more.

So if you know someone who is moving to Delaware, call Alice Kelley, Bank of Delaware's Newcomer Service Coordinator, at (302) 429-1522 or send the coupon below. She'll take care of the rest! The Newcomer Service is just one more of the many convenient services from Bank of Delaware.

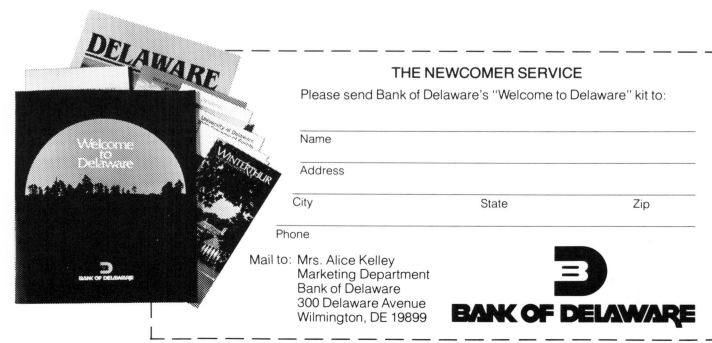

THE NEWCOMER SERVICE

Please send Bank of Delaware's "Welcome to Delaware" kit to:

Name

Address

City   State   Zip

Phone

Mail to: Mrs. Alice Kelley
Marketing Department
Bank of Delaware
300 Delaware Avenue
Wilmington, DE 19899

BANK OF DELAWARE

GOLD

Bank of Delaware buys and sells precious metals in a variety of forms, at the lowest bank commissions in the State. South African krugerrands and Canadian maple leafs are in stock. All other gold bullion coins such as U.S. gold coins, Austrian coronas, Mexican pesos, British sovereigns, etc., may be purchased on order.

Gold bullion is available in bars weighing from 1 ounce to 400 ounces. Silver bullion is available in bars from 1 ounce to 1,000 ounces. U.S. silver coins (90% silver content) are traded by full or half bags.

On all precious metal purchases you may take delivery or store with us at reasonable rates. FDIC insurance coverage excludes precious metals held for safekeeping. Metals in our possession are insured for theft or loss by Bank of Delaware. No sales tax is charged in Delaware.

For information or ordering, call our International Department at (302) 654-7377.

BANK OF DELAWARE

Note: Precious metals are highly volatile commodities whose market prices must increase to provide a financial gain. For this reason, Bank of Delaware takes no advisory position on precious metals as an investment.

MEMBER FDIC

The easy way to get into Gold...

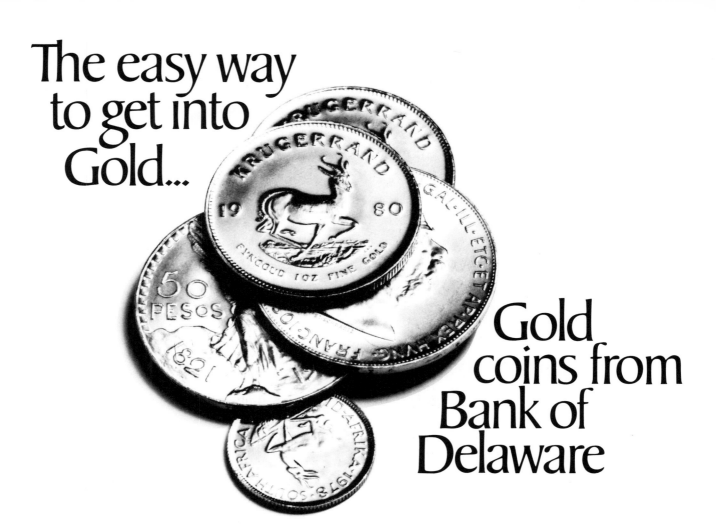

Gold coins from Bank of Delaware

Many Americans are discovering that gold coins are a sensible way to preserve a portion of their income. Yet many who have considered purchasing gold coins have hesitated because they didn't know how to go about it or whom to trust.

We have eliminated that stumbling block. It's easy to purchase gold coins directly through our bank. And you pay no sales tax in Delaware.

At Bank of Delaware, you'll find many widely recognized bullion coins from which to choose, including the popular Krugerrand and the Canadian Maple Leaf. You can store them here in safety too.

And since gold coins are remarkably liquid, you can sell them quickly and easily.

If you've made the decision to buy gold coins, you'll find our bank a reliable source.

NOTE: Due to significant price fluctuations, we take no advisory position on gold coins as an investment. Although FDIC insurance coverage excludes gold coins held for safekeeping, the gold coins in our possession are insured against theft or loss by Bank of Delaware.

For a free brochure "Gold Coins: A Practical Guide", return this coupon to:

Bank of Delaware
Marketing Department-Gold Coins
300 Delaware Avenue
Wilmington, DE 19899

Name _____

Address _____

City _____

State _____ Zip _____

Business Phone _____

Home Phone _____

G-1

BANK OF DELAWARE

"THANK YOU BARNEGAT"

As many of you know, on October 4 we celebrated our grand opening in Barnegat. To commemorate the occasion we invited all of you to come and celebrate with us. And you did, by the thousands. In fact, it was one of our most successful openings. We were delighted. Naturally, Bob Graham, our Branch Manager, and the rest of us at Carteret Savings are pleased with this great turnout. But, we are also very pleased with the friendly way we have been welcomed into your community. Thank you very much.

Robert B. O'Brien, Jr.
President and Chief Executive Officer

Gifts are still available for opening a checking account, savings account or savings certificate.

CARTERET

CARTERET SAVINGS AND LOAN ASSOCIATION
New Jersey's Largest State-Chartered Savings and Loan Association
West Bay Ave. and Barnegat Blvd., Barnegat, N.J. 08005 • (609) 698-1110
Hours: Mon. thru Thurs. . .9 a.m. to 4 p.m.
Friday . . . . .9 a.m. to 8 p.m.   Savings insured to
Saturday . . . . . .9 a.m. to 12 p.m. $100,000 by FSLIC.
Main Office: 866 Broad St., Newark, N.J. 07102 • (201) 622-8010
Assets over one billion dollars

FUN IN BARNEGAT.

At the Grand Opening of Carteret Savings, Saturday, October 4, 9 a.m. to 3 p.m.

It's a Carteret Carnival—a Grand Opening to top all openings. Celebrating the new Carteret Savings and Loan office in Barnegat. Savings accounts and savings certificates that pay top interest and Great Gifts. Checking accounts that pay 5% interest and Great Gifts—and a Carnival of Fun Events for everyone...so bring the whole family.

And how about this exciting vacation sweepstakes! Eastern Airlines 7-21 day "Unlimited Mileage" holiday for two (or $1,000. cash).

Have yourself an international whirl or jet up, down and across the U.S.A. Or do both! The choice is yours. And what a choice! Pick from the 100 cities and 13 countries served by Eastern Airlines. The length of your vacation is up to you—from one to three weeks. So you can set your own pace. All this plus $300. spending money for indulging yourself in the fun and sun pleasures of Mexico, Bermuda, the Bahamas, the Caribbean, Puerto Rico, the Virgin Islands and the greatest land of all—our very own U.S.A. Imagine! It can all come true just by filling out a sweepstakes entry blank or a facsimile and either mail or drop in our box at Carteret's new Barnegat Full Service Branch. There's nothing to buy. No account to open. No jingles to write or puzzle to solve. So enter today. Win an "Unlimited Mileage" vacation for two!

It's a fun-filled Saturday!

- At 10 a.m., WJRZ-FM Radio will broadcast the morning program from our new Carteret office.
- From 9 a.m. to 3 p.m. Choco the Clown will regale kids big and small.
- Talented Ginger Cole will perform her quick-pix sketch artistry for dozens of lucky subjects.

It's a kick-off for the real event!

The real big event is Carteret itself!
Carteret Savings and Loan, bringing to Barnegat a wide and diversified assortment of personal financial services:
- Personal Checking accounts that pay interest of 5% a year and you pay no monthly service or per check charges (on balances of $50. or more).
- Savings accounts and savings certificates insured up to $100,000., all at the highest interest the law allows.
- Personal loans, mortgage loans, auto loans, home improvement loans.
- Check cashing privileges at Carteret's 35 offices statewide.
- And a stunning array of gifts when you open a new account.

- Youngsters will have 60 seconds to seek out coins for their piggy bank in the Sand Box Penny Game.
- Free piggy banks! Free balloons! Free high-flying kites to the first 100 early birds!
- And, if your Carteret Magic Card (check your mail box for it this week) comes up with the right number, you could win a valuable prize.

It's all by way of expressing our pleasure in joining your community. Come in and celebrate with us. Bring the kids. There's fun—and profit—for everyone at Carteret in Barnegat.

A super gift is yours when you open a 5% checking account, a savings account, or invest in a savings certificate.

Open an account for $250. to $999. and select one of these fine gifts.

Designer Check Purse   Sunbeam Alarm Clock   Eveready Lantern   Hanson Bathroom Scale   Luggage Carrier

Open an account for $1,000. to $4,999. and select one of these fine gifts.

Northern Heating Pad   Photo Bulletin Board   Canvas Tote Bag with Umbrella   G.E. 24-Hour Timer   St. Mary's Machine-Washable Blanket

Open an account for $5,000. or more and select one of these fine gifts.

Farberware 3-Piece Stainless Steel Mixing Bowl Set   Calculator (credit card size)   Teakettle Lamp   Tote Bag   Twin-Size Comforter   Magnavox AM/FM Portable Radio   Conair 1200 Watt Hair Dryer

The following gifts are also available in this category but not shown: Man's or Woman's Totes Umbrella, Proctor-Silex Steam and Dry Iron and Proctor-Silex Toaster.

Regulations prohibit our giving a gift for funds transferred from an existing Carteret account. One gift per depositor while supply lasts during Opening Celebration. If demand exceeds supply, depositors may choose from any of the remaining gifts in the appropriate category. We reserve the right to substitute a gift of comparable value.

A complete range of savings plans.

Optional Money Market Certificate.
Only $500. minimum deposit, guaranteed interest and you choose the month of maturity from 30 months to 10 years. Interest is compounded daily and paid monthly. Rate based on the average 30-month yield of U.S. Treasury Securities.

12.137% annual yield on 11.30%

T-Plus Six-Month Money Market Certificate ($10,000. min.).

11.545% equivalent annual yield on 11.074%
Rate available September 25 thru October 1.

Free Checking (with $50. minimum balance).

- No monthly service charge • No per check charge • 5% interest from Day of Deposit to Day of Withdrawal. Also, Free Bank by Mail, Free check storage and a Free initial supply of fully personalized checks (150).

MORE! Statement Savings Account.
Interest compounded daily, credited and paid monthly.

5.73% annual yield on 5.50%

Prime Passbook Savings Account.
Interest compounded daily, credited and paid monthly ($100. min.).

5.73% annual yield on 5.50%

CARTERET

⬟ CARTERET SAVINGS AND LOAN ASSOCIATION
New Jersey's Largest State-Chartered Savings and Loan Association

West Bay Ave. and Barnegat Blvd., Barnegat, N.J. 08005 • (609) 698-1110
Hours: Mon. thru Thurs., 9 a.m. to 4 p.m.; Friday, 9 a.m. to 8 p.m.; Saturday, 9 a.m. to 12 p.m.

Main Office: 866 Broad St., Newark, N.J. 07102
(201) 622-8010
Savings insured to $100,000 by FSLIC
Assets over one billion dollars

FSLIC   EQUAL HOUSING LENDER

Interest on T-Plus Certificate is expressed as an equivalent annual rate which is based on a reinvestment of both principal and interest at the same rate upon maturity. However, the interest rate may change at the time of reinvestment. T-Plus Certificate subject to forfeiture of all interest if withdrawal prior to maturity. Federal regulations require that a penalty be invoked if funds (excluding interest) are withdrawn from a Savings Certificate prior to maturity. Qualifying deposit must remain in a T-Plus Account for 6 months and for a year in all other savings instruments or a charge for the gift will be made. A balance of $50. must remain in MORE! Statement Savings Account. A balance of $100. must remain in Prime Passbook Savings Account to earn interest. $100. is needed to open a checking account.

BE A MILLIONAIRE FOR A WEEKEND.

**Enter Carteret's big "Millionaire Weekend Sweepstakes".
Nothing to buy. No accounts to open. No jingles to write.**

Here's a chance for the two of you to live the most luxurious weekend of your life.
   You'll stay at one of New York's poshest hotels for two nights. You'll wake up to breakfast in bed—with champagne if you like. Do the town in your own chauffeured limousine. Lunch at a world famous, celebrity-studded club. Dine by candlelight at one of the most elegant New York restaurants. Take your pick of two tickets to any hit on Broadway.
   There's more! A $500. gift certificate at a fashionable New York store of your choice. And for spending money, two days' interest on a million dollars— that's about $602. at 11% per year!

   A millionaire's weekend—all on Carteret! Entry blanks are available at any Carteret office. Simply fill one out or a facsimile, and drop it in the special sweepstakes box at any Carteret office or submit by mail. Then cross your fingers...and dream a little.
   In any event, try tucking away a few dollars regularly in a high interest Carteret savings account. It's a good start to becoming a real millionaire.

Only one entry per person. All federal, state and local regulations apply.

10.11% annual yield on 9.50%	8.280% equivalent annual yield on 8.003%
Current rate available for 2½-Year Certificate ($500. min.).	T-Plus Six-Month Money Market Certificate ($10,000. min.). Rate available May 29 to June 4 is higher than that of any commercial bank.

You get a super gift when you deposit $5,000. or more in a new savings account, add-on deposit or savings certificate.

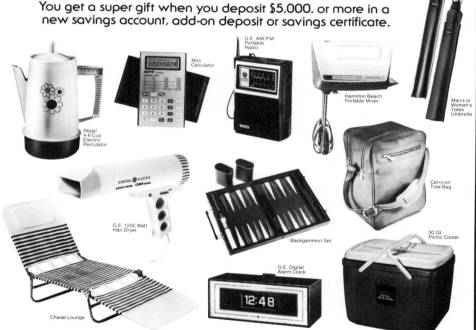

Regal 4-8 Cup Electric Perculator

Mini Calculator

G.E. AM/FM Portable Radio

Hamilton Beach Portable Mixer

Man's or Woman's Totes Umbrella

G.E. 1200 Watt Hair Dryer

Backgammon Set

Carry-on Tote Bag

30 Qt. Picnic Cooler

Chaise Lounge

G.E. Digital Alarm Clock

Gifts available immediately at all full service branches.

CARTERET

CARTERET SAVINGS AND LOAN ASSOCIATION

Assets over a billion dollars.

Main Office: 866 Broad Street, Newark, New Jersey 07102 • (201) 622-8010

Savings insured to $100,000 by FSLIC.

NOW CHECKING WITH 5% INTEREST AT ALL OUR OFFICES.

OFFICE LOCATIONS: Bernardsville • Brick Town • Cliffwood • East Orange • Haddon Heights • Hamilton Township Hazlet/Holmdel • Hillsborough • Hillside • Keansburg • Livingston • Livingston ShopRite • Madison • Matawan Metuchen • Morris Township • Newark (866 Broad Street, 744 Broad Street, Penn-Central R.R. Station, 487 Orange Street, 500 Bloomfield Avenue, 829 Sandford Avenue 712 Springfield Avenue) • Oradell • Phillipsburg Rockaway • South Orange • South Orange Pathmark • Springfield • Union • Verona • Westmont • Woodbury

Does your bank provide these services?

24-Hour Banking.
Seven days a week — 24 hours a day. All day every day, Sundays, and holidays too. 7-24 Banking lets you make deposits, withdraw cash, make loan payments or transfer funds from one account to another, *anytime* of day or night at *your* convenience! It's ready when you are!

Checking Services.
A choice of checking plans tailored to your needs . . . regular checking . . . Chek + Plus — your own personal line of credit . . . Chek-Sav — provides you convenient checking plus the interest of savings . . . no service charge checking for senior citizens . . . no service charge with minimum balance . . . FREE personalized checks — and more!

Loan Services.
Loans for any worthwhile purpose. Long and short-term loans at low cost bank financing.

You can borrow for reasons such as: Automobile, Home Improvement, Vacation, Education, Property, Farm Equipment, Personal, Recreational Vehicles, Boats, Travel Trailers, Mortgage, Health and more! You can even arrange your loan in advance and have your cash ready *before* you buy! A bank loan is the economical way to buy.

Savings Plans.
A number of savings plans to fit your needs . . . Treasury Certificates, Long-term Certificates of Deposit, Short-Term Certificates of Deposit, Golden Savings, and Regular Savings. There's a plan to suit you . . . and each account is insured up to $40,000 by the Federal Deposit Insurance Corporation.

Full-Service Banking.
. . . what you really need in a bank! Services designed to fulfill your *every* need . . . and then some! Services like Drive-in Windows; Direct Deposits; Trust Services; Free Notary Services; Travelers Checks; Money Orders; Cashiers Checks; Christmas Clubs; Individual Retirement Accounts; *plus* friendly, sensible advice on all your money matters!
If your answer is YES to all the above . . . Thanks, for banking with The Energy Bank! If you couldn't answer Yes to all the above — Come to The Energy Bank and discover what you're missing!

Bank of Oak Ridge

Main Office Downtown / Jackson Square / West End / Clinton / Lake City

When it comes to you and your money, we get personal.

Come to the Energy Bank.

Yes, when it comes to you and your money, we get *very* personal! Because your money is a very personal thing, and we're a very personal place!

We believe in providing you the personal service and attention you deserve. *You* are someone special to Bob Petrey, our Branch Manager, and to all the people at the Clinton office. Bob knows the importance of providing you banking services that you just won't find anywhere else. When you walk in, he'll greet you with a smile, a warm handshake, call you by your first name, take a few moments to chat. And that's only the beginning to the personal service and attention you'll get in all your banking needs! With Bob, it's a way of life!

Come in today, and make arrangements for your needs of tomorrow.

Like Bob Petrey, all our people devote all their energy to finding new ways to serve you better! Come to a personal way of banking.

The Energy Bank

Clinton
Bank of Oak Ridge

MAIN OFFICE DOWNTOWN/WEST END/
JACKSON SQUARE/CLINTON/LAKE CITY

OUR 25th YEAR   Member FDIC

210

1978 ADVENTURE ADVERTISING AGENCY

A bank is a bank. But the people in it make a difference.

People like Lynn Phillips.
He sure helps keep our bank running. And he's as friendly as he looks! He'll always take the time to serve you and make you feel right at home. All our people do. He knows the importance of friendly, person-to-person service. Lynn has been with The Hamilton since 1971. He's a friendly Assistant Vice President at our Main Office. We know you'll like him because he's "home folks", just like you. Consider The Hamilton your "hometown bank." We've been serving Morristown for three generations, providing you with the very best in full-service banking. If you're not already a Hamilton customer, come in soon. Let one of our friendly folks help you with your banking needs. We care about you!

"Helping You Build A Better Life"

Hamilton Bank

Morristown, Tennessee
Main Street/Lakeway/Plaza/
Radio Center/Skymart

211

212

A statement for better banking.

Maybe you thought a balanced checkbook existed only in theory. At the end of the month, you get out your checkbook, your bills, your receipts, pencils, paper, and your calculator. Then you work feverishly at your juggling and balancing act, trying to get the figures to cooperate with your cancelled checks.

Sound familiar? If so, you're going to love the Hamilton's computerized statement. It helps to make life simple again, with complete and accurate listings of your monthly transactions.

It lists all your deposits and withdrawals. It lists your checks, and the date we paid them. It shows, at a glance, everything you need to see to balance your account quickly and easily. You don't have to be a mathematician to have a well-balanced account at the Hamilton!

Our computerized statement includes all your banking transactions . . . savings, loans, Club accounts, and more. You can even transfer funds from checking to loan accounts or make deposit transfers.

If there's a better way of doing things, the Hamilton finds it for you. And even in the days of computerized bank statements, you can count on the Hamilton to give you that friendly, personal, "hometown" service you've become accustomed to. Come to the Hamilton . . . there's a world of banking services awaiting you!

"Helping You Build A Better Life"

Hamilton Bank

Morristown, Tennessee

WRAP UP 1980 CHRISTMAS SHOPPING NOW!

New! Automatic Transfer of Funds. *The Hamilton lets you "wrap up" your 1980 Christmas shopping now! It's so convenient! You no longer need make weekly visits to the bank to make your Christmas Club deposits. "Christmas+Plus" at the Hamilton lets you transfer funds from your checking account to your Christmas+Plus account - automatically!*

Here's How It Works. *Tell us how much you want to save on a*

regular basis for next year's Christmas shopping . . . we'll take it from there!

You make 50 payments . . . we make the 51st! And your regular monthly statement reflects your Christmas+Plus balance right along with all your other banking transactions! Christmas+Plus — with automatic transfer of funds — it helps you keep Christmas 1980 in the green!

Start yours now!

"Helping You Build A Better Life

Hamilton Bank HB

Christmas Plus

"HAMILTON BANK HELPS ME GET MORE OUT OF LIFE."

"You wouldn't know it by looking at me now, fishing with my grandson here, but I've taken care of a lot of banking today.

"First, my retirement check was deposited to my account at the Hamilton automatically. They've got direct deposit, you know. Took care of it with no effort from me at all.

"Lessee, then I paid all my bills by mail with Hamilton checks. That just took a minute, and I never left home.

"And, 'course, I made a little money, too, with interest from my savings account at the Hamilton. I even opened a new savings account for my grandson.

"That's somethin', isn't it? Hamilton Bank saved me all that time so I could spend my time at another bank—the creek bank.

"Helpin' you get more out of life. To my way of thinkin', that's what the Hamilton Bank does best."

"Helping You Build A Better Life"

Hamilton Bank ⊞

Morristown, Tennessee

Member FDIC

PEOPLE
HELPING PEOPLE
IS WHAT
BANKING IS
ALL ABOUT.

When you bank with The Citizens Bank, you get the best personal banking services available! You will find that we <u>practice</u> good banking services as well as talking about them – <u>every day</u>! Our people offer you the very best in experience, personal service, and genuine understanding. We provide you with the one-to-one personal service and attention that you rightfully deserve!

The Citizens Bank is proud of our community, our citizens, our employees, and the services they provide you. But most of all we're thankful for the opportunity the community has provided us to serve our customers' needs in all their financial matters. We are truly dedicated to providing you with the best possible banking services available!

Come see us. We'll take good care of you!

CITIZENS BANK
NEW TAZEWELL/TAZEWELL/HARROGATE

218

219

220

222

223

Our new 5-lane Autotellers help you win the race against time.

With a zillion things to do—and not enough time to do them—you need all the time-saving advantages you can get. We've got some dandies at First Bankers.

To help you get in and out quicker, we expanded the Autoteller facilities at our downtown office from 2 to 5 lanes. You can even do your personal banking at the "commercial" Auto-teller lane when it's not being used for business. We're also determined to help you beat the clock inside the bank. We'll soon be expanding our teller capacity from 5 to 10 windows. And the parking space around the bank has been increased so you'll be able to park quick and come right in.

To save you even more time, our Autoteller policy is to open early and close late: 7:30 am to 5:30 pm, Monday thru Thursday; until 7:00 pm on Friday.

Drive in and use our new 5-lane Autoteller system. It's the fastest stop you'll make today.

THE FIRST BANKERS
FIRST NATIONAL BANK
OF VOLUSIA COUNTY
MEMBER FDIC

NEW SMYRNA BEACH BANKING CENTER   PORT ORANGE BANKING CENTER

Person-to-Person.

Only Gulfstream Bank offers individual IRA Rollover Management. Call John Girard at 997-1349.

Some banks think more about numbers than about people. But not Gulfstream Bank. To us, "Person-to-Person" means just that.

It's easy to get a lot of conflicting viewpoints when it comes to your financial future, so we'd like to take a minute to set the record straight. Let's examine some of the choices available to you when it comes to IRA Rollover.

You can take your IRA Rollover funds to a big brokerage firm. Regardless of the firm you choose, you'll probably be dealing with courteous, professional people. And it's true that you'll be offered a choice of where to put your funds. You might choose an equity fund. Or an income fund. But, you'll just be a part of a big money pool, co-mingling your future with everyone else's.

Or, you can deal with a Savings and Loan. You'll still be dealing with friendly, helpful people. But, about all a Savings and Loan can do is put your IRA Rollover funds into Certificates of Deposit. Sometimes good, sometimes not-so-good.

Or, you can come to Gulfstream Bank. We can manage each and every account on an individual basis. Your very own financial counselor will design your very own investment program, working hard to maximize your overall rate of return. Without co-mingled funds or money pools.

So if you've got $100,000 or more that qualifies as an IRA Rollover that you'd like to have individually managed, call John Girard at 997-1349.

We think you'll like our exclusive IRA Rollover management service. And you'll like the way we mind your business.

Gulfstream Bank
Putting ideas into action.

NAPLES FEDERAL ANNOUNCES ANOTHER NEW LOCATION.

THE NEW YORK STOCK EXCHANGE.

Getting listed on the New York Stock Exchange isn't easy. If your company can pass the tough financial requirements, you make application, and maybe the NYSE accepts you. Maybe.

Naples Federal passed with flying colors. But it didn't happen overnight.

Think of us as NAF.

In November, 1979, our customers voted by an overwhelming majority to go public, and many of these same customers chose to become stockholders. (Thanks again for your enthusiastic response!).

Then in February, 1980, Naples Federal officially became one of only three S & L's in Florida to get on the Big Board. (Our stock symbol is NAF).

Generating money.

Of course, if you read our Annual Report, you know that our assets of over $450 million, and our objective to keep the momentum going in the years ahead, more than qualify us for the New York Stock Exchange. But it's the bottom-line aspect of it that we're most happy about. Namely, how the additional funds generated will benefit our customers, and generally strengthen the economy of our Southwest Florida community.

Putting money to good use.

We will have more mortgage money available for home loans to people in our local community—even when the money market gets tight and other financial institutions are hard-pressed for cash.

We'll be better able to expand and improve our customer facilities where and when they're needed.

Money will be available in the 1980's to keep pace with the growth and expansion along Florida's Gulf Coast.

Additional money will also enable us to expand present services, institute new services and explore new high yield investment programs, for people who want the kind of safety with their savings that Naples Federal provides.

The New York Stock Exchange with a friendly smile. Imagine that.

Naples Federal
More than just a friendly smile.

Naples Federal comes to San Carlos with more than just a friendly smile.

Walk into the new Naples Federal office in San Carlos, at 19060 Cleveland Ave. SE (U.S. #41), Monday, May 5th thru Friday, May 9th, and you'll get more than just a cheery hello and a friendly smile.

Super Prizes.

Register with us and you may win one of these valuable prizes: a 19'' Sony Trinitron color TV, or $100 and $200 gift certificates for groceries from Publix. You don't have to make a deposit with us to be eligible. You don't even have to be present to win. So, come in and register anytime, Monday, May 5 thru Friday, May 9.

A "thank you" gift.

We'd like to see you win a big prize at Naples Federal, but we'd also like you to be our permanent customer. So, if you open a savings account with us for $100 or more, we'll thank you with a free gift, to show our appreciation.

Wait, there's more.

Behind Naples Federal's friendly smile is a modern drive-in facility for convenient in-car service. We offer a non-stop source of mortgage money to people who need home loans. We have a variety of high-yield, no-risk Money Market programs to choose from. And if size is important where you save, you should know that Naples Federal is the largest Savings and Loan in Southwest Florida, and is one of only four Savings and Loans in the United States directly listed on the New York Stock Exchange.

Sure, at Naples Federal we're all smiles. Come into our new San Carlos office and find out what's behind it all.

Naples Federal
More than just a friendly smile.
Naples Federal Savings and Loan Association, a New York Stock Exchange Company, with offices throughout Southwest Florida.

What good is a bank that turns off when you need it?

Times are tough. And lots of banks are turning off lots of services. Just when you need them most is just when they offer the least.

Not at The First Bankers. We've made a commitment to serve our customers in bad times as well as good. That means with all the services that attracted our customers in the first place.

There's another way we serve our customers. By helping them turn tough times into opportunities. How? With the new high-return specialized investments you may have been hearing about. It's our business to understand them and to understand the financial ins and outs that make the difference between profit and loss.

At The First Bankers, we look at these times a little differently. It's not a time to stop offering services. This is the time to work together. If we help you now when things are tight, you'll still be our customer when things loosen up. It's good business. It's good banking. It's good sense. Just stop in at any First Bankers office to open your account.

THE FIRST BANKERS
MEMBERS FDIC

We want to work with you.

MONEY SECRETS FOR WOMEN

A FIRST NATIONAL SEMINAR FOR WOMEN ON COMPLETE MONEY MANAGEMENT.

MAY 1, 8 and 15

10 a.m. to noon and 1:30 to 3:30 p.m.
MoneyTree Room I First National Building

There is a wealth of information waiting for you at First National Bank's special seminar, "Money Secrets for Women." You'll learn how to manage your money, make and protect your investments, plan for your retirement, handle an estate, how to establish credit, how to apply for loans, how to choose a savings account, how to keep records, how to deal with inflation, how to set up a budget, how to stick to a budget, how to understand stocks and bonds, how to invest in real estate, how to set up trusts and wills, how to handle taxes and much, much more.

The seminar will be held in two sessions each day on May 1, 8 and 15 in MoneyTree Room I in the First National Building at Capitol & Broadway. The morning session is from 10 to 12, and the afternoon session is from 1:30 to 3:30.

The $10 registration fee covers all materials as well as a two-volume set of Sylvia Porter's New Money Book for the 80's, which is yours to keep. Attendance is limited, so registration is on a first come-first serve basis. You may register by filling out the coupon and mailing it to First National, or you may call us at 371-7269.

Yes, register me for "Money Secrets for Women" May 1, 8 and 15.

Name _____

Address _____ Telephone _____

City _____ State _____ Zip _____

My $10 registration fee is enclosed.

Mail to: First National Bank, Attn: Linda Couch, Retail Banking, P.O. Box 1471, Little Rock, AR 72203

When you think of money, think First.

 FIRST NATIONAL BANK IN LITTLE ROCK

OUR FIRST RESPONSIBILITY.

Bank President William L. Cravens presents an American flag to children from Fair Park School as part of the bank's participation in the Adopt-A-School Program.

 FIRST NATIONAL BANK IN LITTLE ROCK

MEMBER FDIC

"I don't leave things to chance—like my will. That's where First National Trust comes in."

Consult your attorney and a First National Trust officer about your will and estate planning.

When you think of money, think First.

"First National has the know-how my money deserves."

When you think of money, think First.

FIRST NATIONAL BANK IN LITTLE ROCK

235

"First National?
The best.
My bank."

When you think of
money, think First.

 FIRST NATIONAL BANK IN LITTLE ROCK

"Money matters. First National understands that."

When you think of money, think First.

 FIRST NATIONAL BANK IN LITTLE ROCK

"No bank has all the answers. But First National gives me intelligent choices."

When you think of money, think First.

 FIRST NATIONAL BANK IN LITTLE ROCK

"First National handles my money."

When you think of money, think First.

FIRST NATIONAL BANK IN LITTLE ROCK

"First National makes sense. And that makes money."

When you think of money, think First.

 FIRST NATIONAL BANK IN LITTLE ROCK

MEMBER FDIC

241

For want of a dollar, a fortune was lost.

Of course, we realize it takes years of neglect for a house to get into this condition.

But we wanted to make a point. To remind you that your home is a major investment.

If the want of ready cash is keeping you from making some necessary improvements, come in and see us.

Even if they're not so necessary, but will add to your enjoyment of your home, we'd like to help out.

The new law allows us to lend you up to $10,000 for home improvements, with new, longer repayment terms. Our loan experts can give you all the details when you come in.

We know the value of your home will increase with a new addition, or remodeling, or just plain fixin' up, so we have every reason to approve your loan.

This part of the country is a beautiful place to live. We want to do our part to keep it that way.

242

Who says we're a "stuffed shirt" bank?

Every now and then you'll hear someone refer to us as "stuffed shirt."

Could be because we've been in business since 1854 and back in the olden days banks were expected to be "stuffed shirt" and "fuddy-duddy."

It meant "stable". . . "conservative". . . "pillar of the community."

But there's another side of us too. Besides growing into the largest bank with the greatest number of branches in this county, we've evolved into a progressive, innovative, pace-setting bank.

We were the first bank around to offer simple interest loans and the first to give you interest on your checking.

And we pay the highest interest rates the law allows on savings accounts and certificates of deposit.

Since all our loan officers can approve credit up to certain limits, your loan application doesn't have to go before a grand

jury and you'll often have an answer the same day.

Our JiffyBank is a machine, but everyone else is human. In fact, HCNB bankers are so human we cheat on our diets, get the hiccups, and even cry at weddings. We have a sense of humor, too, and can poke fun at our "stuffed shirt" image.

Right now we're selling them. T-shirts, that is. Unstuffed. For the incredibly low price of $2.50 each.

They're USA-made of 50% polyester and 50% cotton and they machine wash and dry beautifully. Get one for everyone in the family. We have children's and adults' sizes.

We never had any old bags at Hunterdon County National Bank. All our bags are brand new and we're selling them, too. Just $2.00 each.

Where else can you get a 13" square tote bag made of sturdy cloth with waterproof lining for only $2.00?? Roomy enough for books and sneakers, tough

enough for wet towels and swimsuits.

If you each get one, watch out that the kids don't swipe them to use as schoolbags. They're so reasonable, get them their own.

Both the T-shirts and totes are beige with contrasting brown design and they're top quality.

We wouldn't put our symbol on any product we didn't think was quality and wouldn't own ourselves. In the photo above, all our management people (including our president) are wearing HCNB T-shirts.

Fill out the coupon below and mail along with your check or money order.

Or — if you'd like to see and feel the quality before buying, come in to any of our ten branches.

We want to be your bank and we're hoping you'll open an account or ask about our services when you come in.

Then we can prove that WHEATREAT YOU GOOD is more than just a jingle.

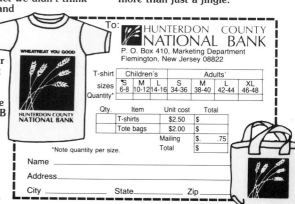

To: **HUNTERDON COUNTY NATIONAL BANK**
P. O. Box 410, Marketing Department
Flemington, New Jersey 08822

T-shirt sizes	Children's			Adults'			
	S 6-8	M 10-12	L 14-16	S 34-36	M 38-40	L 42-44	XL 46-48
Quantity*							

Qty.	Item	Unit cost	Total
	T-shirts	$2.50	$
	Tote bags	$2.00	$
		Mailing	$. .75
		Total	$

*Note quantity per size.

Name _____

Address_____

City _____ State_____ Zip _____

MEMBER FDIC

243

We Don't Do a Single Thing for Farmers.

Sometimes we do three things. Sometimes five things. Maybe eight, ten, or more!

Because we're a full service bank, we can do lots of financial chores for our farm customers. Things a specialized lending agency can't do. And that makes it a lot easier and convenient for you.

- Farm improvement loans
- Production financing
- Savings plans
- Convenient checking plans

- Trust services
- Safety deposit boxes
- Personal loans

.....and much much more. Have a financial need? Then.....

See Our Man in Farming. Chuck Souder.

FIRST SECURITY BANK +TRUST COMPANY

Charles City, Marble Rock, and Ionia   Member FDIC

WHO CAN START FINANCIAL WHEELS TURNING?

You have questions. About checking and savings accounts. 24-hour tellers. Safe deposit services. Or any of a hundred other topics people ask a bank every day.

You need answers. You need Fourth National. Seasoned professionals who can deal with every type of banking question. Including yours. And our professionals are backed by the latest and most conveniently-located automated tellers.

As you skate through life's financial obstacles, remember Fourth National. We're here to smooth out the rough spots.

Who can start financial wheels turning? Fourth National.

SEE FOURTH NATIONAL

THE FOURTH NATIONAL BANK OF TULSA
515 SOUTH BOULDER
TULSA, OKLAHOMA 74103
(918) 587-9171

MEMBER FDIC

FIRST. THE BANK THAT APPLAUDS FINANCIAL SUCCESS.

Sometimes money seems to cause more problems than it's worth. With all the complications and confusion that arise from having more than a little, you'd think that it was something to be uncomfortable about.

Not, however, at First.

First applauds financial success. In fact, First is the bank that supports your success every hour of the day, every day of the week.

With financial insight that is critical to your personal success and to the success of your business. With hard-hitting savings plans, investment options and trusts. With knowledgeable banking professionals who help you meet your needs. And reach your goals.

You worked hard to get where you are. At First we work hard to keep you there. Find out how in our new brochure, "How to buy a bank."

First. The bank that applauds financial success.

THE FIRST NATIONAL BANK AND TRUST COMPANY OF STILLWATER

246

At Columbia, we're building a full-service reputation.

With the introduction of our full-service Banking Packages, a lot of people are deciding not to bank at a bank anymore.

After all, there's a Columbia Banking Package that's just right for you and the way you live today. It features 5¼% daily interest on checking, and many other services you used to expect only from a bank.

And when you consider that Columbia is with you with higher interest on savings, a William Teller network and more branches than any one bank, it just doesn't make sense to bank anywhere else.

So come to Columbia. From the new Columbia Plaza home office at 17th and Broadway to our more than 40 full-service locations statewide, we're with you more than ever.

Columbia Savings

We're with you. In more places, more ways than anyone.

Columbia Plaza, newest addition to Denver's skyline.

No bank in Charleston offers longer hours than KB&T's MiniBank.

Now we're open even longer than before-- from 7:30 a.m. till 7:00 p.m., Monday through Saturday.

For quite a while now our MiniBank Center has offered the longest banking hours in Charleston.

And now we've made it even more convenient to bank there. Because we're now opening at 7:30 every morning instead of 8:00.

So if you'd like to do your banking before work, we can have you on your way in plenty of time.

With our unique drive-in system, the MiniBank offers the fastest banking in town. You face your teller head-on. And with six wide lanes to choose from you can move right through the system

in just a few minutes.

There's plenty of free parking for our walk-in customers, too.

In addition, the KB&T MiniBank has an outdoor QuickBank money machine that handles your check cashing, withdrawals, deposits or whatever, fast—no matter what time it is.

So drive in and visit our MiniBank Center at Virginia and Laidley Streets. You'll discover what some people already know—KB&T's MiniBank Center has the fastest, most convenient banking in town.

We are the bank that has time for you.

KB&T

Member FDIC

248

"The Trust Department at Hospital Trust. They're people who take the time to listen. They respect the fact that I have some ideas about my financial well-being. So they work *with me* to help maintain my lifestyle today. And to give me a more financially secure tomorrow.

"I learned a lot about becoming successful in business from my Dad.

"WHO DO I TRUST?"

But he also taught me how to have faith in the right people. And *people* is what the Personal Trust Department at Hospital Trust is all about.

"After all, *financial management is a matter of personal trust.*"

For more information, call Jim Sullivan at (401) 278-8348, Rhode Island Hospital Trust National Bank, One Hospital Plaza, Providence, RI 02903.

You feel better banking on Hospital Trust.

Total Trust Assets $2.8 Billion

Member F.D.I.C.

Nex
your Central
won't be wh

If you're lookin
6 Common Stre

We're moving!
CentralBank/W
opposite the St.
Armory). Our r
parking space,
handi
to

S
C
int
poss
toda
free
Keo
mor
Wat
ann
Ope

Central Cooperative

Other offices in: Arlington, Burlington, Cambridge, Chestnut H

WE'VE ADDED SEVEN BRANCHES AND A NEW NAME.

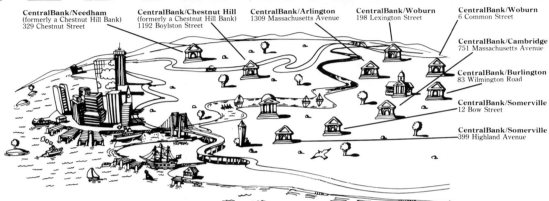

CentralBank/Needham
(formerly a Chestnut Hill Bank)
329 Chestnut Street

CentralBank/Chestnut Hill
(formerly a Chestnut Hill Bank)
1192 Boylston Street

CentralBank/Arlington
1309 Massachusetts Avenue

CentralBank/Woburn
198 Lexington Street

CentralBank/Woburn
6 Common Street

CentralBank/Cambridge
751 Massachusetts Avenue

CentralBank/Burlington
83 Wilmington Road

CentralBank/Somerville
12 Bow Street

CentralBank/Somerville
399 Highland Avenue

We're CentralBank. We used to be known as Chestnut Hill Cooperative Bank, but recently we became partners with Central Cooperative Bank. We both wanted to grow. We also wanted to be able to offer expanded services in more locations. So we merged. And rather than have you call us Chestnut-Hill-Central-Cooperative-Bank, we decided CentralBank would be easier to remember.

CentralBank has nine offices that circle the Metropolitan Boston area. Two in Somerville, two in Woburn, and one each in Arlington, Burlington, Cambridge, Chestnut Hill, and Needham.

We're now one of the largest cooperative banks in Massachusetts with over $140 million in assets. This enables us to offer loans of all types at competitive rates. Whether you need a home mortgage, a personal loan, or money for remodeling, education, or a new car — we can probably be of help.

We also have 6-month Money Market Certificates, and brand new 2½ Year Certificates... each paying the highest rate allowed by law. And we can show you how to retire in style with a Keogh or IRA account.

Drop by any of our nine branches to see what we can do for you. At CentralBank, we're making a name for ourselves.

CHESTNUT HILL COOPERATIVE BANK AND CENTRAL COOPERATIVE BANK ARE NOW...

CentralBank

CentralBank is a trade name of Central Cooperative Bank.

You can't help but win with your new CentralBank/Woburn.

Great banking and great prizes can be yours just for stopping in at the new CentralBank/Woburn office. We're now at 275 Main Street, opposite the St. Charles Church and the Woburn Armory.

We're having a Grand Opening Celebration where everybody wins! All you have to do is walk in the door to get a **free 6 oz. jar of Smucker's Strawberry Preserves.** (Limit one jar per family please, while supply lasts.) And that's just for starters.

The biggest prize of all is seeing what it's like to be a "Millionaire for a Week." Just take a guess at the amount of cash in the "House of Money" in our lobby. If you're the closest, you'll receive one week's interest on a million dollars!*

We're also giving away over 60 other special prizes in the "House of Money" contest**, to make this the the biggest bank celebration in Woburn's history. Prizes include: a 19″ Remote Control Zenith Color T.V., Tappan Microwave Oven, 3 Zenith Multiband Radios, 10 Sharp Calculators, and 50 pairs of General Cinema Movie Tickets.

When you visit the new CentralBank/Woburn office, you'll see banking has never been more convenient. Our mid-town location has lots of free parking, 2 drive-up windows, and extended service hours... so your bank is open when you need it to be.

Come on down and celebrate with us. At the new CentralBank/Woburn Grand Opening Celebration you can't lose.

1st Prize
"Millionaire for a Week"*

2nd Prize
Zenith 19″ Color T.V.

3rd Prize
Tappan Microwave Oven

4th Prize(s)
3 Zenith Radios

5th Prize(s)
10 Sharp Calculators

6th Prize(s)
50 Pairs Movie Tickets

Central Cooperative Bank is now... CB CENTRALBANK

Other offices in: Arlington, Burlington, Cambridge, Chestnut Hill, Needham, and Somerville.

*One week's interest on $1,000,000. deposited in a regular savings account paying 5.50% annually.
**Entries limited to adults 18 and over. One entry per person. Contest ends on March 29th. Winners announced April 14th.

provided the loan that launched S&E Shipping Corporation's new ore carrier, the Kinsman Independent.

analyzes the composition of Dow Chemical's shareholders to keep their records up-to-date and accurate.

AmeriTrust. The Bank that

lent the money to Farmland Industries to reap bumper crops throughout the midwest.

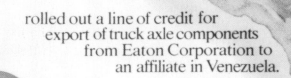

rolled out a line of credit for export of truck axle components from Eaton Corporation to an affiliate in Venezuela.

helps Pickands Mather spotlight its cash position with daily computerized updates.

/AmeriTrust®
Headquarters: Cleveland, Ohio
Making things happen in MidAmerica.

254

The Western Pay-&-Save System.

(Say so long to plain, old checking and earn interest at the same time.)

You get payment orders that look like checks and work like checks.

And you can pay your bills by phone, too. We do all the work and we pay all the postage.

The Western Pay-&-Save System. It pays you interest while it pays your bills.

Here's how it works.

You keep money in your Pay-&-Save Account. We make transfers from savings as you need them. That money earns a healthy 5¼% interest (that's the highest allowed by law) right up to the day you spend it.

And you can spend it two ways.

(1) You get payment orders to pay your bills. They look like checks and work like checks. The only difference is we can't call them checks.

(2) Or you can pay some or all of your bills by phone, too. Just tell us who you want us to pay. And when. We do all the work. And we pay all the postage.

Every month, of course, we send you a Pay-&-Save System statement. It shows all deposits, transfers, interest earned (shown quarterly), savings balance, payment orders and telephone payments. Everything.

So get the convenient Western Pay-&-Save System. And say so long to plain, old checking.

Western
SAVINGS BANK
Member FDIC

Funny, nobody's laughing at Atlantic City anymore.

But at First National State we're all smiles.

The glory of Atlantic City is gone forever, they said, and casino gambling won't help.

But the doom-sayers were wrong. Casino gambling has brought new life to that great resort. Atlantic City is booming and bustling and bursting with pride. And all because the forward-looking people of New Jersey took a positive stand on behalf of a vital area of the State.

First National State has been a primary force in the drive for growth and pride in Atlantic City and throughout the Garden State. And we put our money where our enthusiasm is.

We provided financing for the first casino built in Atlantic City by Resorts International. And we're actively involved in many other vital Atlantic City projects.

We were the lead bank behind the financing of the Meadowlands Sports Complex. We have strongly supported responsible development of off-shore oil recovery. We have continually reflected the pride we have in our state through active support of thousands of growing New Jersey businesses, both large and small.

That's why we're all smiles about the rebirth of Atlantic City. Because that rebirth is only a part of an exciting new era of growth for the entire state of New Jersey.

And you can count on First National State to continue to provide the kind of financial leadership you'd expect from New Jersey's largest commercial bank. In Atlantic City and throughout our great state.

To learn more about our financial and banking expertise and the depth of our knowledge of the New Jersey business and financial marketplace just drop a note on your letterhead to Edward D. Knapp, Senior Executive Vice President.

First National State®

A great bank can make a great difference.

First National State Bank of New Jersey, 550 Broad Street, Newark, N.J. 07102, (201) 565-3200 Member FDIC

The Tower Clock, Waterbury

Big Ben, London

We keep bankers hours. All around the world.

At Colonial Bank, we don't just make things happen in Connecticut. We make things happen all around the world.

Our International Department has relationships with banks throughout the world to help Connecticut businesses of all sizes with their foreign exchange, credit and trade transactions.

Our London office provides Colonial's customers with the capability of borrowing in the International marketplace, and an on-the-scene complement to Colonial's staff.

Our Cayman Islands Branch places and receives deposits in Euro-dollars and other major world currencies, serving both foreign

and domestic clients doing business in Connecticut.

To get the complete story on the kind of bankers hours Colonial keeps throughout the world, just call Charles B. Barlow, Senior Vice President, at (203) 574-7434 or Telex: 96-2405, Cable Address: COLONIAL WBY. He'll give you all the up-to-the-minute details.

International Banking Department
81 West Main St., P.O. Box 2791
Waterbury, Connecticut 06720

We make things happen in Connecticut and around the world.

Member FDIC

Has your cash flow frozen up?

That's where Colonial Business Finance Corporation can make a real difference for your company.

If traditional credit sources simply can't help you meet all of your cash needs, let us explore other possibilities. As a subsidiary of Colonial Bank, we have a proven record of providing flexible commercial financing to meet the most complex requirements.

For example, you most likely have considerable assets which are presently in accounts receivable, inventory or expensive equipment. We can show you how to use those assets to create a continual cash availability and give you the cash flow you need to improve sales and profits. And, we can provide expertise in mergers, buyouts and acquisitions, as well.

To learn more about how we can help you turn assets into cash flow, just give us a call at (203) 574-7538. We'll set up an immediate meeting to break the ice.

Colonial Business Finance Corporation

Waterbury, Connecticut 06720
Subsidiary of Colonial Bank

Seven special thin

Newark! It's a city rich with history and culture. Yet most people in New Jersey don't know the real Newark. And have no idea of the riches it has to offer. Newark has been home for First National State since 1812. And we've come to know our home town well. Here are just a few of the surprising things there are to do in New Jersey's largest city, if you just take the time.

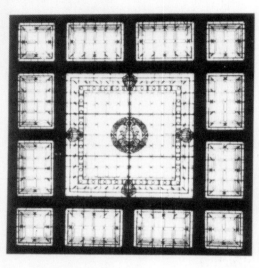

ORIENT YOURSELF

This huge ceramic dragon from the Ming Dynasty Period is just a sample of the exceptional collection of Oriental art on view at the Newark Museum. See it for yourself along with the rest of the treasures of this marvelous cultural institution.

SAY HELLO TO YOUR FATHER

This bronze likeness of the Fath of our Country, George Washingto fine works of sculpture you'll find Park right in the heart of New

LOOK UP

Go to the main branch of the Newark Public Library. Look straight up. You'll see a magnificent stained glass skylight. And while you're there check out some of the resources of one of the country's finest libraries.

MAIL A LETTER

The New Jersey Bell building on Broad Street is one of the finest examples of art deco period architecture in America. If you have occasion to walk into the lobby, address your attention to the extraordinary bronze mailbox. It isn't often you can drop a letter in a work of art.

ǵs to do in Newark.

JAZZ THINGS UP

Jazz is probably our country's only true native art form. And Newark has been a center of jazz music activity since World War I. So it's appropriate that the Rutgers University Newark campus be the home of the Institute for Jazz Studies. The Institute provides scholars and jazz lovers access to a remarkable collection of jazz records, literature and artifacts.

BLOSSOM FORTH

Branchbrook Park is one of six county parks in Newark. Each Spring over 3500 pink and white cherry trees—more than you'll find in Washington, D.C.–come to beautiful and scent-full blossom. It's an experience you'll never forget.

GO BACK TO SCHOOL

George Washington spoke to the students at Lyons Farms Schoolhouse almost two centuries ago. It's been moved from its original location on Elizabeth and Chancellor Avenues to a cozy spot in the Newark Museum Garden. Visit it. You might learn something new.

We hope you'll take our advice and do a few of these very special things in Newark. And while you're in town, stop by First National State's Executive Office at 550 Broad Street, and say hello. We're always pleased to welcome visitors to our wonderful home town.

one of many
ington

First National State

First National State Bank of New Jersey,
550 Broad Street, Newark, N. J. 07102, (201) 565-3200.
A First National State Bancorporation Bank/Member FDIC

We can help you find the most precious commodity in the jewelry business.

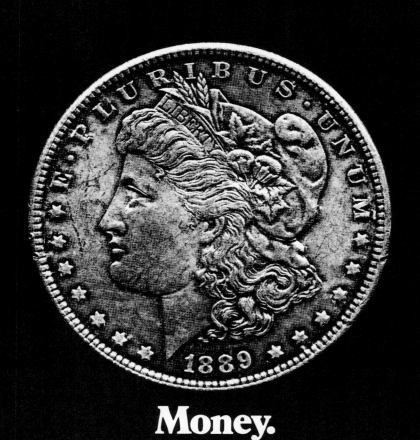

Money.

We offer you a full range of credit services, along with a complete staff that has made it their business to understand yours.

That's because we've established a division devoted exclusively to the unique financial needs of the jewelry business.

So when you deal with InBank, you get more than good financial advice. You get financial assistance that's tempered with a sound knowledge of your industry. From a bank that's located in the jewelry center of the world.

We also have extensive capabilities, like leasing, fixed asset and real estate appraisal, data processing and international services, precious metals financing and pension and profit-sharing services through InCorp, our multi-billion-dollar parent company.

For more information, contact Jewelry Group Head Gene Gasbarro, Vice President, at (401) 278-6507, or write: Jewelry Group, InBank, 111 Westminster Street, Providence, RI 02903. Contact us today. We can show you that a precious commodity doesn't have to be rare.

We make it our business to understand yours.

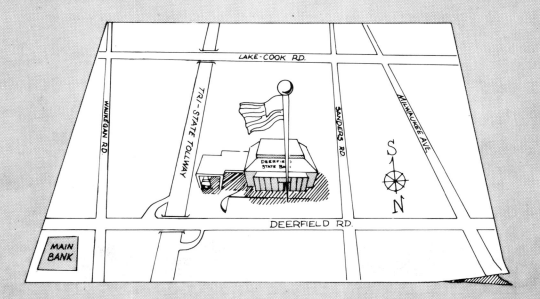

264

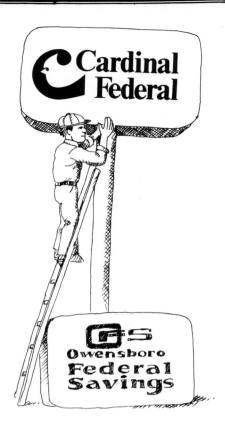

Why would Owensboro's largest savings and loan change its name?

For more than 67 years, we were known as Owensboro Federal. But as we grew, we outgrew our name.

As one of Kentucky's leading financial institutions, we needed a name that would better reflect our importance to the people of our region.

Our new name — Cardinal Federal — reflects our position as one of Kentucky's leading savings and loan associations.

But, in case you're wondering, that's all that has changed. We still have our same five locations, the same people and the same local board of directors.

The only thing we've changed is our name.

Five locations: 700 Frederica Street   Wesleyan Park   Towne Square Mall   Hawesville   Calhoun

Why we changed our name to Cardinal Federal

For more than 67 years, we were known as Owensboro Federal. But as we grew, we outgrew our name.

Our new name — Cardinal Federal — reflects our importance as one of Kentucky's largest savings and loan associations.

As we continue to grow and serve more areas, our new name will serve us better. For your financial needs, you can look to Cardinal Federal in the future, just as people looked to Owensboro Federal for more than 67 years.

Five locations: 700 Frederica Street   Wesleyan Park   Towne Square Mall   Hawesville   Calhoun

How to set up a sweet tax shelter without being filthy rich.

There was a time when you had to be at least fabulously well-to-do to qualify for a genuine tax shelter. No more. Because today there's the Individual Retirement Account, a personal, tax-sheltered retirement savings plan available to people of all incomes. Here's how it works.

Defer taxes on up to 15% of your income. If you're not covered by any pension plan except for Social Security, you can tuck away up to 15% of your income or $1500.00 (whichever is less) — before taxes. If neither you nor your spouse has a pension plan and only one of you has a taxable income, you can set aside up to $1750.

Save more now. Pay less later. As your retirement fund builds, taxes on both the principal and the interest are deferred until you retire. By that time, chances are you'll be in a lower tax bracket, eligible for more deductions. And your tax savings should be considerable.

It's easy to start. Opening an Individual Retirement Account is as easy as opening a savings account. Just stop in at any Citizen's Central office or write for the necessary forms to get your fund started. If you're self-employed, ask about our Keogh retirement plan, too.

So stop by soon. Nibble some complimentary candy while you let Citizen's Central help you set up your own sweet retirement fund now.

Citizens Central
The country bank with big city services.
Arcade, Delevan, Rushford, Silver Springs, Yorkshire, Elba, Lyndonville.

Member F.D.I.C.

EVERY YEAR WE GO FURTHER INTO THE BLACK.

5-Year Performance Review and Statement of Condition

Assets	Dec. 31, 1979	Dec. 31, 1978	Dec. 31, 1977	Dec. 31, 1976	Dec. 31, 1975
First Mortgage Loans	384,042,789.10	323,756,606.20	248,724,326.68	180,003,346.93	128,922,964.87
Other Loans	7,924,621.00	5,978,688.14	4,020,823.55	1,980,007.75	670,765.38
Real Estate Owned	none	none	62,506.82	none	3,743.41
Cash on Hand And In Banks	15,672,759.69	1,163,334.33	1,014,120.77	1,342,640.88	43,355.40
Investments and Securities	33,965,637.50	35,050,198.34	24,536,903.25	19,808,478.35	15,729,571.81
Federal Home Loan Bank Stock	2,702,400.00	2,059,000.00	1,499,500.00	1,114,700.00	882,000.00
Fixed Assets Less Depreciation	8,233,356.86	6,322,512.52	6,036,673.26	4,702,303.49	3,369,539.35
Deferred Charges and Other Assets	1,860,117.80	3,724,177.43	1,102,321.22	989,474.10	866,449.60
Total Assets	**$454,401,681.95**	$378,054,516.96	$286,997,175.55	$209,940,951.50	$150,488,389.82

Liabilities And Net Worth					
Savings Accounts	390,605,567.43	326,354,803.25	251,584,980.46	188,700,346.67	137,181,182.40
Federal Home Loan Bank Advances	24,750,000.00	1,150,000.00	5,760,000.00	1,760,000.00	1,760,000.00
Other Borrowed Money	209,000.00	1,531,000.00	897,741.00		
Loans in Process	14,945,619.73	24,686,286.38	15,757,798.84	10,045,552.57	4,787,549.19
Other Liabilities	2,966,007.25	3,930,397.52	1,675,910.53	1,051,413.35	541,749.60
Deferred Income	3,048,807.48	6,838,035.70	1,406,804.23	1,006,481.35	448,253.83
Specific Reserves	32,000.00	34,900.00	21,000.00		
General Reserves	12,414,875.44	9,647,202.51	7,498,034.36	5,840,849.19	4,388,988.28
Surplus	5,429,804.62	3,881,891.60	2,394,906.13	1,536,308.37	1,380,666.52
Total Liabilities And Net Worth	**$454,401,681.95**	$378,054,516.96	$286,997,175.55	$209,940,951.50	$150,488,389.82

Note: Blanks in 1975 and 1976 indicate account titles not used in those years. FSLIC

Naples Federal
More than just a friendly smile.
Naples Federal Savings and Loan Association with 12 Offices throughout Southwest Florida.

Why we changed our name to American Federal

ANDERSON FEDERAL SAVINGS

For more than 55 years, we've been serving this area. And for most of those years, we've been known as Anderson Federal Savings & Loan Association.

But, as we grew, we outgrew our name. Our new name — American Federal Savings & Loan Association — reflects our impor-

tance as one of the leading financial institutions in our region.

As we continue to grow and serve a larger area of Indiana, our new name will serve us better. For your financial needs, you can look to American Federal in the future, just as people have looked to Anderson Federal in the past.

American Federal
Savings & Loan Association

Some answers about our name change

Some common questions about
our name change
from Anderson Federal
to American Federal

ANDERSON FEDERAL
SAVINGS

Q. Why did you change your name to American Federal?

A. As we grew, our old name — Anderson Federal — was no longer appropriate. We needed a name which reflected our importance as one of the leading financial institutions in our region of Indiana.

Q. What about the people? Are they the same?

A. Yes. The people are the same. We have the same employees, the same local board of directors. The only thing we've changed is our name.

Q. What about my certificate of deposit which says "Anderson Federal." Do I have to get it changed?

A. No. Anything with the name "Anderson Federal" is still valid. You don't have to make any changes.

Q. Has someone acquired Anderson Federal? Has there been a merger or something?

A. No. Nothing has changed except our name.

American Federal
Savings & Loan Association

273

Bank Cards

"The Met offers you <u>both</u> VISA and MasterCard, for those quaint places that might honor only one."

Not many banks offer both of the most widely honored credit cards in the world. And many places still don't <u>accept</u> both. Play it safe. Carry both cards for emergencies, and get them from one bank. You'll only get one convenient statement and make one simple payment each month, too. Simplify your life. Come to . . .

St. Paul Federal told me to take my business elsewhere.

I have nothing against financial institutions, theoretically.

It's just that whenever I need some money, or have to cash a check, there's never a financial institution handy.

I'm usually elsewhere. I spend a lot of my time in supermarkets, actually.

Now, St. Paul Federal has come out with a card that lets me cash checks or make deposits or withdrawals in a number of supermarkets around town, and obtain cash at many out-of-town locations.

It's called the "Yes" card and it lets me transact my financial business from 8 in the morning to 12 midnight, most places.

And, since I tend to run out of money on Sundays, it's a relief to know that the "Yes" card lets me do my banking 7 days a week.

I can't tell you how delighted I was to hear about the "Yes" card.

Because, although I've always been a loyal customer of St. Paul Federal, it's a lot more convenient to be someplace else.

 St. Paul Federal Savings

We give you more for your money than money.

CHICAGO HOME OFFICE: 6700 W. North Ave., 60635/(312) 622-5000 FRANKLIN PARK, 10035 W. Grand Ave., 60131/455-4300 BARTLETT, 140 S. Hickory St., 60103/837-2000 CHICAGO, 2159 W. 18th St., 60608/226-1021 ROLLING MEADOWS, 3901 Kirchoff Rd., 60008/398-0090 HANOVER PARK, 1301 Irving Park Rd., 60103/289-2800 BLUE ISLAND, 11960 S. Western Ave., 60406/388-8400 WHEATON, 923 E. Roosevelt Rd., 60187/668-4700 CHICAGO, 6348 W. Diversey Ave., 60639/622-8877 MOUNT PROSPECT, 940 E. Rand Rd., 60056/259-7575 BERKELEY, 5401 St. Charles Rd., 60163/547-5300 DOWNERS GROVE, 400 W. 75th St., 60515/963-7575 OAK PARK, 6020 W. Roosevelt Rd., (Tri City Division) 60304/383-6650 LOMBARD, 45 W. Roosevelt Rd., (Tri-City Division) 60148/620-0300 ELMWOOD PARK, 7312 W. Grand Ave., 60635/452-8500 WESTCHESTER, 1901 S. Mannheim Rd., 60153/344-8575 MORTON GROVE, 9330 Waukegan Road, 60053/967-1500 ADDISON, 540 W. Lake St., 60101/543-4322

Member Federal Savings and Loan Insurance Corporation

 EQUAL HOUSING LENDER

278

AFTER THE SHOW DOUGH.

Make a deposit, withdrawal, transfer money from one account to another...The Time Machine automatic teller is open 24 hours a day, 7 days a week. It puts time on your side.

THE FIRST BANKERS
MEMBERS FDIC

THE TOW-TRUCK TRANSFER

Make a deposit, withdrawal, transfer money from one account to another…The Time Machine automatic teller is open 24 hours a day, 7 days a week. It puts time on your side.

THE FIRST BANKERS
MEMBERS FDIC

THE WAITING WAITER WITHDRAWAL

Make a deposit, withdrawal, transfer money from one account to another...The Time Machine automatic teller is open 24 hours a day, 7 days a week. It puts time on your side.

THE FIRST BANKERS
MEMBERS FDIC

We never close.

ComBank at the airport

Full service banking. 16 hours a day.

Our office at Orlando International Airport is open 16 hours a day, seven days a week. So, any time between 7:00 a.m. and 11:00 p.m., you can talk to our courteous, bilingual staff about checking and savings accounts, loans, foreign currency exchange, travelers checks, Visa or Master Charge card cash advances, a full range of financial services.

24-hour banking. At your Command.

Even when the staff isn't on duty, our Command 24 automatic teller machine is. So, you and your Command 24 card can complete deposits, withdrawals, transfers and payments any time of the day or night. You can even use your ComBank Visa or Master Charge card to get a cash advance.

Stop by the airport's main lobby one day soon. Get to know our staff. Get acquainted with our Command 24 services. And get the first class bank service you deserve.

Member FDIC

ComBank

ComBank/Pine Castle
Orlando International Airport
West End of Main Lobby/646-6103

At ComBank, you are in command!

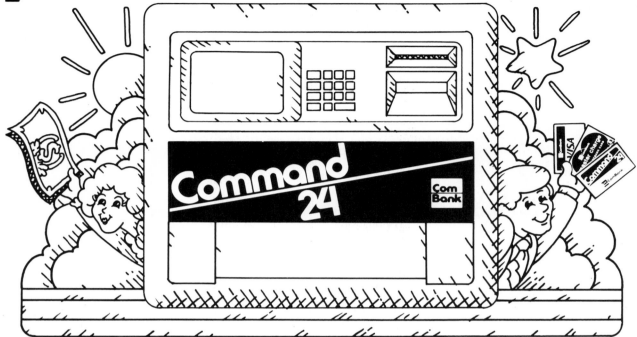

Bank whenever you like with Command 24.

You command. We obey.

Command 24, our new automatic teller machine, puts you in command of your banking 24 hours a day, seven days a week. You can make deposits, withdrawals, transfers and payments in seconds with a Command 24 card. With a magnetic striped ComBank Visa or Master Charge card, you can do even more.

Win a free burger and a chance to see Broadway!

From now through March 7, 1980, you'll get a special bonus when we mail your secret Command 24 number: a coupon for a free Whopper Jr and small soft drink at any participating Burger King restaurant in Orange and Seminole Counties.

If you apply for your card before March 8, you can register for our grand prize drawing March 10, when some lucky Command 24 customer will win a three-day vacation for two in New York City, including a Broadway show.

Second prize is two tickets to three 1980 Broadway shows at Bob Carr Municipal Auditorium. Third, fourth and fifth prizes are $50 savings accounts. And we'll give "I'm in command" T-shirts to 50 other winners.

We can put you in command.

Stop by any ComBank office soon. Request your Command 24 card or magnetic striped Visa or Master Charge card, pick up a copy of our Command 24 information folder and register for our big drawing. (You needn't be here to win.) Then bank whenever you like at ComBank...where you are in command.

Request your Command 24 card at any ComBank office.

Command 24 locations
Altamonte Mall
Palm Springs Dr. & Route 436
Casselberry
Highway 17/92 & Route 436
Longwood
801 E. State Road 434
Orlando International Airport, West end of Main Lobby
Pine Castle
6001 Hansel Avenue
Union Park
9541 E. Colonial Drive

Winter Park
750 S. Orlando Avenue

Other ComBank offices
Apopka
345 E. Main Street
Colony Gardens
329 Park Ave. S., Winter Park
Fairvilla
2250 N. Orange Blossom Trail
Orlando
44 E. Central Boulevard

Com Bank

Where you are in command.
Member FDIC

284

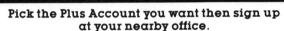

We recently sent
our customers a questionnaire
in order to find out
their needs…

WE
HEAR
YOU.

JIFFYBANK
OPEN **24** HOURS
is coming!

Why our card and not their card should be your card.

Our checking card.

Their credit card.

You might say the shift from credit cards to our checking card reflects what's happening with the economy. Credit's definitely tighter. And may cost you more as banks recalculate the finance charges on unpaid balances.

When you figure out what their card is going to cost you, you may not want to use it as much. Or at all. And that's why we offer our card — FirstCard Plus.

FirstCard Plus is the perfect alternative to their credit card. It looks like a credit card. It's accepted like one. But unlike their credit card, the amount you purchase is deducted from your checking account.

So it's like paying with a check, but without any identification hassle. Or put another way, it's like paying with their card's convenience, but without all the new credit card restrictions.

FirstCard Plus may just be the perfect combination of checking and convenience. And it's affordable convenience too, because with FirstCard Plus, you pay just a flat charge of $1.00 per month no matter how many times you use the card, plus any checking charges you would normally incur.

No wonder so many people are changing from their card to our card. It's almost hard not to. If you qualify for their card, just move your checking account to First National and you can have our card. And since FirstCard Plus is only one of the extra features you'll have with a First National checking account, you'll really be ahead. Any of our First National branch managers can give you full details.

FIRST NATIONAL BANK
OF LOUISVILLE
Member Federal Deposit Insurance Corporation

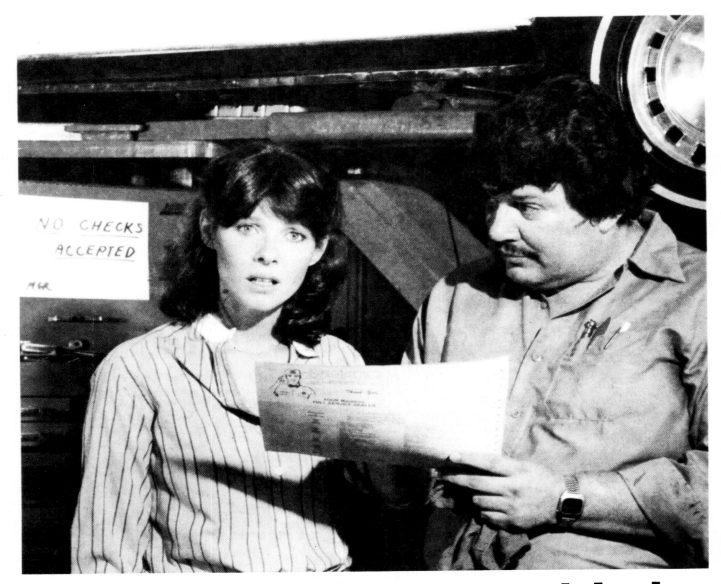

"They wouldn't take my personal check, but they took my plastic one: FirstCard Plus."

FirstCard Plus is instantly accepted wherever you see the blue, white and gold Visa symbol. But it's different than a credit card, because the money comes out of your checking account.

So it's really a plastic check that you can use at most stores and restaurants. You can even use it to get cash from any of our Teller/24 machines or at any of our 52 neighborhood branches.

And all your FirstCard Plus conveniences cost only a dollar a month, plus any checking charges you'd normally incur. That's a real bargain when you consider the trouble it saves and the purchasing freedom it offers.

You've always had a big choice of reasons to use a First National checking account. Paying bills with a simple, time-saving phone call is one. Getting cash any time of day or night with Teller/24 is another. And FirstCard Plus is the newest.

Only First National offers FirstCard Plus. And it's only one of the extra features you can have with First National checking. Any of our branch managers can give you all the details.

FirstCard Plus
VISA
4410 0012 3456 7891
GOOD THRU
LAST DAY OF 10-80
WALKER SMITH

FIRST NATIONAL BANK
OF LOUISVILLE
Member FDIC

288

When You've Got The Governor In Your Pocket... People Take Notice

The Governor's Account. New from Andrew Jackson.

Now, you can get 5¼% interest for your money, plus the prestige of many special services available exclusively to Governor's Account card holders. A minimum balance of $500. is required.

Call on the Governor When You Need to Transfer Money.

The Governor's Account lets you transfer funds from your savings account to your checking account, or from checking to savings with just a phone call and at no charge. It's an excellent way to keep all of your funds working to earn you a maximum return. (Minimum transaction amount is $100.)

The Governor Guarantees You Emergency Cash Nationwide.

With the Governor's Account you get the peace of mind of guaranteed emergency cash, nationwide, simply by showing your card at any participating savings and loan. It costs you nothing, but it's worth a lot.

The Governor Promises You Special Favors.

When you're a Governor's Account card holder you get American Express travelers checks at no charge and notary services free when you need them. Plus, you get the special attention of our staff on all your financial needs.

The Governor's Statements Tell All.

The Governor's Account provides you with a monthly statement that keeps you informed of all activity on your account, including deposits, withdrawals, transfers and interest paid. It makes keeping track of your money very convenient. The Governor's Account. It's the Prestige™ way to make the most of your money.

Andrew Jackson Savings & Loan Association

2000 Apalachee Parkway/
Tallahassee, FL/(904) 878-6105
Member FSLIC

290

Get a new bank.

The Huntington.

We'll waive the fee on your credit card. Either VISA or Master Charge. Just open a Huntington Personal Checking Account *and* a Huntington Savings Account or Certificate of Deposit and maintain a minimum balance of $500 in your checking *or* $1000 in your savings or CD.

Of course, you must also qualify for VISA or Master Charge credit. But then, you probably already do.

What's more, you'll also qualify for our No Service Charge Checking by maintaining these minimum balances. So the money you'll save on your everyday banking service charges can really add up.

If you already are a Huntington checking, savings or credit card customer, obviously now is the best, most economical time to consolidate all your banking business with us. Because then you won't have to pay a $20 service charge on our VISA or Master Charge cards either. All it takes is one quick visit to tell us which combination of Huntington accounts you want to use to qualify.

So, whether you're a new or existing Huntington customer, all you have to do is open both, and maintain either the checking or savings minimum balance and your VISA or Master Charge is yours for no fee. Should you not maintain your qualifying balance one month – you'll only be charged the $1.65 credit card service charge for that month and your normal checking account service charges.

Stop by the Huntington today. Don't just get mad at your bank for charging you what we'll give you for no charge. Get even.

Huntington Banks

We're never satisfied until you are.

291

WHEN MINUTES COUNT, COUNT ON US!

In a hurry?
It only takes a minute to do your banking with our Valley-24 automatic teller at Valley Bank. It doesn't have to be one of our minutes, though, because our Valley-24 works any time, not just during regular business hours.

You can get cash whenever you need it, make a deposit, transfer funds from one of your accounts to another, even make loan payments—all with the touch of a button.

When minutes count— count on Valley Bank to give you banking when you need it ... with Valley-24!

"The Leader"
Valley Bank

VALLEY FIDELITY BANK & TRUST COMPANY
KNOXVILLE, TN
MEMBER FDIC

292

NOW OPEN

FARRAGUT VALLEY 24 IS READY WHEN YOU ARE!

Valley 24 is now open in Farragut to serve you. Located adjacent to the Kroger parking lot, just across Kingston Pike from the new Farragut High School, our Farragut Valley 24 is one of nine Valley 24 banking centers that are conveniently located throughout Knoxville and Knox County.

This is our second Valley 24 in West Knox County. The other is at our Cedar Bluff office at 9123 Executive Park Boulevard in the Cedar Bluff Shopping Center.

Valley 24 is push-button quick and easy! It only takes minutes for you to make cash with-drawals, deposits, transfer funds, and you can even make loan payments.

At Valley Bank, you can bank when you want to— any time of day or night. Get your Valley 24 Card NOW . . . so when minutes count, you won't have to give it a second thought!

"The Leader"

Valley Bank

Valley Fidelity Bank & Trust Company
Knoxville, TN

293

WE CARRY ON ALL HOURS OF THE DAY AND NIGHT.

Beginning January 2, the bank that offers you more banking services will also give you more hours to bank.

First National Bank in Weatherford.

The new hours for our main lobby will be 9-3, Monday-Thursday, and 9-6 on Friday.

Coupled with our new motor bank, open 7:30-6:30, Monday-

Friday, and our 24-hour teller, BanCash 24, you'll be able to transact business with us anytime you want.

Our better hours are another reason why you should bank at First National. We're going to be your bank in 1980.

1st National Bank in Weatherford 220 Palo Pinto Weatherford, Texas 76086 594-7481 Member FDIC, Member Federal Reserve System.

NOW
Accounts

FACT: A LOT OF PEOPLE IN DENVER ARE JUST GETTING CHECKS WITH THEIR CHECKING ACCOUNTS.

WE MAKE CHECKING ACCOUNTS DO A LOT MORE BY ADDING THE PLUS SYSTEM.®

When you're a Colorado National Bank customer, you can get a Plus System Card with your checking account. The Plus symbol means access to cash 24 hours a day, every day of the year at 71 Plus System Automated Banking Machines at shopping centers and banks all over the Rocky Mountain region.

As part of your checking, you may qualify for a VISA® Banking Card that lets you make purchases without writing checks at over 2.5 million locations around the world. And it gives you check guarantee, as well as 24-hour, 7-day-a-week access to the entire Plus System for instant cash.

You get No-Service-Charge Checking when you maintain just a $200 minimum balance in your checking account, or it's free when you maintain just $1,000 in any of our savings accounts.

We also give you plenty of easy ways to transfer funds between your checking and savings accounts. You can do it anytime with our 24-hour Teller-Phone® service. Or bank-by-mail . . . we pay the postage both ways. You can arrange for our Automatic Transfer Service. And, of course, there are convenient drive-up and express tellers downtown.

893-1862, EXT. 4332 IS THE NUMBER TO CALL.

We'll give you all the details and answer all your questions. We can mail you our simple checking and savings application forms and an authorization form to transfer funds from other financial institutions. Or you can stop by our Family Banking Center, downtown at 17th and Champa, Denver, CO 80202. No other bank in Denver makes so much effort to make your banking so easy.

COLORADO NATIONAL BANK
WE MAKE BIG IDEAS HAPPEN.

Member FDIC

Member Plus System

WAITING TO EARN INTEREST ON CHECKING?

PARK'S CHECKING-WITH-INTEREST PLAN IS HERE AND NOW.

Perhaps you've heard about the N.O.W. (Negotiable Order of Withdrawal) account. Beginning Jan. 1, 1981, N.O.W. accounts will pay interest on checking account funds. But there's really no need to wait. Park's Checking-With-Interest Plan puts your idle dollars to work for you now.

So if you're waiting around for N.O.W.'s to become legal, you're wasting a lot more than time. You're wasting money.

EARN ALL YOU CAN ON ALL YOUR MONEY.

At Park all the benefits of a N.O.W. account are available to you right now through automatic transfer.

Our Checking-With-Interest Plan gives you the check writing conven-ience of a checking account—plus your money earns 5¼% daily interest right up to the day you spend it.

You get one easy to reconcile monthly statement. And your money is in one safe, convenient Park location.

DON'T DELAY...EARN TODAY.

Park's Checking-With-Interest Plan works on a simple principle. The money that would normally remain idle in a regular checking account is put in a separate, interest-earning account. When your checks clear the bank, we transfer just enough money to cover them. That way, your checking account dollars work for you. And, best of all, you don't have to wait.

So why mark time? Make money. Get the extra earning power of Park's Checking-With-Interest Plan today.

Call or visit any of our 12 conven-iently located offices. Park will answer all your questions. Now when it's important to make every dollar count, our Checking-With-Interest Plan makes a lot of sense.

PARK
Park National Bank
Knoxville, Tennessee
MEMBER F.D.I.C.

297

Announcing the

Introducing the <u>Investment Checking Plan.</u>

The perfect way to keep your money earning interest until your check clears the bank.

Investment Checking is a new First National State plan which combines a checking account, a savings account and "Automatic Transfer System." Together they make it possible for you to keep all of your money in your new Savings Account right up to the time a check reaches the bank. Then we *automatically* transfer the exact amount you need to cover the check into your new Checking Account. Which means your money keeps earning interest right up to the last minute.

It's almost as though we were paying interest on your checking account. And, legally, Investment Checking is the closest we can come to doing just that.

One simple statement, one account number.

We've made certain that the Investment Checking Plan will simplify your everyday banking needs. For one thing, you'll have just one account number. And all of your transactions will be shown on one simple monthly statement. You'll be able to see the date each check cleared the bank, the date of all transfers from savings to cover checks written, the dates you made deposits, how much your money earned in interest and what your savings balance is.

Earn 5.20% Effective Annual Yield on 5% Annual Interest.

The money you keep in the savings portion of your Investment Checking Plan will earn an Effective

nd of lazy money.

Annual Yield of 5.20% on 5.00% Annual Interest with interest compounded continuously on collected balances.* And that's the highest rate any commercial bank is allowed to pay on regular savings.

Of course you'll be earning that high rate of interest on money you *used* to keep in your checking account. Which is the beauty of Investment Checking.

No passbook, no unnecessary trips to the bank.

With Investment Checking there's no need for a passbook for your savings. And there's no need to visit the bank to transfer money from savings to checking.

It is necessary to keep a minimum Investment Checking Plan balance of $500 to earn interest in any given month. Investment Checking is for individuals only.

At last! A dollars and sensible way to bank.

Investment Checking lets you keep your money working for you all the time. The costs are not much more than that of a regular First National State checking account. And if you keep a minimum balance of $2,500 or more in your Investment Checking Plan we'll waive charges. There are no charges for transfers, no interest penalties, no minimum transfer amounts. Each day we transfer the amount of those checks which have arrived at the bank. You write checks and pay bills just the way you always have. And earn interest in the bargain.

So put an end to lazy money today by visiting the First National State office nearest you and applying for Investment Checking. It's the dollars and sensible way of getting the most out of your money.

First National State®

- First National State Bank of New Jersey 201-565-3200
- First National State Bank of Central Jersey 609-396-4060
- First National State Bank—County 201-567-5000, 201-391-4000
- First National State Bank—Edison 201-985-0500 Middlesex County; 201-449-5500 Monmouth County; 201-364-1100 Ocean County
- First National State Bank of Northwest Jersey 201-584-6700; 201-347-6637
- First National State Bank of West Jersey 609-386-0091 Burlington and Atlantic Counties; 201-766-1000 Somerset and Morris Counties

Members First National State Bancorporation
550 Broad Street, Newark, New Jersey 07102.
Members FDIC

It pays interest
like a savings account.

Use it like a
checking account.

Interest Checking is American Federal's checking account that pays you interest.

You will earn 5¼% interest on your checking account.

If you maintain a $500 minimum balance, there's no monthly service charge. If your balance falls below $500, you pay a $5 service charge for that month. Either way, you still earn interest on the account.

Sign up today for **Interest Checking** at any American Federal office.

American Federal
Savings & Loan Association

Earn interest on money you used to just pay bills with.

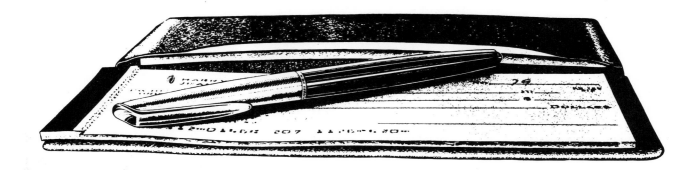

Interest Checking. At American Federal.

Interest Checking lets you earn interest on money that is in your checking account.

With an **Interest Checking** account, you earn 5¼% interest on your checking account.

By maintaining a $500 minimum balance, you will have no service charge on your account. Should your balance fall below $500, you will have a $5 service charge for that month.

Earn interest on your checking acccount-with **Interest Checking** from American Federal.

American Federal
Savings & Loan Association

301

NOW*

PAYING

*INTEREST ON CHECKING

Earn 5¼% Interest on Checking Accounts.

Now you can earn interest on all your money, checking and savings! We'll pay you 5-1/4% interest on every dollar in your checking account—right from the date we collect it until the date you spend it. And the interest is compounded daily and paid monthly. A Hamilton Bank NOW* account is a great way for you to consolidate your savings and checking accounts.

The cost of this service is low, and can even be FREE.

There is no service charge for our NOW* account if you maintain a minimum monthly balance of $1,000. If your balance falls below the minimum, the service charge is $2.00 plus 25¢ per check. If your balance falls below $500, the service charge is $3.00 plus 25¢ per check. There are many ways a NOW* account can save you money and make you money. Come see us—let us tell you more about NOW*!

"Helping You Build A Better Life"

(*Negotiable Order of Withdrawal*)

Hamilton Bank

Morristown, Tennessee

CITIZENS BANK HAS THE ANSWER TO YOUR CHECKING NEEDS FROM NOW* ON.

Regular Checking—FREE at Citizens Bank. Keep check on all your spending with a checking account at the Citizens Bank. You get the freedom from worry about carrying cash when you shop; makes it easy to pay your bills by mail; and your cancelled checks are a legal receipt of payment. Your monthly statement from us lets you know where your money's going. PLUS you get personalized checks in your choice of styles and colors! Check into Citizens Bank—get the best checking services to be found—FREE!

NOW*. Citizens Bank's 5¼% Interest-Checking Account. Earn 5-1/4% on every dollar in your Citizens Bank NOW* Checking Account—right from the date we collect it 'til the date you spend it. And, you will get your cancelled checks back with your regular monthly statement.

NOW* accounts are FREE if you maintain a monthly balance of $1,000. If your balance falls below the minimum, there is a service charge of $3.00 plus 20¢ per check. A Citizens Bank NOW* account can save you money and make you money.

(*Negotiable Order of Withdrawal)

"We'll take good care of you!"

CITIZENS BANK

NEW TAZEWELL/TAZEWELL/HARROGATE

Member FDIC

Interest on your checking and a free calculator. With NOW accounts at 18 St. Paul Federal locations.

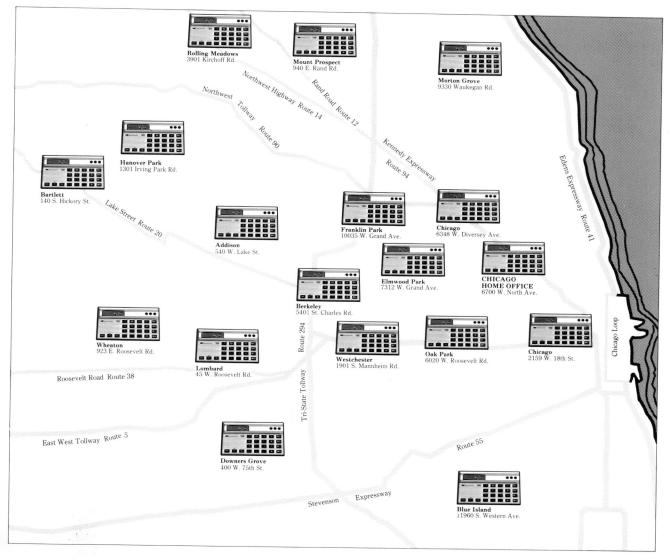

There are a lot more reasons than ever before to do your banking at St. Paul Federal. Because now, we not only give you the highest interest allowed by law on both your savings and your checking, but for a limited time we'll also give you a free N.S.C. super-thin calculator just for opening a NOW account with us.

All you have to do to get 5¼% interest on your checking and a free credit-card-size calculator is to visit any one of the 18 conveniently located St. Paul Federal offices around town.

When you open your NOW account with $500 or more the calculator is yours. It's that simple. And the account is free as long as you maintain that balance. If you wish to keep less than a $500 balance, the monthly charge is small—only $3 if you write 12 checks or less a month or $5 if you write more than 12 checks. Even if your

monthly balance is less than $500 you still collect interest compounded daily.

If you already have or if you open a regular savings account with St. Paul and keep a balance of at least $2,500, your checking account is free. And if you're a senior citizen and sign up for direct deposit of your social security check, there is never a service charge on your NOW account.

So just follow the map at the top of this page. You'll not only find a free calculator, you'll also discover where you can earn interest on money that never could earn interest before.

St. Paul Federal
We give you more for your money than money.
Member Federal Savings and Loan Insurance Corporation

305

306

Leonardo da Vinci couldn't get a checking account that paid interest. You can starting Jan. 2nd at St. Paul Federal

Savings and Loan Association

Ask for more information about the new NOW account at any of our 18 St. Paul offices. Or call 622-5000.

EQUAL HOUSING LENDER

Member Federal Savings and Loan Insurance Corporation

We give you more for your money than money.

308

INTEREST + CHECKING
FIRST ACCOUNT
WHAT A PEACH

How sweet it is when you find the right checking/savings plan that gives you interest plus checking. And First National's new First Account fills the bill.

THE PEACHES

Open your First Account with a $1,000 minimum deposit, maintain a $1,000 minimum balance, and you get free checking and 5¼% interest* on all your money. If your balance falls below $1,000, you are charged a $7.50 service charge, but you still get 5¼% interest on all your money.

THE CREAM

Keep $2,000 in a daily savings account at First National and there is no charge on your First Account, regardless of your balance.
Open your First Account at any First National location today.

When you think of money, think First.

FIRST NATIONAL BANK IN LITTLE ROCK

*Annual rate of simple interest.

Member FDIC

NOW, EXPLAINED.

A NOW account is the answer to earning interest on checking.

The question is, is a NOW account right for you?

Could be the answer to that is in the questions and answers here. So look them over. Then, if you have more questions, give us a call or come see us.

Not only will we be glad to tell you everything you need to know about NOW accounts.

We'll be glad to help you open one.

Piedmont Bank's NOW Checking With Interest

Q. What is a NOW account?

A. A NOW account is simply a checking account that earns interest.

Q. Why have banks not offered NOW accounts before?

A. Because federal regulation has previously prohibited the payment of interest on checking accounts.

Q. What is the interest rate for Piedmont's *NOW Checking With Interest*?

A. 5¼% with interest compounded daily for an annual effective yield of 5.39%.

Q. What is the difference between Piedmont's *NOW Checking With Interest* and a regular checking account?

A. A NOW account earns interest. A Piedmont regular

checking account does not.

Q. Are there any costs for Piedmont's *NOW Checking With Interest*?

A. There is no charge for *NOW Checking With Interest* if: a $500 minimum balance is maintained in the NOW account or $1,000 in a Piedmont regular savings account. If neither requirement is met, a $4.00 monthly fee and 20¢ per check are charged.

Q. Is a Piedmont NOW account right for me?

A. Because of the minimum balance required, a Piedmont NOW account isn't for everyone. To see if it's the best plan for you, look at the chart above. Compare

Daily Balance	Monthly Interest Earned*	Monthly Service Charge
$1,000	$4.43	$ 0
750	3.32	0
500	2.22	0
400	1.77	4.00**
300	1.33	4.00**
*Estimated interest calculation based on a 30 day month.		
**Plus $.20 per check.		

for yourself.

Q. Will all Piedmont checking account customers automatically begin receiving interest on checking on December 31, 1980?

A. No. Only those Piedmont customers who come in and sign up for a NOW account will receive interest.

Q. If I sign up for Piedmont's *NOW Checking With Interest*, will I have to open a new checking account?

A. No. Your existing Piedmont checking account converts to a NOW account. You continue to use your same account number and checks.

Member FDIC

Write checks now... earn interest January 1st. It's time for Freedom*NOW*!

FreedomNOW is a brand new Freedom Savings account which gives you all the convenience of a checking account (plus 5¼% interest on your money beginning January 1, 1981).

FreedomNOW brings you other services, too, including 24-hour Freedom Machines and Prestige® emergency cash. And if you open your account now, we'll give you a set of starter checks. Free.

It's time you got more for your money. It's time for FreedomNOW.

THE TODAY™ ACCOUNT

CHECKING CONVENIENCE PLUS INTEREST

Now it's yours on a free silver platter.

Majestic takes pride in bringing you the TODAY account, a new service that offers you the convenience of checking PLUS you earn daily interest.

Open a Majestic TODAY account, select your personalized drafts and write as many as you need to pay bills, to shop, to get cash. Your funds will be transferred from your TODAY interest-bearing savings account to cover the exact amount of your drafts.

5¼% Interest Compounded Daily.

Chances are, your present checking account isn't earning you a penny. With your TODAY account, your money earns 5¼% compound interest until it's transferred to cover your drafts.

No Service Charge.

The TODAY account is yours without monthly charges when you (1) maintain a balance of $300 or more; or (2) maintain a minimum deposit of $1,000 in any other Majestic account; or (3) are 60+ years old; or (4) take advantage of Majestic's direct deposit services.

Free Silver Platter.

With an opening deposit of $300 or more, Majestic will give you a free silver platter! Or you can choose from 60 other name-brand gifts.

Convenient Statewide Branches.

Open a TODAY account and you open the doors of convenience to the largest network of branches in Colorado.

Now earn interest on all your money!

Majestic Savings C
WE TAKE PRIDE

Akron • Arvada • Aurora (Mall, Buckingham Square, Chambers Plaza) • Boulder (Mall, Crossroads) • Brighton • Brush • Canon City •
Colorado Springs (Downtown, Broadmarket) • Denver (Cherry Creek, Downtown, East 8th, University Hills, So. Sheridan, Lincoln St.) • Englewood •
Florence • Ft. Collins • Ft. Morgan • Glenwood Springs • Greeley • Holyoke • Julesburg • Lakewood (Villa Italia, Westland) • Littleton • Longmont •
Pueblo • Sterling • Thornton • Wheat Ridge (Applewood, Lakeside) • Wray • Yuma

MEMBER
FSLIC
Federal Savings & Loan Insurance Corp.
Your Savings Insured to $100,000

314

315

IT'S BACK. IT'S BETTER. CHECKING CONVENIENCE PLUS 5½% INTEREST.

Majestic authorized to re-offer TODAY™ with new, higher interest!

Now you can earn 5½% interest on funds that would normally be earning you nothing.

That's a full ¼% higher than has ever been offered before on similar accounts. And it's compounded daily.

No Service Charge.

Under many circumstances, the TODAY account can be yours without a monthly service charge. Ask about our no-service-charge provisions when you open your TODAY account.

Get TransAction, Too.

With every new TODAY account comes the optional convenience of TransAction—the card that lets you deposit or withdraw from your Majestic account any time of day, any day of the year, in 33 convenient locations.

All on a free silver platter.

If you open your account with $500 or more, we'll hand you your TODAY account on a free silver platter. Or you can choose from 60 other name-brand gifts.

Come in today.

Majestic Savings
WE TAKE PRIDE

Would
a checking account
that pays
interest you?

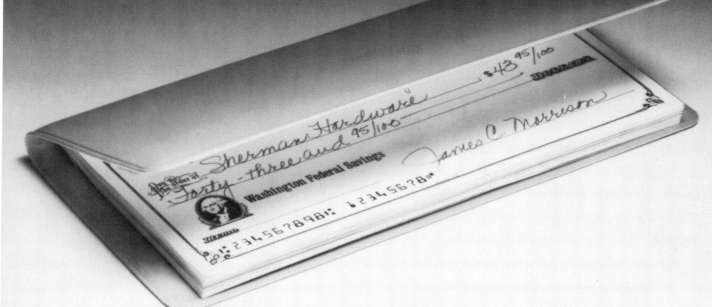

"Checking with Interest"
is coming on December 31, 1980.

Washington Federal Savings' new "Checking With Interest" does something most bank checking accounts do not. It pays.

Because "Checking With Interest" lets you earn the highest interest allowed by law on money that normally sits idle in your checking account. And it's compounded daily.

Simply by keeping a low minimum monthly balance, "Checking With Interest" is available free of charge.

Other than that, it functions just like a regular checking account. The FSLIC insures each account up to $100,000.

Ask one of our Customer Service Representatives (C.S.R.'s) soon for details about "Checking With Interest".

We honestly believe you'll notice the difference at . . .

Washington Federal Savings

August 10, 1980

Mr. Henry Czerwinski
FEDERAL RESERVE BANK
925 Grant Street
Kansas City, Missouri 64198

Dear Mr. Czerwinski:

I wish to register my protest on your arbitrary action in the
refusal of the Federal Reserve Bank to accept drafts presented
for payment by the Majestic Savings and Loan Association of Denver.

I have carried a "Today" account at Majestic since its inception
and have had no difficulty with their handling of my account.

I have carried "checking accounts" at commercial banks for 55
years and in all that time the commercial banks have used my
money for loans, etc., receiving high interest, and I have
received nothing from them for the use of my money. Majestic
has offered 5¼% on a "checking account", which I took advantage
of. It is something that should have been done years ago.

I am 75 years old and to me every dollar counts. If I can get
a few extra dollars on my checking account it is my prerogative
to do so. I believe that it is an infringement on my rights
for a few men to say what I can do with my money.

The commercial banks are apprehensive about the competition,
they are threatened by the loss of millions of dollars in revenue
that they receive from their "checking accounts". It is my hope
that you will see fit to convince the board to rescind their
recent decision and allow the Savings and Loan Associations to
continue their checking accounts.

It is no wonder that there are so many rebellions and protest
demonstrations in the world today. Are we a free enterprise
country or a dictatorship?

                              Sincerely,

                              Leslie M. Mugford
                              Englewood, Colorado

cc: Majestic Savings & Loan

N.O.W. AND IMPROVED.

TULSA'S MOST CONVENIENT CHECKING ACCOUNTS ARE ABOUT TO GET 5¼% BETTER.

Something new has been added to Fourth National Bank's full-service checking accounts. Beginning December 31, Fourth National N.O.W. Accounts will pay the highest rate of interest permitted by law on checking account balances.

The Fourth National N.O.W. Account, we call it *Interest on Checking*, is easy to open or convert from an existing Fourth National account. And it can be accessed through any of the seven convenient Teller Anytime locations across Tulsa.

Fourth has been successfully managing checking accounts for more than fifty years. That's over half a century of good, solid experience.

N.O.W. *Interest on Checking* at Fourth National. Once again, our experience is about to come in very handy.

For more information about *Interest on Checking* call a new accounts representative at 587-9171.

THE FOURTH NATIONAL BANK
OF TULSA
BOULDER AT SIXTH
TULSA, OKLAHOMA 74101
(918) 587-9171

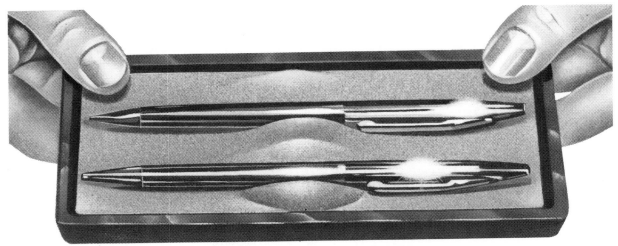

Get Columbia's Checking with Interest and write off your bank.

When you open a Columbia Checking with Interest account with $100 or more, you'll receive a beautiful chrome pen and pencil set, free.*

And when you look into Columbia's new full-service Banking Packages — and 42 convenient branches — you may decide not to bank at a bank anymore.

Our four new Banking Packages are designed to go way beyond Checking with Interest. You can qualify for a line of credit, credit cards, check guarantee and overdraft protection. Opt for safe check storage, direct deposit services and free checking plans. And count on Columbia's William Teller network, 24 hours a day.

Come to Columbia, and see for yourself. When you look into banking, you'll end up at Columbia.

* Pen and pencil set offer good through 3/31/81.

 **Columbia Savings**
We're with you. In more
places, more ways than anyone.

320

Only First National offers you maximum interest... maximum convenience.

First National is now offering Interest on Checking. And that means your checking dollars can be earning 5-1/4% interest compounded daily— the maximum annual rate any financial institution can pay. And depending on the monthly balance you maintain, your checking can be virtually free, too.

You'll not only be earning the maximum rate, but with these First National checking options, you'll have maximum convenience, too.

FirstCard Plus— The VISA checking card.

It has the instant acceptance of a credit card, and yet the money for your purchase comes out of your checking account.

30 Teller/24 machines.

No bank gives you as many places to bank around the town and around the clock.

Bank from home with Pay-by-Phone.

One call with Pay-by-Phone and you can transfer funds or pay bills, all right from the comfort of your home or office.

The time savings of direct deposit.

In many cases, we can arrange with your employer to have your paycheck automatically deposited to your First National account.

Customer service.

At First National, you have a Customer Service hotline. Just call 581-7525 and we'll answer questions and take care of any problems.

First National gives you more.

Only First National checking offers you maximum rate and maximum convenience. It's a combination no one else can match. That's why you should be checking with us.

It's easy to do because with 50 neighborhood branches there's always a First National Bank close by. Just stop in and ask for Interest on Checking.

50¢ a week was enough allowance for you. It ought to be enough for him.

Of course 25 years ago a pack of baseball bubblegum cards cost a nickel and a quarter got you into a double feature with three cartoons and a serial to boot. Nowadays, a piece of penny candy costs a nickel.

Inflation has changed the value of that 50¢ dramatically. And, that's something you and your family have to face every day.

At Colonial Bank, we have some ways to help you fight inflation. Here are just a few:

1) Colonial NOW Account. With a Colonial NOW Account your money earns 5% interest until a check is drawn against it. So you get the convenience of checking and the interest of savings. And, if you keep a minimum balance of $500, you pay no service charges.

2) Colonial Checkmate. If you keep a minimum balance of $300 in your Checkmate checking account or in a Statement Savings Account earning 5% interest or in a 90 Day Investment Savings Account* earning 5½% interest, you pay no service charges.

3) Colonial Savings Accounts. All savings accounts earn interest which is compounded continuously for maximum yield. In addition, our Regular Statement Savings Account pays interest monthly.

Colonial's no-service-charge checking and high interest earnings on savings won't stop inflation. But, they can help you save money and increase the spending power of the whole family. Why not stop by the Colonial office nearest you today and open the accounts that make the most dollars and sense for you.

*Federal regulations permit you to withdraw your deposit before maturity; however, regulations also require that an interest penalty be incurred.

Colonial Bank

We'll help you fight inflation. NOW.

Member FDIC

322

Wilbur's legacy.

When Wilbur Smedley invented the checking account, little did the eager young teller's assistant realize the far-reaching implications of his brilliant creation.

Today, though Smedley is forgotten, his legacy lives on at Citizens Central. Because here at Citizens Central Bank, we've designed the ultimate tribute to Smedley and an extremely sensible service to our customers who can keep at least $500 in their accounts: Interest On Checking.

With Interest On Checking, Citizens Central introduces the convenience of a checking ac-count that actually pays you interest. Every Citizens Central Interest On Checking account pays five percent interest on its average monthly balance. That's the highest interest rate on checking accounts allowed by law.

If your balance should fall below the $500 minimum, you pay only a modest service charge of $4.00 for that month. For the full Interest On Checking story, call or stop by any office of Citizens Central, the country bank with big city services. And tell them Wilbur sent you.

Checking with 5% interest at Citizens Central.

Irving Bank
Corporation

Citizens Central

Member F.D.I.C.

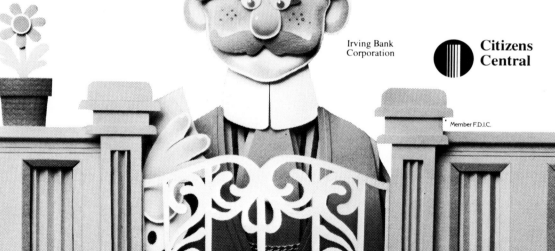

Announcing the end of lazy money.

Introducing the Investment Checking Plan.™ The perfect way to keep your money earning interest until your check clears the bank.

Investment Checking is a new First National State plan which combines a checking account, a savings account and "Automatic Transfer System." Together they make it possible for you to keep all of your money in your new Savings Account right up to the time a check reaches the bank. Then we *automatically* transfer the exact amount you need to cover the check into your new Checking Account. Which means your money keeps earning interest right up to the last minute.

It's almost as though we were paying interest on your checking account. And, legally, Investment Checking is the closest we can come to doing just that.

One simple statement, one account number.

We've made certain that the Investment Checking Plan will simplify your everyday banking needs. For one thing, you'll have just one account number. And all of your transactions will be shown on one simple monthly statement. You'll be able to see the date each check cleared the bank, the date of all transfers from savings to cover checks written, the dates you made deposits, how much your money earned in interest and what your savings balance is.

Earn 5.20% Effective Annual Yield on 5% Annual Interest.

The money you keep in the savings portion of your Investment Checking Plan will earn an Effective Annual Yield of 5.20% on 5.00% Annual Interest with interest compounded continuously on collected balances.* And that's the highest rate any commercial bank is allowed to pay on regular savings.

Of course you'll be earning that high rate of interest on money you *used* to keep in your checking account. Which is the beauty of Investment Checking.

No passbook, no unnecessary trips to the bank.

With Investment Checking there's no need for a passbook for your savings. And there's no need to visit the bank to transfer money from savings to checking.

At last! A dollars and sensible way to bank.

Investment Checking lets you keep your money working for you all the time. The costs are not much more than that of a regular First National State checking account. And if you keep a minimum balance of $2,500 or more in your Investment Checking Plan we'll waive charges. There are no charges for transfers, no interest penalties, no minimum transfer amounts. Each day we transfer the amount of those checks which have arrived at the bank. You write checks and pay bills just the way you always have. And earn interest in the bargain.

So put an end to lazy money today by visiting the First National State office nearest you and applying for Investment Checking. It's the dollars and sensible way of getting the most out of your money.

First National State®

*It is necessary to keep a minimum Investment Checking Plan balance of $500 to earn interest in any given month. *Investment Checking is for individuals only.*

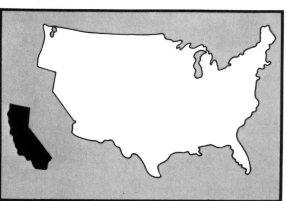

It's
not exactly a checking account and not exactly a savings account.

But it does pay bills. And it does pay interest on everyday money until you need it.

The time has come to earn interest on the everyday money you use to pay bills. Regular checking accounts don't pay interest. The Moneystore pays you the maximum interest permitted by law until the day you need to pay bills.

And the Moneystore pays your bills direct—after you authorize payment by telephone. No more checks to write, no envelopes to address, no stamps to buy. Just call the Moneystore, tell us who to pay and how much and we'll pay your bills.

Moneystore is new. It's completely safe, it's confidential, it saves time and it earns interest on everyday funds until you need them.

For information about Moneystore,
call or visit:

BRAZOS
Savings

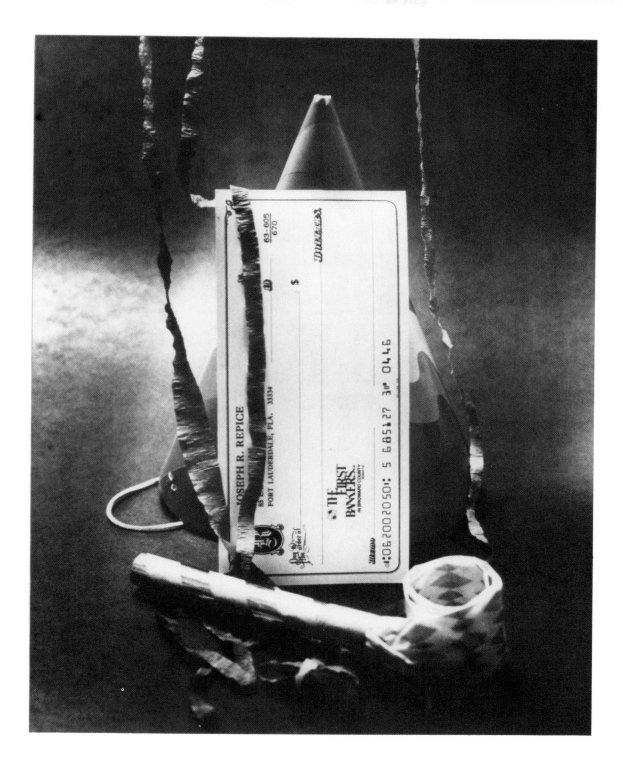

HAPPY NOW YEAR!

There's a lot of talk about these new checking accounts. They can make a big difference in how you handle your money.

At First Bankers we have tried to make it all as easy as possible for you. Our new Interest On

Checking accounts are designed to be simple and effective.

To further help, we have produced a special, easy-to-read booklet which will help you understand all about these new accounts. We invite you to stop in at any First Bankers Banking Center and pick up a copy.

At First Bankers, we want to work with you.

THE FIRST BANKERS

MEMBERS FDIC

FOR YOUR DIRECT DEPOSIT WE'LL GIVE YOU FREE CHECKING PLUS 5¼% INTEREST.

Save time, save money and earn 5¼% interest when you Direct Deposit your government check at Naples Federal.

With Direct Deposit, you won't have to worry about your check being stolen or lost in the mail. Or the valuable time you used to spend driving to the bank and standing in line. With Direct Deposit at Naples Federal your check is automatically credited right to your account. And it's working for you, gathering interest immediately instead of waiting for you to deposit it. With Direct Deposit, your worries are over.

Along with the convenience of Direct Deposit, you get a free Advantage Checking℠ account and no minimum balance requirement. It could save you

an average of $60.00 in yearly service charges, depending on where your checking account is now. At Naples Federal, you can save on service charges and add up all the other advantages you get with Advantage Checking.

The "extra's" include free Barclays/VISA travelers checks. Free American Express money orders. Itemized monthly statements and carbonless check copies for easy balancing. Free check safe-keeping and microfilming service. Telephone bill paying. And a free Prestige Card with out-of-town emergency cash privileges.

And, at Naples Federal, one of the biggest advantages of Direct Deposit is the 5¼% interest that is compounded daily and credited monthly to your account. You earn interest on all of your deposits, while Direct Deposit gives you Advantage Checking absolutely free! And, all the time you save getting your check to us is yours to enjoy.

At Naples Federal, we're making it easy for you to get more for your money. Just come in and ask for Direct Deposit, plus free Advantage Checking. We'll help you fill out the necessary forms and answer all your questions for you.

Just bring in your next check to get your free Direct Deposit Advantage Checking account. At Naples Federal. Where you save time, earn interest on checking, and save costly checking account service charges. Come in and sign up for your free Direct Deposit Advantage Checking account today. Only at Naples Federal.

FSLIC
Insured to $100,000

Naples Federal

Naples Federal Savings and Loan Association, a New York Stock Exchange Company, with offices throughout Southwest Florida.

Free Checking!
Interest on Checking!

Introducing 5 new Checking Plans(one is just right for you)!

At Platte Valley Federal we recognize that everyone's checking account needs are different. So, to better serve the people of the Nebraska Panhandle, we're offering you a choice of five distinct checking plans.

You can select the one that's just right for you. If you want free checking, you can have it. If you want to earn interest on your checking funds, you can do it. Whether you write a lot of checks a month, or just a few, you'll find a plan that's perfect for your needs.

PVF Free Checking Plan: No service charges, no minimum balance.

Write as many checks as you want without any monthly service charge or minimum balance requirements. Think back on the service charges you pay for your present checking account and then think about the money you'll save with this plan.

PVF Basic Checking Plan: Earn interest; pay flat fee of $2 a mo.

This checking plan pays you 5¼% continuous compound interest on all the funds in your account, regardless of your balance. In addition, you can write as many checks as you want for a flat fee of $2. Remember, too, that the fee will probably be offset by the interest you earn.

PVF Economy Checking Plan: If you write less than 20 checks a month.

Simply stated, you pay 10¢ for every check we process. So if you write less than 20 checks a month, this plan costs you less than $2. Then consider that you earn 5¼% continuous compound interest on your funds, so the cost could be a lot less than $2. No minimum balance required.

PVF Unlimited Checking Plan: Write as many checks as you want.

Some people write a large number of checks each month, and this has cost them plenty in service charges over the years.

Now they can write unlimited checks, earn 5¼% interest, and eliminate monthly service charges just by maintaining a minimum balance of $300 in the account. Even when they don't, the monthly charge is only $3.

PVF VIP Checking Plan: Free for seniors, direct deposits, IRA/Keogh.

Good news for those 62 years old or older—you can write as many checks as you want without paying any service charge and earn 5¼% interest! The same holds true for others who arrange for the direct deposit of social security, other regular government payments, retirement or payroll checks. It also applies if you have an IRA or Keogh account with us. All VIP accountholders must be qualified for the PVF "Money Line" (See below).

Everyone can apply for "Money Line" personal line of credit.

Regardless of the checking plan you choose, you can make application for our valuable "Money Line"—a service that provides you with a substantial line of credit and overdraft protection. "Money Line" lets you write yourself a loan for the things you need. "Money Line" covers you when you make a mistake in arithmetic and inadvertently write a check without sufficient funds in your account. It saves you the embarrassment of having your check returned and saves you the related service charge.

Checks returned with convenient monthly statement.

With all of PVF's checking plans your cancelled checks are returned for convenient record keeping. Plus each month you receive a monthly statement that's simple and easy to balance.

PVF Checking has other benefits too!

Every PVF checking accountholder is welcome to the following services at any of our branches.
• Free traveler's checks
• Free money orders
• Free notary service
• Free automatic transfer between accounts at PVF
• Free bank by mail
• Free direct deposits of social security, payroll, retirement and regular government payments
• Drive-up window service

Every account is insured to $100,000.

All checking and savings accounts at Platte Valley Federal are insured to $100,000 by the Federal Savings and Loan Insurance Corporation. For more information on how to insure larger amounts, contact your PVF branch.

Open your account now and discover a better way to do your banking.

After you've selected the checking plan that's just right for you, visit your nearby PVF branch. We're looking forward to serving you and we'll do everything we can to make your financial life easier. If you have questions, just ask. In person, or on the phone, we'll treat your personal inquiries with the strictest confidence.

COMPARE! SELECT THE PLAN THAT'S RIGHT FOR YOU.

NEW CHECKING PLANS	MONTHLY SERVICE FEE	INTEREST EARNED
1. PVF FREE CHECKING	Free No minimum balance	None*
2. PVF BASIC CHECKING	Flat fee of $2 a mo. No minimum balance	5¼% No minimum balance
3. PVF ECONOMY CHECKING	10¢ a check No minimum balance	5¼% No minimum balance
4. PVF UNLIMITED CHECKING	Free when balance is $300 or more; $3 a mo. when balance is less	5¼% No minimum balance
5. PVF VIP CHECKING	Free for seniors (62+), Direct Depositors, IRA & Keogh Accountholders who qualify for "Money Line."	5¼% No minimum balance

*Bonus interest of 5¼% paid if your balance stays above $1500 for the month.

PLATTE VALLEY FEDERAL

Gering: 1740 10th Street. 436-3111.   Scottsbluff: 119 East 16th. 632-3200.   Chadron: 316 Main. 432-2858.
Hours: Lobby— Mon-Thurs, 9 to 4; Fri., 9 to 6 (Chadron 9 to 5) Drive-up— Mon-Thurs, 8 to 5; Fri., 8 to 6 (Chadron 8 to 5)

Act before Jan. 31! We'll buy back your old checks and give you new ones.

Our new checking accounts go into effect on December 31, 1980. However, when you open your account early we'll help you three ways. We'll pay you 5½% interest from your date of deposit to December 31. We'll give you 50 personalized checks free. And we'll even buy back the unused checks from your old account ($2 minimum, $5 maximum). Don't wait any longer for the checking account that's just right for you.

329

Checking

Can Your Business Afford Its Checking Account?

Can It Afford Not To Have Ours?

In these days of double-digit inflation, it's important for business owners, professionals, and not-for-profit organizations to get the most out of every dollar. Our Vermont Heritage Business Account can help.

Compare our monthly service charges (or lack of them) with what other banks offer:

0–50 Transactions	No Service Charge
51–100 Transactions	$1.00 Service Charge
101–200 Transactions	$2.00 Service Charge
More than 200 Transactions	$3.00 Service Charge

Not-for-profit and governmental agencies pay no service charges.

Your firm or organization can also earn 5½% interest, compounded continuously and credited monthly, on dollars in the savings side of the account not required for immediate checking needs.

You can maximize your interest earnings by using 24-hour Bank-by-Phone service and automatic teller machines to make transfers from the savings to checking side of the account or vice versa. You also have the flexibility of 16 convenient locations, and night depositories at many of these locations.

Finally, there is the advantage of having your account with one of northern New England's largest and most respected financial institutions, one capable of providing most anything you would ever want from a bank.

Check the cost of your checking account today and see why it might be advantageous to have ours.

Burlington Savings Bank

MEMBER FDIC

Sixteen Convenient Locations
Brattleboro Office
132 Main Street 257-7747

BURLINGTON: Main Office, 148 College St.; 52 Church St., 1123 North Ave., Corner College/Pine Streets. OTHER OFFICES: Brattleboro, Essex Center, Essex Junction, Middlebury, Milton, St. Albans, South Burlington, Winooski. All have automatic teller machines. FREE-STANDING AUTOMATIC TELLER MACHINES: Brattleboro-Fairfield Shopping Plaza, Colchester-Colchester Square Shopping Center, Shelburne-Shelburne Shopping Park. **Call toll free from anywhere in Vermont 1-800-642-5154.**

GEORGE'S LAW:

You've had a fair amount
of money in the bank for years,
but every month you still get
billed for checking account charges.

Don't get upset. Come to The Met…and
be a Met Bank Smart Saver.™ It's the only
checking account around that gives you
credit for the money you have in your
checking account and/or StateMET Savings Account…credit that can reduce or
even *eliminate* checking account service
charges. And the credits you earn for
your savings alone more than offset the
slightly higher interest rates offered by
other types of financial institutions.
Smart Saver. The Smart new way to bank.
Only from The Met.

THE MET

The Metropolitan Bank of Lima, Ohio, Member F.D.I.C.

"Now it's a lot easier to live without checking service charges than to live with them."

Many banks have established minimum checking account balance figures for you to qualify for no-service-charge checking. But some are pretty steep, and it's sometimes easier just to pay the charges. But at The Met a $300 minimum balance gets rid of checking service charges for you. Only $300. It makes your banking a lot easier. And it's from…

THE MET *of course*

The Metropolitan Bank of Lima, Ohio Member F.D.I.C. Deposits insured to $100,000

HERE'S A SAVINGS-TO-CHECKING TRANSFER PLAN THAT YOU DON'T HAVE TO BE J.P. MORGAN TO UNDERSTAND.

You've probably noticed that many banks have been advertising account transfer plans with paragraph after paragraph of financial-ese.

We can't blame you if you don't want to read all that, or if you're a little confused about just what's being offered.

So we'd like to explain the Bank of Highwood's plan in three simple sentences:

1. You can have 100% *free* checking as long as you keep at least a thousand dollars in your savings account.

2. You simply make all deposits to your savings account and we'll transfer money to your checking account as needed.

3. Good news—money that would have been sitting in your checkbook now earns 5% interest while it's in the bank.

If your balance should drop below a thousand dollars there will be a $5 service charge.

That's it. At the Bank of Highwood we like to keep things understandable. And we like to keep your money working for you every way possible.

Don't you?

Why not come in now, or call us at 433-3000 and we'll help you set things up.

THE BANK OF HIGHWOOD

Neighborhood bank for the whole North Shore

Member FDIC

335

How does your checking account stack up?

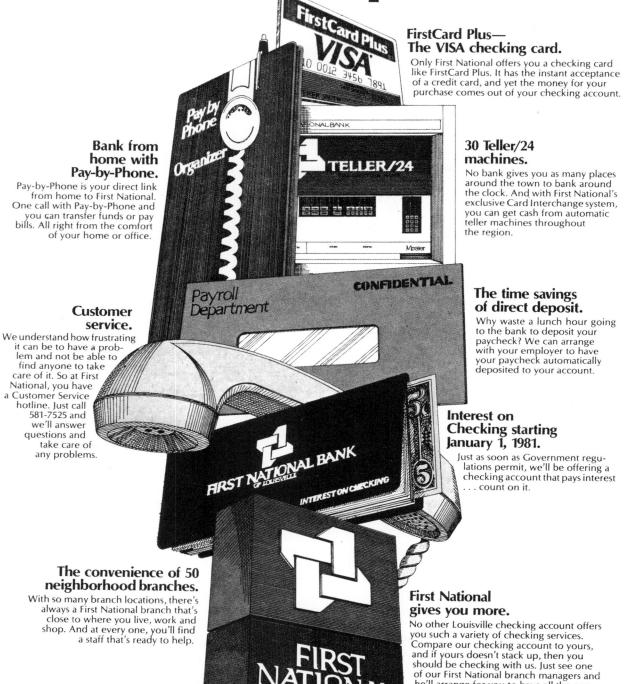

FirstCard Plus—The VISA checking card.
Only First National offers you a checking card like FirstCard Plus. It has the instant acceptance of a credit card, and yet the money for your purchase comes out of your checking account.

Bank from home with Pay-by-Phone.
Pay-by-Phone is your direct link from home to First National. One call with Pay-by-Phone and you can transfer funds or pay bills. All right from the comfort of your home or office.

30 Teller/24 machines.
No bank gives you as many places around the town to bank around the clock. And with First National's exclusive Card Interchange system, you can get cash from automatic teller machines throughout the region.

Customer service.
We understand how frustrating it can be to have a problem and not be able to find anyone to take care of it. So at First National, you have a Customer Service hotline. Just call 581-7525 and we'll answer questions and take care of any problems.

The time savings of direct deposit.
Why waste a lunch hour going to the bank to deposit your paycheck? We can arrange with your employer to have your paycheck automatically deposited to your account.

Interest on Checking starting January 1, 1981.
Just as soon as Government regulations permit, we'll be offering a checking account that pays interest . . . count on it.

The convenience of 50 neighborhood branches.
With so many branch locations, there's always a First National branch that's close to where you live, work and shop. And at every one, you'll find a staff that's ready to help.

First National gives you more.
No other Louisville checking account offers you such a variety of checking services. Compare our checking account to yours, and if yours doesn't stack up, then you should be checking with us. Just see one of our First National branch managers and he'll arrange for you to have all the convenience of Louisville's most popular checking account.

FACT: MANY PEOPLE IN DENVER ARE PAYING TOO MUCH FOR NO-SERVICE-CHARGE CHECKING.

WE MAKE IT MORE ECONOMICAL WITH A $200 MINIMUM BALANCE.

Compare the banks in and around Denver. You'll find checking charges of $3, $4 and $5 a month. At Colorado National Bank, service charges on your checking account are a simple $2 a month if your minimum balance falls below $200. If you maintain a monthly minimum balance of $200 or more at Colorado National Bank, there are no service charges on your account, no matter how many checks you write. Many other banks require $400 and $500 minimums for No-Service-Charge Checking.

And if you want to turn your checking account into real savings, that's where consolidating your banking with us really pays off. $1,000 in any Savings Account, Bonus Savings, Certificate of Deposit or Individual Retirement Account (IRA) will get you free checking, plus a free safe-deposit box for one year (a $12 value). Some other banks require that you maintain $2,000 or $2,500 in savings for free checking.

WE MAKE IT MORE CONVENIENT WITH 5 WAYS TO MANAGE YOUR MONEY.

We also give you plenty of easy ways to transfer funds between your checking and savings accounts. You can do it anytime with our 24-hour Teller-Phone® service. Or bank-by-mail . . . we pay the postage both ways. You can arrange for our Automatic Transfer Service. And, of course, there are convenient drive-up and express tellers downtown.

You'll also get our Plus System® Card that gives you access to the Plus System , providing you 24-hour cash availability from 71 Plus System Automated Banking Machines all over the Rocky Mountain region.

893-1862, EXT. 4332 IS THE NUMBER TO CALL.

We'll give you all the details and answer all your questions. We can mail you our simple checking and savings application forms and an authorization form to transfer funds from other financial institutions. Or you can stop by our Family Banking Center, downtown at 17th and Champa, Denver, CO 80202. No other bank in Denver makes so much effort to make your banking so easy.

COLORADO NATIONAL BANK
WE MAKE BIG IDEAS HAPPEN.

Member FDIC

Member Plus System

337

This simple device gives you a receipt for every bill you pay.

Open a C&S checking account.

C & S Bank

The Commercial & Savings Bank

25 Court Street   Silver Bridge Plaza   Spring Valley   Member FDIC

The Business Barometer

When you place your business account with Bank of Delaware, you get a lot more than a business checking account.

What you really get is a business barometer.

Economic information is made available to you, so your business decisions will be made on better, more up-to-date financial data.

Every three months, for instance, you'll receive a copy of our exclusive "Business Perspectives" newsletter. It contains informative articles on such topics as management techniques, financial reporting procedures, tax deductions, investment strategies and a wealth of other vital information.

Find out all about our business services. Return the coupon, or call 429-1125. Do it today!

BANK OF DELAWARE

MEMBER FDIC

Here's one time when putting all your eggs in one basket makes sense

Who says you should never put all your eggs in one basket? We've put ten of our most popular banking services in one basket and you're going to love it! It's called the Big Plus Account and all ten services are provided to customers who meet normal credit requirements and keep $500 or more in a savings account. You'll find the Big Plus Account is a more convenient, money-saving way to bank. Come to any Bank of Delaware office, or return the coupon for an informative brochure. We'll be glad to answer all your questions and help you open a Big Plus Account of your own.

340

The Thorp Thrift Bird's favorite "Branches" are mailboxes.

8.33% Open an account by mail and earn up to 8.33%. We're as close as your nearest mailbox. You can even open an account by mail. Your transactions are confirmed by mail with postage paid both ways. When you Thrift by mail, you earn higher interest than saving at banks or savings and loans. And it's just as easy!

Interest Rate	Description	Minimum Amount	Effective Annual Rate
6%	Passbook Thrift Accounts	None	6.18%
6½%	One Year Thrift Certificates	$ 500.00	6.66%
7½%	Three Year Thrift Certificates	$1,000.00	8.33%*

*Effective annual yield when held to maturity and compounded quarterly.

Write or call your nearest Thorp office listed below for a "Thrift by Mail" Kit and Prospectus today. Thorp Credit & Thrift Company is the right slot for you. Let the postman bring your deposits to Thorp.

THORP CREDIT & THRIFT COMPANY [THORP]

A financial service of ITT

In St. Paul
21 West Sixth Street
Phone 291-1919

In Minneapolis
510 Marquette Avenue
National City Bank Bldg.
Skyway Level
Phone 339-4853

In Brainerd
700 Front Street
Phone 829-3518

This announcement is not an offer to sell or a solicitation of an offer to buy these securities, which are not insured by any agency of the federal government. This offering is made only by the Prospectus to Minnesota residents only.

343

You won't find better checking services anywhere else.

Most people sooner or later start checking around to find the most for their money in a checking account. It does make sense for something as indispensable as a checking account to be as attractive, convenient, and economical as possible. Most banks offer quite an array of options these days, including a potpourri of fancy checks and checkbook styles (often at extra cost to you). Naturally, you may think that one bank will offer you a better checking plan than another.

Well, one bank will. It's the Hamilton. That's why you can stop going from bank to bank, and check with us instead. We have the latest looks in check styles, and a sensible variety of checking plans, designed especially to offer you maximum checking services. You just won't find better checking services anywhere else. It's that simple.

Another thing you'll notice, is that the Hamilton is a very friendly bank. It just comes natural with us. We've served the Morristown community for three generations, so our customers are our friends and neighbors. We consider our customers the most important aspect of our business. And that means YOU, when you choose to bank at the Hamilton. Enjoy the best banking services available, and the friendliest bank in town. Visit us today. You'll be glad you did.

You can stop checking around.

"Helping You Build A Better Life"

Hamilton Bank **HB**

Morristown, Tennessee
Main Street/Lakeway/Plaza/
Radio Center/Skymart
Member FDIC

Check with us. We have a checking account plan that's just right for you! A checking account at the Citizens helps you keep check on all your spending— and it serves as proof of payment too! No need to carry cash when you carry your

Citizens checkbook! See us today. Check into the many types of plans available. Plus personalized checks in your choice of styles and colors.

A Citizens checking plan pays— *Write on the money!*

OUR PERSONALIZED CHECKING SERVICES FOR YOU ARE

WRITE ON THE MONEY!

"We'll take good care of you!"

CITIZENS BANK

NEW TAZEWELL/TAZEWELL/HARROGATE

Member FDIC

Installment Loans

The way to the best deal on your home loan.

A lot of people are coming to Olive Hill to get the best deal on their home loan. The Peoples Bank of Olive Hill has very good rates on their home loans, and when they tell you your rate, it remains the same throughout the mortgage period. Come to Olive Hill and find out that you can get the best deal on your home loan at the Peoples Bank.

EQUAL HOUSING
LENDER

Peoples Bank
Olive Hill

Member FDIC

Do you need a good reason loan?

- ☐ Buying a new car
- ☐ Buying a good used car
- ☐ Buying some new furniture
- ☐ Buying a major appliance
- ☐ Planning a special vacation
- ☐ Paying college tuition
- ☐ Getting braces on a child's teeth
- ☐ Consolidating your bills
- ☐ etc. ....

Get a good reason loan from the Peoples Bank.

Peoples Bank
Olive Hill

349

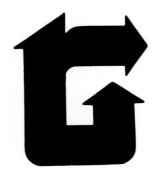

350

GEORGE'S LAW:

By the time you're financially able
to take that big vacation,
the thought of all those bills
exhausts you.

Thank goodness for The Met. Because we
can help you develop a financial plan
that will get you on your way without facing a monumental struggle when you get
back. And without waiting all your life
to go see the wonders of the world. Your
plan could be as simple as one of our
9 savings plans. Or a Met Equi-Loan,
where you get back some of the money
you've already put into your home. Or
an installment loan. Or any combination
of those services. Whatever is easiest
for you...and on you. Do you have big
plans? So do we. Let's talk about how
the two can work together...now.
Because life is for living. Not waiting.

THE MET

The Metropolitan Bank of Lima, Ohio, Member F.D.I.C.

We finance great escapes.

THE FIRST BANKERS

First National Bank
of Broward County

First Citrus Bank
of Indian River County
MEMBERS OF F.D.I.C.

352

Smile.
Gulfstream Bank just lowered the cost of living.

Now. A 14% annual percentage rate on all personal installment loans.

Cheer up! Gulfstream Bank has just made Personal Installment Loans a lot simpler. And a whole lot easier to repay.

Gulfstream's streamlined loans now feature a 14% annual percentage rate. And it doesn't matter what kind of personal installment loan you apply for — home improvement, education, car, boat, whatever. We keep it simple. The same 14% rate still applies.

It's not just another way of putting our money where our mouth is. It's also another good example of our direction. By putting our resources into action for the people in our area.

So if you've been biding your time to apply for an installment loan, your time has finally come. Right now.

The 14% Annual Percentage Rate Personal Installment Loan. It's another personal service from Gulfstream Bank. And it's really something special to smile about.

 **Gulfstream Bank**

In the Boca Raton Area	In the Boynton Beach Area	In the Ft. Lauderdale Area
Gulfstream First Bank & Trust, N.A.	Gulfstream Bank of Boynton Beach, N.A.	Gulfstream American Bank & Trust, N.A.
395-4420	737-7711	763-6300

Equal Opportunity Lender

Members FDIC

353

If you're serious about buying a home we'll get you over the money hurdles.

Plenty of mortgage money.

One of the sad effects of an uncertain economy has been the scarcity of mortgage funds. This has left a lot of people out in the cold. Unless they came to Naples Federal. Through economic ups and downs, we've managed to give Southwest Florida home buyers a non-stop source of mortgage money since 1953. So just ask. We can easily supply you with the money you need.

Easy qualification.

We are not in business to turn down home loans. We want you to have that new home as much as you do. So we make the ``qualifying process'' as simple, quick and easy as possible. We'll work with you to get the amount you need, with terms suited to you.

Interest rates are down.

If you've been holding off buying a home because interest rates were sky high, look again. Interest rates on mortgage money have come down.

So check with us. We'll explain how you can buy the home you want without having to pay an unnecessary premium to get it.

We work with Realtors.

Home buying is a cooperative venture. If everybody does their job right, you'll have the home you want and be a satisfied customer.

That's why Naples Federal works closely with the Realtors in this area. We help Realtors help you in any way we can. Like keeping them informed that we have an ample supply of mortgage money available. Working with them on the technicalities and paperwork involved in buying a home. Making sure that there will be no snags in the transaction which could unnecessarily hold up getting your home. Teamwork. That's our style at Naples Federal.

15 offices to help you.

We don't just make mortgage money easy to get. We also make it easy to get to. How? By having Naples Federal offices in strategic locations up and down Southwest Florida's growing Gulf coast. Today, we have 15 offices to meet your home loan needs, and more offices are planned for the near future.

So if you're serious about buying a home, we're serious about helping you. Stop at any Naples Federal office and let's jump those hurdles.

Naples Federal
More than just a friendly smile.

MORTGAGE MONEY TO GO.

When economic times get tight, money gets scarce. When money is scarce, loans are hard to get, and tough to make. And people who need mortgage money for a new home are suddenly out in the cold.

Not so at Naples Federal. We've got it. Plenty of money to lend qualified people who have a new home in their sights. Or refinancing on their mind. Or a home improvement up their sleeve.

How come we've got money when others don't? Because we don't work like others. With careful financial planning and money management, economic ups and downs seldom seriously cut into our money supply. So, we've been able to give Southwest Florida a non-stop source of mortgage money since 1953. And we don't intend to stop now.

If you've been to places that are short on funds, don't get discouraged. Anybody who wants to talk turkey about mortgage money, is always welcome at Naples Federal. We've got it. And it's hot to go.

FSLIC

Naples Federal
More than just a friendly smile.

Naples Federal Savings and Loan Association with 12 Offices throughout Southwest Florida.

A Gem City PIL is easy to take.

Every home, new or old, needs a little doctoring up from time to time. It's a good investment too. The problem is, home improvements cost money – and that seems like a tough pill to swallow.

Gem City can make things a whole lot easier. We can lend you the money to make almost any improvement in and around your home. Anything from adding a family room or remodeling a kitchen, to central air conditioning, energy saving items, or siding. Borrow what you need, from $300 to $15,000. And Gem City gives you up to 12 years to repay.

So, visit any full service Gem City office and let us prescribe a PIL. A Gem City Property Improvement Loan.

EQUAL HOUSING LENDER

Gem City Savings

making things happen for you.

Loan is not a 4-letter word.

Not at The Huntington.

If you've been kind of apprehensive about applying for a loan, you needn't be anymore.

You see, at The Huntington we know that everyone, at one time or another, can use a little financial help. Money to consolidate bills, make some home improvements, buy a new car. Whatever.

What's more, we know that when you need a loan, what you really want from your bank is a quick, simple *yes*.

We'll do everything we can to see that you get it.

We'll give you a loan agreement that's written in plain, simple English. We'll only charge you simple interest so you could actually save money in interest payments should you elect to pay off your loan before the end of its term.

What we won't give you is the old run-around about needing a loan. Because at The Huntington we have a 3-letter word for loan. Yes.

Huntington Banks
We're never satisfied until you are.

COMMERCIAL FINANCING. WHO STARTS FINANCIAL MACHINERY MOVING?

Growth and change. Two allies of a successful business. They demand financial flexibility and expertise. They demand Fourth National.

Building a new plant. Leasing additional equipment. Increasing credit lines. Issuing letters of credit for an expanding market. Fourth creates innovative financial services specifically for you.

To commercial customers, large and small, regional and local, Fourth has become a source of funds and knowledge for meeting the demands of growth and change.

Who starts financial machinery moving? See Fourth National.

SEE FOURTH NATIONAL

THE FOURTH NATIONAL BANK OF TULSA
SIXTH AT BOULDER
P.O. BOX 2360
TULSA, OKLAHOMA 74101
(918) 587-9171
MEMBER FDIC

Your house is good as gold.

It could get you $25,000 at Third National Bank.

Think how much your home has increased in value through the years. Think of all the improvements you've made to it. Most likely, they add up to a tidy sum.

That tidy sum can do some neat things—with a Home Equity loan from Third National Bank. We can lend you up to $25,000 or more, based on the current market value of your home. Less the balance of your mortgage.

That's right, $25,000. Or more. With it you might want to con-

solidate your bills. Pay tuition costs. Take the family on vacation. Or make even further home improvements, like a new pool, for example.

You might even want to invest in a second home. In any case, there are all sorts of wonderful possibilities.

You'll find the rates at Third National Bank extremely attractive. And your first mortgage rate will not be affected.

Talk to one of our loan specialists at any Third National Bank office.

They'll show you how to make a Home Equity loan you can live with.

Borrow This Much	And You'll Pay in 96 Months	
$ 5,000.00	Mon. Pay	$ 85.41
	Tot. Pay	8,199.36
10,000.00	Mon. Pay	170.83
	Tot. Pay	16,399.68
25,000.00	Mon. Pay	427.08
	Tot. Pay	40,999.68
Annual Percentage Rate on 2nd Mortgages is 13.50%		

Third National Bank

We know how to help.

An equal opportunity lender

Member F.D.I.C.

359

Farming is not a game... neither is your financing

You take farming seriously... and White® Motor Credit knows this. They often know your operation overhead is hard to meet. And sometimes getting equipment you need just isn't possible. That's where White Motor Credit* financing can help you out in a pinch.

Jump from season to season without worry with White's flexible payment plan. By paying monthly, quarterly, semi-annual or annual, you buy your White equipment at the starting line and use White's finance plan through to the finish.

One move is all it takes. So see your White Dealer today.   *Available at participating dealers.

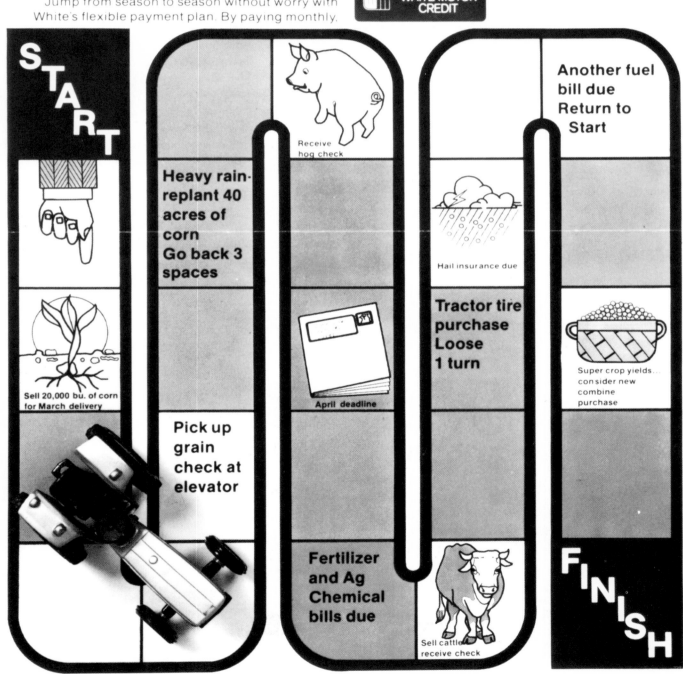

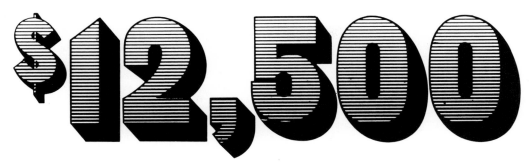

362

There are a lot of good $30,000 houses around. Trouble is they cost $90,000.

Inflation. It's a household word these days. If you can afford to buy a house. But chances are the split-level your parents paid $30,000 for will run you about $90,000 today.

At Colonial Bank we can't bring down the asking price of your dream house. But we do have lots of ways to help you wage the day-to-day battle against inflation. Here are just a few:

1) Colonial NOW Account. The sensible way to bank. Because it gives you the convenience of checking and the interest of savings. Your money earns 5% interest right up to the day a check is drawn against it. And, if you keep a minimum balance of $500 or more, you pay no checking service charges.

2) Colonial Checkmate. A Checkmate checking account is waived of normal service charges if you maintain a minimum balance of $300 in a checking account or in a 5% Statement Savings Account or a 5½% 90 Day Investment Savings Account*.

3) Colonial Savings Accounts. All savings accounts earn interest which is compounded continuously from day of deposit to day of withdrawal for maximum yield. In addition, our Regular Statement Savings Account pays interest monthly.

Of course, Colonial's no-service-charge checking and high interest savings don't spell the end of inflation, but they do add up to extra dollars to help you keep your financial house in order.

Why not stop by the Colonial Bank office nearest you today and talk to a Colonial banker about the checking and savings accounts that make the most sense for you.

*Federal regulations permit you to withdraw your deposit before maturity; however, regulations also require that an interest penalty be incurred.

Colonial Bank

We'll help you fight inflation. NOW.

PICK $1110 FROM THE HOME FEDERAL MONEY TREE

In the lobby of Home Federal's beautiful new Eastland branch, you're going to see something you've always dreamed about — A 6 foot tall money tree! And it could be yours to pick. Just drive your car displaying a WBT Superstar sticker to the Drive-In window at our new Eastland area branch, and our teller will hand you a registration card that enters you in the Cash Grab sweepstakes. Specially marked registration cards could make you an instant $11 winner.

Don't have a Superstar sticker? You can get one at any of our branches, including Eastland.

Then on August 13 we'll draw a winner from all the registration cards entered and that lucky person will have 110 seconds to pick all the money he can from our money tree — up to $1110 in fresh green!

So drive into the new Eastland branch of Home Federal before August 10th and register for your chance to pick our money tree clean. Why wait to rake in some money when you can pick it while it's still fresh.

HomeFederalSavings

Eastland branch conveniently located at Central Avenue and Reddman Road, across from Eastland Mall.
Additional branches at Cotswold, Park Road Shopping Center and Uptown.

Take a good look at our little house on the corner.

It tells a lot about Home Federal...and you

EQUALITY
At Home Federal, we make home and home improvement loans at regular rates and loan fees. To qualified buyers. That's our only criterion. Marital status, sex and race are not considerations. If you qualify, you get the loan. No matter who you are. No matter where you want to live.

ADVICE
There's no way of finding out whether you qualify if you don't ask. At Home Federal, we're here to answer your lending questions. Free. When you take advantage of our willingness to help, you'll also find it's easier to qualify than you think. Try us.

SINCERITY
We built our business by helping families buy and improve their own homes. This help also improves neighborhoods and makes our city a better place to live. So, we care about every question you have, and your plans for the future. You are important to us . . . and that's important to you.

HOME FEDERAL SAVINGS
and Loan Association of San Diego

Arcadia 445-6080 • Bolsa-Golden West 898-0934 • Glendale 240-3741 • Huntington Beach 536-9338 • Irvine 752-5435 • La Cañada 790-0411 • Laguna Hills 770-7171 • Lincoln Heights 223-1164 • Los Angeles/Downtown 625-2099 • Playa del Rey 822-9001 • Redondo Beach 376-8966 • San Juan Capistrano 493-7711 • Santa Ana 835-4336 • Seal Beach (714) 898-3488 or (213) 431-6581 • Thousand Oaks 497-9588 • West Covina 960-1981 • Woodland Hills 340-4464

EQUAL HOUSING LENDER

WHEN STATE FEDERAL LOANS MORE MONEY IN SHAWNEE THAN IT TAKES IN SAVINGS, IT'S NO WONDER WHY THIS CITY GROWS ON YOU.

It's a fact. State Federal in Shawnee puts more money into this community than what it receives in savings, thanks to State's commitment to Oklahoma. And its collective resources in savings through offices in Tulsa and Broken Arrow.

No one has to tell you Shawnee's getting bigger and better. With more industry. More agricultural output. More business. And especially more people.

State Federal is proud of this growth because our involvement has put a lot into this town — with home loans, home improvement loans, equity loans, and commercial loans. In short, money to help build a growing Shawnee.

Shawnee and State Federal Savings and Loan. When it comes to our city's growth, we've got common grounds to be proud.

State Federal Savings
AND LOAN
120 North Bell 275-1771

WE LEND MORTGAGE MONEY TO PEOPLE, ENABLING THEM TO HAVE A HOME WITH A PORCH WHERE THEY CAN TAKE THE NEWSPAPER.

State Federal Savings
AND LOAN

372

MONTANA RANCHERS AND FARMERS ARE NUMBER ONE UNDER THE SUN.

THAT'S WHY OUR AGRI-BANKERS WORK HARD TO HELP YOU RAISE CATTLE, CROPS, AND PROFITS.

In businesses as complicated as raising cattle and farming, it's nice to know you can talk with someone who can speak your language. That's why the specialists in our agri-business department are more than just qualified bankers. They're also experienced ranchers, farmers, and livestock producers. People who can understand your problems and needs.

They can work closely with you to help forecast agricultural trends, help plan for sufficient working capital, and provide any specific financial service you need. And just as important, our loan officers have the authority to make decisions fast. So you can take advantage of changing conditions and growth opportunities.

In farming, livestock production, or any commercial venture, we think the best opportunities for success come when knowledgeable, experienced people in your business work with knowledgeable, experienced people in ours. It's another way we make you number one under the sun at Security Bank.

YOU'RE NUMBER ONE UNDER THE SUN.

Security Bank NA

29th & 3rd Ave. N. • Convenient Banking at Security West, 3rd Ave. N. at 31st • Member FDIC

376

Another big idea:
A new availability schedule that minimizes lag time and maximizes your investable funds.

The more efficiently you can use your funds, the more income you can earn on those funds.

You'll find Colorado National Bank's schedule most accommodating. We maximize the use of cash letters. And we offer a 10:00 P.M. cutoff time for general ledger credit. Both to meet our customers' needs rather than our own convenience.

You'll find that we offer the most competitive ways to maximize your investable funds. And to offer you even better service, Colorado National Bank developed one of the most sophisticated regional check processing systems in the nation. Our computers analyze every check and assign availability on a per-item basis.

Our schedule, computer capability, and central geographic location allows us to make full use of an extensive direct-send schedule.

So if your big idea is to make the most of your money, send it through Colorado National Bank. We can make it happen.

Colorado National Bank, P. O. Box 5168, Denver, Colorado 80217. (303) 893-1862.

Car Loans

Put yourself in the driver's seat.

with a new car loan from the Hamilton

We'll leave the driving to you. But when it comes to financing your new car, let the Hamilton get you rolling in the right direction. Our auto loans can help you get those payments down to size; that's as important as the cost of the car itself. We're experts at helping you make ends meet. One of our friendly loan officers will gladly take the time to talk over your new car purchase in dollars and cents. Even if you haven't decided on the kind of car you plan to buy, <u>now is the time</u> to arrange your financing – through the dealer of your choice, or come to The Hamilton. We're ready to help!

"Helping You Build A Better Life"

Hamilton Bank

Morristown, Tennessee
Main Street/Lakeway/Plaza/
Radio Center/Skymart

380

Before we made new car loans, we made horse and buggy loans.

THE BANK
PEOPLES DEPOSIT BANK

Member FDIC

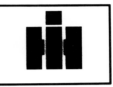

Buy a car from a Charles City dealer.

Save on your financing for the length of the loan.

We'd like to help you buy a car from a Charles City dealer. So we're offering a SPECIAL RATE on loans for autos or trucks purchased from a Charles City dealer prior to January 1.

That's right! With qualified credit, we're offering half a percentage point off the annual percentage rate you'd ordinarily pay.

Visit your favorite dealers—make your selection and agree on the trade— then see us for the financing. You'll save money for the length of the loan!

"GUESS WHAT I BOUGHT WITH MY TUITION MONEY!"

Hospital Trust makes student loans. Car loans. Tuition loans. We'll issue Visa and Master Charge cards to undergraduates. All we ask is that you meet our standard credit requirements. The fact that you're in school is a plus in our book. It demonstrates that you probably want to make something of yourself. So think of us as your rich — but strict — uncle.

YOU FEEL BETTER BANKING AT HOSPITAL TRUST.

Individual Retirement Accounts

At Dollar, you can build a high-yield retirement annuity plan and defer the taxes.

With Dollar Savings new G.I.F.T.™ plan (Guaranteed Income for Tomorrow), you can combine the advantages of high-yielding certificates of deposit with a tax deferred retirement annuity. The G.I.F.T. plan is underwritten by the World Book Life Insurance Co.

S The G.I.F.T. plan is not like the traditional annuity or IRA/KEOGH accounts. You select the term and interest rate for the certificate of deposit, and you can deposit up to $100,000.

S Taxes on the interest on your annuity are deferred until you actually withdraw your money. So the interest you earn today won't be taxed until later…at retirement for example, when you may be in a much lower tax bracket.

S You can start a G.I.F.T. annuity plan with an initial deposit of only $5,000. And you can add to it anytime, in amounts as low as $1,000.

S You can make tax-free withdrawals up to the amount of your original deposit. And your funds are insured up to $100,000 by the F.S.L.I.C.

S If you prefer, you can change beneficiaries at any time in the future. And in the event of death before your annuity matures, your designated beneficiary will receive the proceeds of your G.I.F.T. annuity without the expense or time of probate.

S Call or stop by your nearest Dollar Savings office for complete details. And see why the future of your dollar is looking brighter every day.

Your Dollar works harder.

T. A. Brunzgardner
President

There's a Dollar Savings office near you:

MAIN OFFICE:
Gay at High St.
228-6851

EASTMOOR/BEXLEY:
2951 E. Main St.
236-5065

TRI-VILLAGE:
1177 Olentangy River Rd. at Third
294-6361

ARLINGTON:
1756 W. Lane Ave. at Brandon
481-8187

GERMAN VILLAGE:
673 Mohawk St.
444-6866

HILLIARD:
3750 Main St.
876-9946

PICKERINGTON:
266 Hill Road N.
837-5591

FIFTH/NELSON:
2344 E. Fifth Ave. at Nelson
253-7218

WESTERVILLE:
579 S. State St.
891-1451

WORTHINGTON:
200 W. Wilson Bridge Rd.
436-3653

SUNBURY:
45 E. Granville St.
965-3931

WALNUT HILL:
6121 E. Livingston Ave. at Brice
864-1162

DOLLAR SAVINGS

FSLIC — EQUAL HOUSING LENDER

How to build a nest egg in an economy that's working against you.

There used to be nothing to it. You made a little money. You saved a little money. And, over time, your savings grew.

Unfortunately, things aren't like that anymore. You work like crazy to make a little money. You scrape and scrimp to save a little money. Then inflation takes most of it away. Or bad investments do. Or both. It isn't easy.

But making money in hard times is possible. It takes experience and understanding of our complicated financial situation. It takes the latest information, because the situation keeps changing. It takes knowing just the right balance of lower risk, lower yield investments with higher risk, higher yield investments. It takes a certain amount of liquidity and a whole lot of solvency.

In other words, it takes a financial expert. Someone who has the ability to understand finances and will take the time to understand you. We want to be your somebody. We have experience with those high interest investments you've been hearing about. And a couple you probably haven't heard about. We know what works. We know what doesn't. And we want to help you find what's right for you.

We want to be more than your bank. We want to be your financial advisor. Why? It's a matter of philosophy. At The First Bankers.

THE FIRST BANKERS
MEMBERS FDIC

We want to work with you.

IS UNCLE GETTING FAT AT YOUR EXPENSE?

Sure, we all love Uncle Sam; but he doesn't expect us to contribute more than our fair share in feeding him next April.

<u>TAKE ADVANTAGE OF IRA.</u> It's not only fair—it's smart—to get a deduction of up to $1500 on your 1980 tax return through an Individual Retirement Account (IRA).

IRA is a special tax-deferred *retirement plan* for any employed individual under 70½ years of age not currently covered by a government-approved retirement plan, profit-sharing, annuity or bond purchase program.

Open an IRA at FirstBank, and your money will earn 8%—the highest saving rate allowed by law for any bank or S&L. Compounded daily, your FirstBank IRA offers an effective annual yield of 8.45%. Both your contribution and

interest earned are fully deductible from your gross income.

Learn more about the smart way to keep your fair share through an IRA at FirstBank Evanston. Come in for our free IRA brochure or call a Personal FirstBanker at 866-5682.

Do it today, with Uncle's blessing.

FirstBank Evanston™
We care more.

NOTE: A substantial interest penalty is incurred if money is withdrawn before the age of 59½.

First National Bank and Trust Company of Evanston. A Unit of First Illinois Corporation.
800 Davis Street/901 Grove Street/1900 Central Street/Evanston, IL 60204/866-5500/273-4200/Member FDIC.
All deposits insured up to $100,000 by FDIC.

"An IRA? Who needs one?"

You might. If you don't have a pension or profit sharing plan where you work—or you've changed jobs or your company's retirement plan has been dropped—you should open a Western Individual Retirement Account.

Here are some very compelling reasons why.

Tax savings every year.
You pay no Federal income tax on the money you put in or the interest it earns until you retire—when you'll probably be in a lower income tax bracket. Also, you can get additional tax savings each year by enrolling your non-working spouse.

At least 8% interest.
Contributions to your Western IRA Account can earn at least 8% interest guaranteed for three years up to eight years on contributions of $250 or more. Other Western certificates are available depending on your needs or personal choice.

Interest compounded daily.
From the day each contribution is made, interest is compounded daily. Some banks do not compound as frequently as Western.

Insurance and no fees.
At Western, there are no fees or charges when we set up your IRA. And it's a safe investment, too. It's insured by the FDIC for up to $100,000.

Simplicity and convenience.
We keep things simple. We'll tell you everything you need to know about eligibility, taxes, contributions, withdrawals, and beneficiaries. It's also very convenient, after you've set up your plan, to handle all future contributions by mail.

Retirement, remember, especially your own, is not a frivolous matter. If you have any questions about the Western IRA, or you simply want to open one, call or visit your nearest Western office. You'll find we offer a variety of advantages you simply cannot find in plans offered by insurance companies, mutual funds or many other banks.

Federal Law applicable to all banks requires that certificates in an IRA plan redeemed before their maturity will be subject to substantial penalty unless you have reached the age of 59½ or are disabled.

Western
SAVINGS BANK
Member FDIC

Convenient offices throughout the Delaware Valley

"We know what an IRA is, but what in the world is an IRA Rollover?"

If you will soon be a member of a discontinued pension plan—or a profit-sharing plan—or if you are retiring soon and will receive a lump sum payment from your profit-sharing plan, Western will show you how to tax-shelter that money by placing it in a separate IRA called a Rollover Account.

To take advantage of this, you must complete the transaction no later than 60 days after you receive the funds.

You pay no Federal income tax on the money you put in or the interest it earns until you retire or until you are age 70½—when you'll probably be in a lower income tax bracket.

You can earn at least 8% interest, compounded daily on your contribution from the day the contribution is made. Some banks do not compound as frequently as Western. Also, at Western, we'll set up your IRA Rollover Account free. And it's a safe investment. It's insured by the FDIC up to $100,000.

If you have any questions about the Western IRA Rollover, call or visit your nearest Western office.

You'll find we offer a variety of advantages you simply cannot find in plans offered by insurance companies, money market funds, mutual funds or many other banks.

Federal Law applicable to all banks requires that certificates in an IRA plan redeemed before their maturity will be subjected to substantial penalty unless you have reached the age of 59½ or are disabled.

Western
SAVINGS BANK

Convenient offices throughout the Delaware Valley.   Member FDIC

393

Fall asleep counting 14,900 tax-deferred Keogh dollars

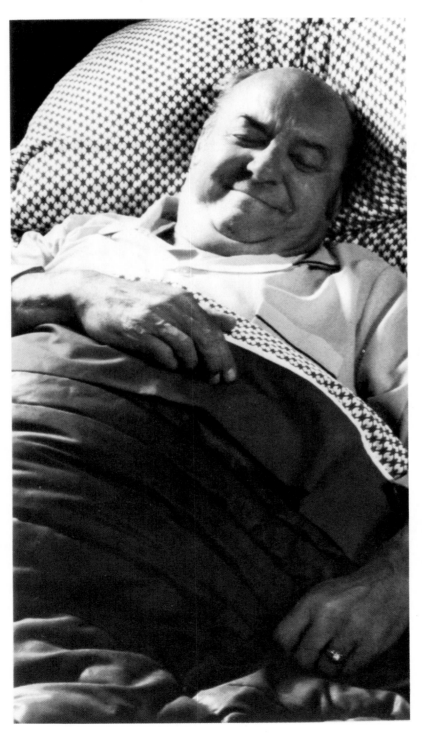

If you're not familiar with Keogh, it's a plan that allows a self-employed person the opportunity to build a tax-deferred retirement fund.

Under Home Federal's defined benefit Keogh plan, you can contribute up to $14,900 to your plan each year — and defer taxes on that contribution until you retire — as early as 59½ or as late as 70½. It's your decision.

In either case, you'll probably be in a lower tax bracket with a comfortable retirement fund. And that's a nice place to be.

Sleep easy tonight. Open your Keogh account today — and don't forget, the administrator does all the paperwork. Your only responsibility is deducting your Keogh contribution from your income tax return. And that's more fun than work.

HOME FEDERAL SAVINGS
of San Diego

Check the Yellow Pages for the office nearest you.

DEEP IN THE HEART OF TAXES?

EARN A HEARTY 1979 TAX DEDUCTION BY OPENING A STATE FEDERAL IRA BEFORE YOU FILE.

THE TAX-DEFERRED INDIVIDUAL RETIREMENT ACCOUNT (IRA) — A BRILLIANT DEDUCTION OF UP TO $1,750.00.

If there's one thing nicer than earning a full 8% on your retirement savings, it's getting up to a $1,750 tax deduction this year, And each year hereafter.

How? With a State Federal IRA . . . a tax-deductible, tax-deferred retirement savings plan for full or part-time workers without an approved pension plan.

With a State Federal IRA, you can deposit up to $1,500 of your annual income (or 15%, whichever is less) before you file, and deduct every cent on your 1979 return. If your spouse isn't receiving a salary, you can make an additional $250 contribution for a total of up to $1,750 of tax deductible dollars each year. And, the interest you receive on these accounts is also tax deductible.

You have until April 15th (or until the date of your tax deadline extension) to open your State Federal IRA for a hearty tax deduction. Meanwhile, your deposits will start earning 8%, protected up to $100,000 by FSLIC insurance.

THE TAX-DEFERRED KEOGH ACCOUNT — AN EVEN BIGGER TAX BREAK-THROUGH OF $7,500.00.

You can earn an even bigger yearly tax deduction if you're self-employed and unincorporated.

State Federal's Keogh account works much in the same way as the IRA: 8% earnings, tax-deferred and tax deductible until you retire, insured up to $100,000 by the FSLIC.

Yet, you can make an ever bigger tax deductible deposit of up to $7,500.00 (or 15% of annual income, whichever is less) each year. Like the IRA, your earned interest is tax deductible.

Talk to your tax or legal consultant today. Then visit any one of State Federal's nearby offices to learn more about the 8%, tax-deferred and tax deductible IRA and Keogh accounts — two tax benefits that are after your own heart.

Federal regulations require an interest penalty for withdrawal of IRA or Keogh funds prior to age 59½.

State Federal Savings
IRA AND KEOGH ACCOUNTS INSURED UP TO $100,000 BY THE FSLIC

TULSA: (918) 583-8111; 610 SOUTH BOSTON, 31ST AND MINGO, 41ST AND DARLINGTON, 6560 EAST 71ST STREET
BROKEN ARROW: (918) 455-9323; 709 WEST WASHINGTON..
SHAWNEE: (405) 275-1771; 120 NORTH BELL.

MEMBER FSLIC

How I retired without worry

Since I retired a couple of years ago, I've really enjoyed myself. Civic Savings really helped, because I started saving regularly a long time ago — back when they were called Citizens Savings.

I'm glad I've found financial security at Civic Savings.

You can, too. Civic Savings has 12 different types of savings accounts. One will be just right for you.

Ohio River Road
Wheelersburg
574-2524

507 Chillicothe Street
Portsmouth
354-6611

507 Emmitt Avenue
Waverly
947-7718

738 East Main Street
Jackson
286-6355

Which stack of money would you rather have when you retire?

The answer is obvious and yet there are many people who will only have the small stack of money when they retire. Why? Because they are putting their retirement money in a savings account and don't realize how their funds are substantially reduced by the income taxes they pay.

If you are one of those people and you don't have a pension plan where you work, we would like to show you how you can make your retirement dollars grow more quickly with a Bank of Delaware tax-sheltered retirement plan.

We have developed an easy-to-read booklet that contains answers to common questions about Individual Retirement Accounts. Send for it today and learn how you can begin building your stack of money.

Federal regulations require a substantial interest penalty for early withdrawal.

The two stacks of money show the difference between how much you would have if you were saving on your own and paying taxes compared to our tax-sheltered Individual Retirement Account if you invested $1,500 per year for 20 years. This example assumes a 25% tax bracket and is based on 8% interest compounded daily with an effective annual yield of 8.45%.

SAVING ON YOUR OWN AND PAYING TAXES
$45,629

WITH A TAX-SHELTERED IRA
$78,242

BANK OF DELAWARE

MEMBER FDIC

397

The answer to these 5 questions about Carteret's IRA/KEOGH Tax-Shrinker Retirement Plans is

Q. My wife and I run a small business together. There are no other employees. Can we each have a tax-deferred KEOGH Plan?

A. Yes.

Q. The company I worked for had a pension plan, but they moved to North Carolina. I didn't, so they paid me a lump sum from their pension fund. Can this be converted into an IRA Account?

A. Yes.

Q. I have elected to take my Social Security at age 62. I have an IRA Account. Can I start drawing on my do-it-myself pension at 62?

A. Yes. Even at 59½.

Q. I have not yet filed my 1979 income tax return. Will Carteret help me get started so I can shrink my 1979 taxes before the deadline?

A. Yes. Free of charge.

Q. If the husband is self-employed and the wife works for a "no-pension" employer, can they maintain separate accounts—a KEOGH for him and IRA for her?

A. Yes.

Obviously there are a lot of questions about KEOGH and IRA Tax-Shrinker Retirement Accounts. Many of them cannot be answered with a simple yes or no. But, whatever the answer, you'll get the right one at Carteret.

Call (201) 239-2772 or stop in at any of our offices soon. Talk to us about the benefits the law entitles you to. For the moment, just remember this:

1. An IRA Account helps provide for your retirement when your employer doesn't.

2. A KEOGH Account helps provide for your retirement when you work for yourself.

3. Both will shrink your federal taxes. How and by how much depends on what you earn.

4. Your Carteret Savings office will be happy to show you how and get you started.

Trusts

The little book with the big ideas for finding a trust department.

Providing investment management is an intensely personal service. So is acting as a trustee or as an executor of your estate. You not only want a bank with experience and professionalism, but one that is right for the needs of you and your family.

Each trust department is unique, however. There are differences in staff, in the approach to investing, in rendering of services, and in management philosophy. On the surface, it is difficult to determine the differences between trust departments.

Our booklet, "How to Select A Trust Department for Personal Trust Services," will help you investigate and determine the differences. It is an insider's objective view, presented by a veteran trust officer. And it will help you choose the best trust department for your individual needs.

We'll be happy to send you a copy.

**COLORADO NATIONAL BANK
WE MAKE BIG IDEAS HAPPEN.**
Member FDIC

COLORADO NATIONAL BANK
COLORADO NATIONAL BANK
COLORADO NATIONAL BANK
COLORADO NATIONAL BANK
COLORADO NATIONAL BANK
COLORADO NATIONAL BANK
COLORADO NATIONAL BANK
COLORADO NATIONAL BANK

How to Select A Trust Department for Personal Trust Services

Send for it.

MAIL TO: Colorado National Bank
Trust Department
P.O. Box 5168 T.A.
Denver, Colorado 80217
Please send me a copy of "How to Select A Trust Department for Personal Trust Services."

Name_____

Address_____

City _____ State_____ Zip_____

"You don't need a bank you can trust. You need a bank you can really trust."

John Jevne is our Senior Trust Officer, because he understands people as well as he understands money.

There is a bank on Wall Street where a Trust Officer
will manage every detail of your financial affairs
as if he were a part of your family.
Its name is The Merchants Bank and Trust Company.
And it isn't in New York.

Merchants.
The Wall Street bank in Norwalk.

Annual
Reports

United Midwest Bancorporation, Ltd. Annual Report 1979

American Bank of Commerce

TIMES

and 1979 Annual Report

Woman of the Year

How do you rate a bank's success?

10th ANNIVERSARY EDITION

Radio Commercials

Farm & Home Savings Assn.

Announcer 1:	Ok, Mr. Abernathy, you've listed 387 dollars as a gift from Sur pass.
Announcer 2:	Well, I like to think of it as a gift.
Announcer 1:	I'm sure you do, but the IRS needs a little more information to go on than that. Is this Sur pass your English relative?
Announcer 2:	Well, not exactly.
Announcer 1:	Then, is Sur pass a close personal friend?
Announcer 2:	Well, not really.
Announcer 1:	A total stranger?
Announcer 2:	No.
Announcer 1:	Ok, I give up.
Announcer 2:	Good, lets go on to the next one.
Announcer 1:	It's not that easy.
Announcer 2:	Well, you see, I get most of my money from certificates at Farm and Home Savings. So I get my interest monthly. And that's where I met Sur pass.
Announcer 1:	At Farm and Home?
Announcer 2:	Right. Farm and Home automatically transfers my certificate interest into my Sur pass account each month. So I earn 5½% annual interest compounded daily while I'm waiting to spend it.
Announcer 1:	Ahhh...
Announcer 2:	More money for my money.
Announcer 1:	So Sur pass is an account.
Announcer 2:	I prefer to think of him as a friend.
Announcer 1:	Dis allowed! Now about these business expenses. Lunch with Sur pass.
Announcer 2:	I can explain that.
Announcer 1:	I bet you can.
Announcer 2:	Here's what you do...

AmeriTrust

"And the Captain has requested that you remain seated."

Announcer 1:	Excuse me. My checkbook fell under your tray table.
Announcer 2:	Oh, yeah, here it is.
Announcer 1:	Thanks.
Announcer 2:	Are these your smoked almonds?
Announcer 1:	They're finished, that's okay.
Announcer 2:	Hey, you're from Cleveland!
Announcer 1:	Right.
Announcer 2:	I was raised there.
Announcer 1:	Where?
Announcer 2:	Rocky River. My folks bought a house on Sharon Drive right after the war.
Announcer 1:	Sharon Drive. You know today that house would be in the fast lane of route 2.
Announcer 2:	Gee, they never tell me anything.
Announcer 1:	About the time you were living on Sharon Drive, we lived in the Alemeda project.
Announcer 2:	I remember that. Those quanset huts on Detroit Ave?
Announcer 1:	Right.
Announcer 2:	Is that a freeway now too?
Announcer 1:	Un huh, a high school, St. Ed's.
Announcer 2:	What about the east side? Euclid Beach?
Announcer 1:	Gone.
Announcer 2:	Oh no! The Derby Racer, the flying turns, the Thriller.
Announcer 1:	The Thriller is gone. You wouldn't recognize Cleveland.
Announcer 2:	I bet. I do recognize your checkbook. Good old Cleveland Trust.
Announcer 1:	Well, that's AmeriTrust now.
Announcer 2:	AmeriTrust?
Announcer 1:	Yeah, I can still use my checks and visa card and everything, but the bank's expanding all over the state, and they want everything under one name.
Announcer 2:	Makes sense.
Announcer 1:	Um hum.
Announcer 2:	Well, at least the Indians are in the same place.
Announcer 1:	Well, if you mean the stadium, yes.
Announcer 2:	I did mean that.

AmeriTrust

AFX:Telephone rings

Announcer 1:	Hallo
Announcer 2:	Hello, Ma.
Announcer 1:	Stafush?
Announcer 2:	Yeah Ma, I got a message, you called.
Announcer 1:	Stafush, stap donie gin, esta ush?
Announcer 2:	Yes Ma, we got the card and the check. Thanks, Mary Ruth is going to use it to buy the baby a new outfit for his birthday party.
Announcer 1:	Rosh emba, shimmi, shen det da getshika.
Announcer 2:	We'll take lots of pictures Ma, I promise.
Announcer 1:	Shumpa check, shumpa shon dombres.
Announcer 2:	I know your check is good.
Announcer 1:	Shebit mouie navao shaba nota check has Cleveland Trust on it.
Announcer 2:	I know Ma. The same thing here in Columbus. My bank was Columbus Trust, now it's AmeriTrust. It's that way all over the state. The only thing that's changed is the name. I can still use my checks, my savings passbook, my Visa card.
Announcer 1:	Yes ma shu-br ru shebit, bunco shapiera nervada.
Announcer 2:	Same people here too Ma, but now it's called AmeriTrust.
Announcer 1:	Mien.
Announcer 2:	And Ma, I sure wish you were coming down for the baby's birthday.
Announcer 1:	Yabenta bich tamie rosen. Ah Stafush?
Announcer 2:	Yes Ma?
Announcer 1:	Shaim eu da Prushiras. Kiss him for me.
Announcer 2:	Yabo pots eliva. I will Ma.

Miscellaneous

"I remember when chuck was 39¢ a pound. That's why I opt for Oppenheimer."

"If you had told me ten years ago that a pound of chuck was going to cost me about $2, I simply wouldn't have believed you.

"Today, it's a fact. Prices are beyond what we could have imagined, and getting worse. Cutting corners and searching for bargains simply aren't enough to keep up.

"We turned to our broker for advice. He suggested we look into mutual funds, and explained several of them to us.

"We liked the Oppenheimer High Yield the best. It's made up of many high yield corporate bonds that the professionals at Oppenheimer think are especially good buys.

"We put some of our savings into High Yield, and let me tell you—so far we've been well satisfied. Those monthly dividend checks sure help us through that checkout counter.

"And with today's inflation, we need all the help we can get.

For more information call free (800) 221-5348. In New York call collect (212) 825-8320.

Oppenheimer High Yield Fund
One New York Plaza, New York, N.Y. 10004

For more complete information, including all charges and expenses, write or call for a free prospectus. Read it carefully before you invest or send money. Minimum initial investment just $2500.

Oppenheimer
Management Corporation

Name

Address

City   State   ZIP

My telephone

White has two ways to "preserve" your cash

During these times of tight money markets, let White® help preserve your cash with White Motor Credit's Rent or Lease Programs. For short term needs, rent new White equipment from a minimum of 100 hours to maximum of 300 hours. Or with White's leasing program, you can lease the piece of equipment with various repayment plans. This is one way to have machinery without making a large capital investment...and you may write off the leasing cost as a business expense.

Regardless of the choice you make...rent, lease, or even financing, the best advantage you have is continuous availability of funds through White's finance plans. And with these favorable plans, White Motor Credit stands ready to help you acquire the machinery you need right now ...while preserving your cash. Talk over the options with your participating White Dealer today.

 WHITE MOTOR CREDIT

Index

111 . . .First National Bank of Chicago . . . . .Foote, Cone, & Belding
112 . . .First National Bank of Chicago . . . . .Foote, Cone, & Belding
113 . . .First National Bank of Chicago . . . . .Foote, Cone, & Belding
114 . . .First National Bank of Chicago . . . . .Foote, Cone, & Belding
115 . . .Delaware Management Company . . . . .Lane, Golden, Phillips Advertising, Inc.
116 . . .Delaware Management Company . . . . .Lane, Golden, Phillips Advertising, Inc.
117 . . .Delaware Management Company . . . . .Lane, Golden, Phillips Advertising, Inc.
118 . . .Delaware Management Company . . . . .Lane, Golden, Phillips Advertising, Inc.
119 . . .Delaware Management Company . . . . .Lane, Golden, Phillips Advertising, Inc.
120 . . .Delaware Management Company . . . . .Lane, Golden, Phillips Advertising, Inc.
121 . . .AmeriFirst Federal Savings & Loan Assn. . . . . .Caravetta, Allen Kimbrough/BBDO
122 . . .First National Bank of Chicago . . . . .Foote, Cone, & Belding
123 . . .AmeriFirst Federal Savings & Loan Assn. . . . . .Caravetta, Allen, Kimbrough/BBDO
124 . . .AmeriFirst Federal Savings & Loan Assn. . . . . .Caravetta, Allen, Kimbrough/BBDO
126 . . .AmeriFirst Federal Savings & Loan Assn. . . . . .Caravetta, Allen, Kimbrough/BBDO
128 . . .AmeriFirst Federal Savings & Loan Assn. . . . . .Caravetta, Allen, Kimbrough/BBDO
130 . . .Citizens Central Bank . . . . .Ellis, Singer, Webb & Associates
131 . . .AmeriTrust . . . . .Lang, Fisher & Stashower
132 . . .AmeriTrust . . . . .Lang, Fisher & Stashower
134 . . .AmeriTrust . . . . .Lang, Fisher & Stashower
135 . . .AmeriTrust . . . . .Lang, Fisher & Stashower
136 . . .AmeriTrust . . . . .Lang, Fisher & Stashower
138 . . .Long Island Trust Co. . . . . .Trout & Rees Advertising, Inc.
139 . . .Brazos Savings Assoc. . . . . .Joe Buser & Associates
140 . . .Brazos Savings Assoc. . . . . .Joe Buser & Associates
141 . . .Brazos Savings Assoc. . . . . .Joe Buser & Associates
142 . . .Girard Bank . . . . .Montgomery & Associates
143 . . .R.I. Hospital Trust Bank . . . . .Creamer, Inc.
144 . . .R.I. Hospital Trust Bank . . . . .Creamer, Inc.
145 . . .Home Federal Savings of San Diego . . . . .Lane & Huff Advertising
146 . . .Home Federal Savings of San Diego . . . . .Lane & Huff Advertising
147 . . .Home Federal Savings of San Diego . . . . .Lane & Huff Advertising
148 . . .Home Federal Savings of San Diego . . . . .Lane & Huff Advertising
149 . . .Home Federal Savings of San Diego . . . . .Lane & Huff Advertising
150 . . .Home Federal Savings of San Diego . . . . .Lane & Huff Advertising
151 . . .Home Federal Savings of San Diego . . . . .Lane & Huff Advertising
152 . . .Home Federal Savings of San Diego . . . . .Lane & Huff Advertising
153 . . .Home Federal Savings of San Diego . . . . .Lane & Huff Advertising
154 . . .Home Federal Savings of San Diego . . . . .Lane & Huff Advertising
155 . . .Home Federal Savings of San Diego . . . . .Lane & Huff Advertising
156 . . .Cass Bank . . . . .Hughes Advertising, Inc.
157 . . .Farmers State Bank . . . . .Hughes Advertising, Inc.
158 . . .Pacificbank . . . . .Ehrig and Associates
159 . . .Pacificbank . . . . .Ehrig and Associates
160 . . .Pacificbank . . . . .Ehrig and Associates
161 . . .Bank of Highwood . . . . .Lubow Advertising, Inc.
162 . . .Western Bank . . . . .Alpine Advertising, Inc.
163 . . .Bank of Highwood . . . . .Lubow Advertising, Inc.
164 . . .Mutual of New York . . . . .The Marschalk Company
165 . . .Mutual of New York . . . . .The Marschalk Company
166 . . .Colonial Bank . . . . .Gianettino & Meredith, Inc.
167 . . .Colonial Bank . . . . .Gianettino & Meredith, Inc.
168 . . .Bank of Commerce . . . . .Hood-Hope & Assoc.
169 . . .Bank of Commerce . . . . .Hood-Hope & Assoc.
170 . . .Bank of Commerce . . . . .Hood-Hope & Assoc.
171 . . .Bank of Commerce . . . . .Hood-Hope & Assoc.

172 . . .Bank of Commerce . . . . .Hood-Hope & Assoc.
173 . . .Home Federal Savings & Loan. . . . . .Shotwell and Partners, Inc.
174 . . .Home Federal Savings & Loan. . . . . .Shotwell and Partners, Inc.
175 . . .Home Federal Savings of San Diego . . . . .Lane & Huff Advertising
176 . . .Security Bank . . . . .Frye Sills, Inc.
178 . . .Home Federal Savings of San Diego . . . . .Lane & Huff Advertising
179 . . .Citizens First National Bank of Tyler . . . . .William F. Finn & Assoc., Inc.
180 . . .Citizens First National Bank of Tyler . . . . .William F. Finn & Assoc., Inc.
181 . . .Merchants Bank & Trust Co.. . . . . .Warren Pfaff, Inc.
182 . . .Merchants Bank & Trust Co.. . . . . .Warren Pfaff, Inc.
183 . . .Merchants Bank & Trust Co.. . . . . .Warren Pfaff, Inc.
184 . . .Farm & Home Savings Assoc. . . . . .Brewer Advertising, Inc.
185 . . .Continental National Bank .Jerre R. Todd & Associates
186 . . .Mercantile National Bank of Arlington . . . . .Jerre R. Todd & Associates
187 . . .Home Federal Savings & Loan. . . . . .Shotwell and Partners, Inc.
188 . . .Colorado National Bank . . . . .Frye Sills, Inc.
189 . . .Colorado National Bank . . . . .Frye Sills, Inc.
190 . . .Colorado National Bank . . . . .Frye Sills, Inc.
191 . . .Continental National Bank .Jerre R. Todd & Associates
192 . . .Bank of the West. . . . . .Bergthold, Fillhardt, Wright, Inc.
193 . . .Bank of the West. . . . . .Bergthold, Fillhardt, Wright, Inc.
194 . . .Civic Savings & Loan Assn. . . . . .David E. Carter Corporate Communications, Inc.
195 . . .Peoples Deposit Bank & Trust Co.. . . . . .David E. Carter Corporate Communications, Inc.
196 . . .Bank of the West. . . . . .Bergthold, Fillhardt, Wright, Inc.
198 . . .Peoples Deposit Bank & Trust Co.. . . . . .David E. Carter Corporate Communications, Inc.
199 . . .Peoples Deposit Bank & Trust Co.. . . . . .David E. Carter Corporate Communications, Inc.
200 . . .Peoples Deposit Bank & Trust Co.. . . . . .David E. Carter Corporate Communications, Inc.
201 . . .The Bank of Santa Fe . . . . .Epstein Communications
202 . . .Bank of Delaware . . . . .deMartin-Marona-Cranstoun-Downes
203 . . .Bank of Delaware . . . . .deMartin-Marona-Cranstoun-Downes
204 . . .Bank of Delaware . . . . .deMartin-Marona-Cranstoun-Downes
205 . . .Carteret Savings and Loan Assn. . . . . .Douglas Turner, Inc.
206 . . .Carteret Savings and Loan Assn. . . . . .Douglas Turner, Inc.
207 . . .Carteret Savings and Loan Assn. . . . . .Douglas Turner, Inc.
208 . . .Bank of Oak Ridge . . . . .AdVenture Advertising Agency, Inc.
209 . . .Bank of Oak Ridge . . . . .AdVenture Advertising Agency, Inc.
210 . . .Bank of Oak Ridge . . . . .AdVenture Advertising Agency, Inc.
211 . . .Hamilton Bank of Morristown. . . . . .AdVenture Advertising Agency, Inc.
212 . . .Hamilton Bank of Morristown. . . . . .AdVenture Advertising Agency, Inc.
213 . . .Hamilton Bank of Morristown. . . . . .AdVenture Advertising Agency, Inc.
214 . . .Hamilton Bank of Morristown. . . . . .AdVenture Advertising Agency, Inc.
215 . . .Hamilton Bank of Morristown. . . . . .AdVenture Advertising Agency, Inc.
216 . . .Hamilton Bank of Morristown. . . . . .AdVenture Advertising Agency, Inc.
217 . . .Citizens Bank . . . . .AdVenture Advertising Agency, Inc.
218 . . .Valley Fidelity Bank . . . . .AdVenture Advertising Agency, Inc.
219 . . .The Metropolitan Bank of Lima, Ohio . . . . .Lord, Sullivan & Yoder, Inc. Advertising
220 . . .St. Paul Federal Savings. . . . . .Doremus & Company
221 . . .St. Paul Federal Savings. . . . . .Doremus & Company
222 . . .St. Paul Federal Savings. . . . . .Doremus & Company
223 . . .St. Paul Federal Savings. . . . . .Doremus & Company
224 . . .St. Paul Federal Savings. . . . . .Doremus & Company
225 . . .The First Bankers Corporation of Florida . . . . .Group 3hree Advertising Corp.
226 . . .Gulfstream Bank . . . . .Group 3hree Advertising Corp.
228 . . .Naples Federal Savings & Loan Assn. . . . . .Group 3hree Advertising Corp.
229 . . .Naples Federal Savings & Loan Assn. . . . . .Group 3hree Advertising Corp.
230 . . .The First Bankers Corporation of Florida . . . . .Group 3hree Advertising Corp.

354 ...Naples Federal Savings & Loan Assn. ....Group 3hree Advertising Corp.
355 ...Naples Federal Savings & Loan Assn. ....Group 3hree Advertising Corp.
356 ...Gem Savings ....Kircher, Helton & Collett, Inc.
357 ...Huntington National Bank ....Kircher, Helton & Collett, Inc.
358 ...Fourth National Bank....................Davis & Nauser, Inc. Advertising
359 ...Third National Bank ....Creamer, Inc.
360 ...White Motor Credit Corp..................Rhea & Kaiser Advertising
361 ...American Savings Bank ....George P. Clarke Advertising Inc.
362 ...New Century Bank ....Lubow Advertising
363 ...New Century Bank ....Lubow Advertising
364 ...Bank of Highwood ....Lubow Advertising
365 ...Colonial Bank ....Gianettino & Meredith, Inc.
366 ...Leader Federal Savings & Loan ....Ward Archer & Assoc., Inc.
367 ...Home Federal Savings & Loan..............Shotwell and Partners, Inc.
368 ...Home Federal Savings of San Diego ....Lane & Huff Advertising
369 ...Home Federal Savings of San Diego ....Lane & Huff Advertising
370 ...State Federal Savings & Loan Assn...........Hinkle-Brown-Bloyed, Inc.
371 ...State Federal Savings & Loan Assn...........Hinkle-Brown-Bloyed, Inc.
372 ...Merchants Bank & Trust Co................Waren Pfaff, Inc.
373 ...Colorado National Bank ....Frye Sills, Inc.
374 ...Security Bank ....Frye Sills, Inc.
375 ...Security Bank ....Frye Sills, Inc.
376 ...Colorado National Bank ....Frye Sills, Inc.
377 ...Colorado National Bank ....Frye Sills, Inc.
378 ...Colorado National Bank ....Frye Sills, Inc.
380 ...Hamilton Bank of Morristown..............AdVenture Advertising Agency, Inc.
381 ...Commercial & Savings Bank ....David E. Carter Corporate Communications, Inc.
382 ...Peoples Deposit Bank & Trust Co...........David E. Carter Corporate Communications, Inc.
383 ...Citizens Bank ....AdVenture Advertising Agency, Inc.
384 ...First Security Bank & Trust Co. ....AdVenture Advertising Agency, Inc.
385 ...R.I. Hospital Trust Bank..................Creamer, Inc.
388 ...AmeriFirst Federal Savings & Loan Assn........Caravetta, Allen, Kimbrough/BBDO
389 ...Dollar Savings ....Lord, Sullivan & Yoder, Inc. Advertising
390 ...The First Bankers Corporation of Florida........Group 3hree Advertising Corp.
391 ...FirstBank Evanston.....................Brand Advertising, Inc.
392 ...Western Savings Bank ....Lewis & Gilman
393 ...Western Savings Bank ....Lewis & Gilman
394 ...Home Federal Savings of San Diego ....Lane & Huff Advertising
395 ...State Federal Savings & Loan Assn...........Hinkle-Brown-Bloyed, Inc.
396 ...Civic Savings & Loan Assn................David E. Carter Corporate Communications, Inc.
397 ...Bank of Delaware ....deMartin-Marona-Cranstoun-Downes
398 ...Carteret Savings & Loan Assn..............Douglas Turner, Inc.
400 ...Merchants Bank & Trust Co................Warren Pfaff Inc.
401 ...Colorado National Bank ....Frye Sills, Inc.
402 ...Merchants Bank & Trust Co................Warren Pfaff, Inc.
405 ...United Midwest/Liberty State..............Desmond & Associates
406 ...American Bank of Commerce ....Vance-Mathews, Inc.
409 ...Farm & Home Savings Assn................Brewer Advertising, Inc.
410 ...AmeriTrust ....Lang, Fisher & Stashower
411 ...AmeriTrust ....Lang, Fisher & Stashower
414 ...Oppenheimer Management Corp............David Deutsch Assoc., Inc.
415 ...Oppenheimer Management Corp............David Deutsch Assoc., Inc.
416 ...White Motor Credit Corp..................Rhea & Kaiser Advertising